Linda Blair: The Works

Charles K. Ashmore

Lovstad Publishing
Poynette, Wisconsin
Lovstadpublishing@live.com

ISBN: 061575130X
ISBN-13: 978-0615751306

Printed in the United States of America

Cover Design by Lovstad Publishing
Cover photos by the author: Al Ringling Theater,
marquee & front entrance, Baraboo, Wisconsin

For Kim, Sally, & Hannah

CONTENTS

LINDA BLAIR:
THE WORKS

Linda Blair
The Movies

In 1973 a petite French-Canadian lassie persuaded me to accompany her to a movie. She was my first love and the relationship lasted for about two years. The movie was the first horror movie that I ever saw and it has been talked about ever since. I loved the girl, but didn't care that much for the movie. The movie of topic is *The Exorcist* and it starred a lovely girl named Linda Blair and she has been in films ever since.

Years passed and I wondered whatever became of the 14 year old girl in *The Exorcist*. I heard rumors that she posed for Playboy, only to discover that she graced not the American, but the cover of the Italian magazine of the famed name. I found out later that she posed for *OUI* magazine and as far as I know, she never did any totally nude modeling. (She confessed that she didn't look good nude.) All good photographers know to show just enough of a subject to make the viewer want to see more. Everyone said that she looked hot. Yet, I was in the dark room as to her acting career until I saw her in the seventh season of *Married With Children* in 1992. It sparked a curiosity concerning this pop-icon's career. Nineteen years had passed since she starred in the classic *The Exorcist* and I wondered what, if anything else she has done in the film industry. To date, I have seen 34 of her movies and am looking forward to the next one. They are just like a box of chocolates, as you never know what you're going to get.

Critically Acclaimed

Linda Denise Blair will always be known as "The Scream Queen." It is a title that she earned and she is the original. She followed up *The Exorcist* with *Hell Night* in 1981 followed by *Witchery* and *Grotesque* in 1988. *The Chilling* in 1989 was close to being scary, but fell short of being a horror film. In 1995 she was one of the starlets in the flick *Sorceress*, but that bordered more on the line of erotic thriller than it did as a horror movie. It hardly seems fair that such a cute kid could be immortalized by one movie as she was in *The Exorcist*.

She was nominated for an Oscar as best actress in a supporting role in *The Exorcist* and many people attempt to minimize this accomplishment because there was a double filling in on some of the most trying scenes. She was awarded the Golden Globe in 1974 for Best Supporting Actress and was nominated for the Golden Globe as The Most Promising Newcomer. If she had been a childhood star like Elizabeth Taylor who starred in *National Velvet* at the age of 12, Linda Blair would have been endeared to the public. Fate takes many strange turns. Taylor would be acclaimed for her acting ability and rightly so. She was the adorable girl on the prize horse. Blair would be sneered and jeered by a large portion of the public because she played the girl possessed. Yet, the reason that she accepted the role in *The Exorcist* was to fund her schooling to fulfill her childhood ambition of becoming a veterinarian. Linda's love of prize riding horses was the motivating force behind her roles in many of her movies.(a) The media portrays Linda Blair, as a bit of a promiscuous tramp, yet she never married. Liz Taylor has been married and divorced several times; twice to Blair's co-star in *The Exorcist II- The Heretic* (Richard Burton).

Some of the functions in *The Exorcist* that were played out by Linda's character were disturbing. Projecting vomit never invokes pleasant memories. The possessed voice is unnerving at best. Masturbating with a crucifix is one of the surest ways to alienate a Catholic. The acting in this movie was convincing enough to make us forget that these were just people playing roles on film. The characters made this all seem real and it disturbed us. It should have. One of the great injustices of this movie is that it typecast Blair into a mold as if she where she was devil herself. It may have been impossible for her to be accepted in a role as a normal teenage girl thereafter. It wouldn't be until 1979 when she played the role of Hank Bradford in *Wild Horse Hank* that she was awarded a role as anything but a victim. *Wild Horse Hank*'s potential was never realized. Linda got to ride a horse, do anything that a man could do and save the day against enormous odds. Yet, *Wild Horse Hank* never scored big at the box office. Once again, maybe the public wasn't ready for a woman to ride off in the sunset as the hero. *Wild Horse Hank* was also lacking in a supporting cast with name recognition. Had this film been as big a success as *The Exorcist*, Linda might have been accepted as a fine actress. It is a claim that fits her, but the girl was still famous for spinning her head.

She tried unsuccessfully again in 1979 to climb out of the shadow cast by *The Exorcist* in the musical *Roller Boogie*. She would no longer be known as the child prodigy after this. She found time to have an off camera affair with soap opera and recording star Rick Springfield and with the new Linda in *Roller Boogie*, a woman emerged. Despite looking as good as she ever would on film from a physical standpoint, no one took this movie seriously. It also seemed that no one took Linda's acting ability seriously either.

Blair would star in the movie *Ruckus* two years later. It was a film before its time. Some say that it was *Rambo* without Sylvester Stallone. After viewing *Ruckus*, it had a stronger resemblance to the *Dukes of Hazard* than to *Rambo*. You might say that it was another bad break for the 21-year-old starlet. In spite of her talent, she would never score as big as she did in *The Exorcist*.

I cannot help but to feel that there is a comedienne trapped in the body of the St. Louis star. She appeared in *Night Patrol, Zapped Again, Repossessed, The Blair Bitch Project*, and *IMPS (The Immoral Minority Picture Show)* but fell short of the laughing appreciations of George Carlin. *Night Patrol* had all of the ingredients for a gut busting comedy. Pat Paulsen (straight man of TV's *Smothers Brother's Show*) and the Unknown Comic along with Billy Barty should have been more than enough to keep us entertained. Due to artistic differences, the film never takes us in any well-defined direction and should have been funnier. She played a kidnap victim in *Double Blast*. The scene that featured her under hypnosis had my eight-year old daughter squealing with laughter. If she had dyed her hair flaming red and never played the part of Regan (in *The Exorcist*) she may have made us all forget about Lucile Ball.

The family friendly *Double Blast* was among the three martial arts movies that featured the talents of Linda Blair. *Silent Assassins* featured martial arts in a positive way. It was one of her movies that rivaled her classic (*The Exorcist*) in its ability to disturb the viewer. A young child was abducted along with a brilliant nuclear physicist. It featured a lot of blood and guts as well as leaving you wondering what they were going to do with the little girl. It needed a little less Kung fu and a little more in-depth character from the cast. She also did a movie dubbed *Prey of the Jaguar*. My eight-year old liked this movie. It is o.k. as a movie targeted for children. The good-guys win again in this one. As karate movies go, these were as good as anything that I have seen; save *The Karate Kid*. I feel that is the reason that the public didn't endear, and *Silent Assassins* was that movies questioned the integrity of the government. Movie critics don't want to be political. Perhaps another reason that these films didn't take off is there were dozens of martial arts flicks out at the time.

Even as a teenager, Linda wasn't afraid to take on social issues in her films. She played the victim of a broken home in *Born Innocent*. The scene where she was raped in the bathroom bothered me. I have three daughters and the thought of any of them being raped is an issue that I never want to be confronted with. She is kidnapped in four of her films. *Red Heat* illustrates the true concern of the American government regarding its citizens abroad. She is hijacked in *Victory at Entebbe* and the day saving rescuers in red, white and blue are barely mentioned. It is an Israeli strike force that liberates most of the hostages. Maybe the public wasn't ready to see an old Jewish lady fall victim to a hostile bunch of bigoted terrorists who happened to be white. *Sarah T: Portrait of a Teenage Alcoholic* is the finest movie made regarding alcoholism. It is poignant. It is chilling and it is dead on accurate. The arrow smacks the bulls' eye when it is revealed that the parents would rather accept that their daughter had a mental disease than have to deal with their little darling being an alcoholic. If you even think that there might be a family member (including you) who suffers from this disease, see the movie. It is a must. Blair is convincing in this role. This movie could change your life for the better. Can you imagine any other childhood star accepting this role? This is a tremendous teaching film and despite this, Blair seems to be remembered only as the head spinning accursed from *The Exorcist*. It took courage to tackle this role. I doubt that Miley Cyrus would take such a bold risk. (Who would pay a scalper $400 for a concert ticket to see someone who played an alcoholic?) Maybe Disney should show this film to their young prodigies. Would it have any impact on the careers of Lindsay Lohan and Brittany Spears?

She brought the plight of the homeless to the silver screen in *Up Your Alley*. Had the language been more tempered, this would be a fine teaching tool. We have always had a homeless section in our society and one of the only other films that come to mind that deal with the dilemma is *The Grapes of Wrath*. And that was made in 1941.

She dares to question the authority of the Milwaukee Police Department in *Calendar Girl, Cop Killer*, also known as *The Heart of the Lie*. She questions the motives of the governing philosophy of Big Brother in *Prey of the Jaguar*. The cop in *Moving Target* is rotten to the core.

So many of the pictures that feature the actress that moved to Connecticut as a two-year old child question the powers that be. They don't always portray the authority figures as the good guy. Most movies are purely for entertainment purposes. Many of the Blair Batch of movies provoke your thoughts. They cause you to look deeper at the dilemma in the plot and ask questions. You wonder and ponder past the plot and past the movie.

She was a prolific youthful starlet. Her role as Regan in *The Exorcist* catapulted her into the limelight. It is difficult to ascertain her place in films without it. It did give her instant name recognition. That in itself can be a good thing and it can be as cursed as the role itself. She said that it was an interesting cross to bear (a). Many people hated her for playing the role of the possessed girl, and would not accept her as anything but a damned devilish thing thereafter. It also put her in demand, as she was attractive and talented enough to fill roles adequately. It turned the girl who was going into her sophomore (b) year in high school into a high profile media giant. It is almost an oxymoron, a five-foot two veteran of three movies being a media giant. Along with putting her in demand and being hated by the intolerants of our society, there were problems that plague the profession like measles on a baby. There was the Hollywood scene and it seemed that the young Linda reveled in it. I have seen photographs of her with the Keith Moon (drummer of The Who) and Linda Lovelace (the actress who headlined in *Deep Throat*). According to the photo in one of the tabloids of that day, she was escorted to Keith Moon's birthday party by Shaun Cassidy. She is also pictured with Pee Wee Herman. There is the photo of her and the King of Pop, Michael Jackson, before he was much more than the singing star in the family band, The Jackson 5. She seemed to be drawn to musicians. One of her first recorded loves was with recording artist Rick Springfield. There was a tint of regret in her interview regarding the affair. Linda was under age at the time (15) and Rick was a young adult (24). He also had a top 40 hit, *Jessie's Girl*. In the interview that Springfield did for A&E, he mentioned that her Hollywood connections contributed to their schism. There also seemed to be regret in his voice for the love that never blossomed into full flower. In an interview with *US Magazine* (March 20, 1982) Springfield said that the press crucified him. She dated Cheap Trick's Robin Zander and had a brief affair with funk master Rick James. At one time she is said to have stated that, "He (James) is the only man I want in my life." She also had a fling or thing with Jim Dandy of the band Black Oak Arkansas during the mid to late 1970s (c). She was a huge fan of bands Lynyrd Skynyrd and Deep Purple. I have seen her pictured with Lynyrd Synyrd band members Artimus Pyle and Allen Collins. She dated bassist Glenn Hughes and guitar player Tommy Brolin of Deep Purple. (Brolin died in December of 1976 from a mix of alcohol, heroine and cocaine.) There were rumors and a legal accusation of drug possession and use. There was an Internet rumor tying her to another actress in a romantic way. Rumors abound in Tinsel Town. Nothing can ruin a good reputation faster than fact fabrication and it is a frequently used weapon of personal destruction. The Swift Boat Veterans ran a smear campaign in an attempt to discredit Senator Kerry and it worked. I cannot help but feel that after *The Exorcist*, Linda had a long line of people in high places that were eager to bring about her demise. Even with that being said, it is still difficult to keep your head screwed on in Hollywood as an adult, let alone a teenager. Linda admits, "I was never your average kid at any point of my life"(e).

In the end, Linda has proven true to herself. She hasn't left any broken homes in the wake of her personal history. She has handled her career as a true professional. The real love of her life, animals, have benefited greatly from her generosity. She has stepped outside of the box as an actress, to be an author *(Going Vegan)* and as an animal rights activist. She is the head of the World Heart Foundation, which is an animal rescue service. Mental images of Linda Blair range from ditsy, scatterbrain, vulnerable to voluptuous and sultry. Although she has mastered all these roles, she is in real life: successful, intelligent and sensitive. Besides the suppressed comedian, there is also a kid caged up in this masterful woman.

Even though most of her movies fell short of the critical acclaim as classics, many were a treat to watch. Enjoy them as you read.

The Sporting Club
1971

I was excited to discover that Linda Blair was in a movie with Jack Warden. He was one of my favorite character actors during the 1970s. Little Linda Blair would have been 12 when this strange production hit the road. Her first movie was *The Way We Live Now* and this followed it up. I have never seen the first flick, but I can honestly say that I wouldn't watch the second (*The Sporting Club*) were I not compiling this work on the movies of Linda Blair.

Jack Warden always appeared as a middle-aged man who had dived into life with all of the enthusiasm of a schoolboy on his first trip to a peep show. He had a rough demeanor, but always possessed a hidden charm that made him seem like the happy-go-lucky drunk that lives next door. He was perfectly cast as the new keeper of the Centennial Sporting Club. His role would provide the contrast needed to pit the classes of the Sporting Club and the local population that tolerated the touring guests who stayed for the three most pleasant months of the year.

Born in the great state of New Jersey, in Newark to be precise, 18 September 1920, Warden received notoriety in the classic *From Here to Eternity* as Corporal Buckley. The 33 year-old work horse found himself working with the likes of Burt Lancaster, Frank Sinatra, Montgomery Clift, Donna Reed and Deborah Kerr as well as Ernest Borgnine in that masterpiece. He was juror #7 in the original *Twelve Angry Men*, which was released two years prior to Blair's birth (1957). He mastered the role of Master Sergeant Saul Rosen in one of the better WWII movies, *Darby's Rangers* (1958.) His tough demeanor won him the job of playing Chicago Bears Head Coach George Halas in *Brian's Song* (1971). He earned an Emmy for Outstanding Performance by an Actor In a Supporting Role in Drama for his role as Halas. It is one of history's most touching sports movies. Warden starred in seven productions that were released in 1971. Besides *Brian's Song* and *The Sporting Club*, he was cast in *In Memory of Two Mondays*, *Summertree, Who is Harry Kellerman* and *Why is He Saying Those Terrible Things About Me? Welcome to the Club, The Face of Fear* and *What's a Nice Girl Like You?* Warden was a very busy man during an era that sported some of the greatest changes in the cinematic field. Partial nudity was being permitted on the screen for the first time, at least legally anyway. *The Sporting Club* sports some exposed upper female torsos as well as some clothed, but tangled bodies heating up. Jack Warden played the role of the soldier in many films and could master the part of the regular dogface soldier better than many stars who gave it their best shot. His resume even includes a part in *The Great Muppet Caper* and he played Mark Twain in *Helen Keller: The Miracle Continues.* Other great men in American history that Jack starred as include J. Edgar Hoover (*The Hoovers vs. the Kennedys: The Second Civil War*), and Joe Kennedy Sr. in *Robert Kennedy and His Times.* He was featured in *Shampoo* and as the judge in *...And Justice For All* (1979 (a).)

His birth name was John H. Lebzelter, and was the son of a Jewish father and an Irish mother. He spent some time as a professional boxer, fighting under the name of Johnny Costello. He also spent some time as a bouncer in a nightclub. He did a tour of duty in the US Navy and Merchant Marine. He tired of the life aboard ship and enlisted in the Army where he became a member of the elite 101st Airborne Division. As luck would have it, he missed the D-Day exercise because he broke his leg while training for that eventful day, landing on a fence (b). Many of his comrades sacrificed their lives for the freedom that permits me to write this and you to read it. He appeared in many other renowned works (*The Bad News Bears, The Asphalt Jungle, The Wackiest Ship in the Navy*) before receiving his eternal reward 19 July 2006 (a).

Unfortunately, this was not even one of Warden's best movies of 1971 or any other time. He played the part of the new caretaker of a sporting club community of debutants in a remote wilderness in Michigan, near Canada. He is mocked and he wholeheartedly retaliates.

The Sporting Club is steeped in tradition. There are three generations featured as members and I feel that Linda Blair's brief appearance as Barby is included for that reason alone. (I don't think that Linda Blair is featured for a full minute in this forgettable feature.) There are the old, but not quite senile. There is the middle aged, from the upper twenties to early sixties who are leading the way, making decisions and demonstrating astonishing new ways to concoct blunders.

His unique brand of vengeance proves that you don't have to be a Rockefeller to rock and roll with the financial heavyweights of the world.

Earl Olive (Jack Warden) celebrates his new calling in life with a barbeque. His friends show up on motorcycles. The occupants of *The Sporting Club* showed up in Lincolns and Cadillacs. Nothing compares to owning a Cadillac. Earl Olive owns a 1960 Chevrolet four-door sedan. It appears to be a Bel Air, as it doesn't have all of the chrome extras of the top of the line Impala of 1960, and the entry level Biscayne featured no chrome at all. They were powered by a 235 cu. in. six cylinder engine from the factory and could be obtained with the 283 cu. in. V-8 for a little more muscle and a little more money. Olive's all-purpose sedan looks like it has seen better days. Most Chevys from this era came with radios, but the sound system was still somewhat prehistoric.

It is just as well. This is one of the few Blair movies whose music is not up to par. It is best described as a mix of Celtic, grunge and blue grass. With the exception of Jerry Lee Lewis' *Great Balls of Fire* it is truly awful as is the movie.

If there is any redeeming factor in *The Sporting Club* it is the scenery.

What else was done in '71? The Baltimore Colts of the American Football Conference won Super Bowl V, nipping the

Dallas Cowboys in the Orange Bowl by the close score of 16-13. The Baltimore Orioles defeated the Pittsburgh Pirates in Roberto Clemente's final World Series by a slim margin of 4 games to 3. *The French Connection* won the Oscar as the Best Movie of 1971. Its director, William Friedkin receive the Oscar for Best Director. Two years later he would be at the director's helm in the most memorable Linda Blair movie, *The Exorcist.*

The Exorcist
1973

Thirty-six years have passed since the green-eyed captor of my heart dragged me to see a cast of yet-to-be-known artists in the movie dubbed the *Exorcist*. I really didn't want to see it. I knew too many people that had bad experiences after trifling with the occult. I figured that once I read the Bible and understood it, I might find out something about the adversary. That same dread came upon me as I convinced myself that it was necessary to view the film one more time before I wrote this work.

I rented the version that had the introductory interviews with it. Director William Friedkin advised the viewers, "That most viewers take out of the Exorcist what they bring to it. If you believe that the world is a dark and evil place, then The Exorcist will reinforce that. But if you believe that there is a force for good, that combats and eventually triumphs over evil, then you will be taking out of the film what we tried to put into it." (a) It was grand advice, as I enjoyed the movie the second time that I saw it. It also helped that I had a better knowledge of how the priesthood works and the power of free choice.

One of the reasons that this is a classic is the teamwork that takes place during the 7½ months that this was filmed. The novel by William Blatty was a great work based on a documented case of an exorcism in 1949. He brings more than verbs and nouns to the table. Director William Friedkin was relentless throughout the filming. Although there were many things out of the ordinary that occurred, Max Von Snydow (Father Merrin) calmly stated that there are bound to be unusual things that happen when a film takes that long to make. (b) They had a fire that completely destroyed the set. There were two deaths involving the crew, the cast or their families. Max Von Snydow lost a family member during the film run and one of the cameramen died while filming.

The film crew and special effects specialists brought this movie from the dregs of just another scary movie to the great work for which it is remembered. The projected vomit is green pea soup thrust out of a sack that is activated inside of Linda Blair's mouth. The dynamic pushing of Regan's mother is done with a harness. In this scene, Ellen Burstyn is yanked back with the cord that is attached to the harness with such force that it caused her a permanent spinal injury as she fell on her coccyx. Like a true trouper, she hung in there and finished filming. Linda Blair also suffered spinal injury during the segment that displayed her thrashing uncontrollably in the bed while she was acting possessed. The screams of pain and terror are not acting, but genuine. She truly did want them to stop the scene because the back brace came loose and it did in fact hurt her (j). There were nine sets of pulleys that made Regan's bed shake. The photography was of excellent quality. The sound was above and beyond the normal acceptable level for movies of that era. Mercedes McCambridge was brought in to do the possessed voice and it was most effective (c). The bedroom that looked cold in the movie was that cold on the set. Computer imaging was unavailable at the time and the cold breath couldn't be added in during the editing. The room on the set was −40 degrees. (d) The cast and crew performed magnificently. The Exorcist made such strong demands on its cast that some of the movie had to be shot in New York because the child labor laws in California were too restrictive. One may ask if all of the unpleasantry was necessary to make this a good movie. In order to bring about the total effect of evil it was done to a tee. If any of the disgusting innuendo had been deleted, we would not have been as convinced of the awfulness of the evil spirit.

This was more than a movie about a girl possessed and the affects that it had on those who were close to her. It is the ultimate tale of good verses evil. An adorable young girl (Blair) becomes possessed when she seriously pondered said possibility. Her mother (Ellen Burstyn) becomes frantic with worry. (Ellen Burstyn was nominated for an Oscar as Chris Mac Neil. The role was offered to Jane Fonda.) She is convinced that the dilemma cannot be remedied with the usual trip to the physiatrist. It is advised that an Exorcist be called in. This is no ordinary task and the movie takes just enough time to explain it. Father Karras (James Mason) is called to do the deed, and needs to have another Catholic priest to assist in the procedure. (In order to perform this procedure in the proper and accepted way,(The Catholic Church's Rituale Romanum) another person from the possessed family of the same sex and a doctor should have been in the room. The family member should have been there to restrain the victim and the doctor needs to be there for obvious reasons. Another priest should have been summoned when Father Merrin could no longer function as an Exorcist.) (e)

James Mason plays the part of Father Karras perfectly. He is young, intelligent, sensitive and dedicated. He once boxed, but this part of his life isn't overdone. He is haunted by the death of his mother. It gnaws at his very soul. Every character in this classic is played so convincingly that you might find yourself searching the credits for the one character who didn't make a physical appearance himself, the devil.

In this epoch tale of good verses evil, there is a price that ultimately must be paid. The movie is so symbolic to the eternal tale of evil's attempt to usurp good. Father Merrin gives his life in order to free Regan from the force of evil. Jesus Christ did the same for us.

The most touching scene in this movie is when Regan kisses the priest near the finale, as she is about to enter the car. When she recognizes the symbol of the priesthood, the collar. It was truly a moving theatrical performance.

William Friedkin stated, "I've always thought that a film should be, first of all, an emotional experience. It should make you laugh or cry or be scared. But it should also inspire and provoke you and make you reflect." (f) Friedkin, who got his start in show business as a 16 year-old boy in Chicago radio's WGN mailroom, also directed *The French Connection.*

Yet, it was an emotion packed film. The characters were convincing. You could feel for Regan's mother. I felt sympathy for Fr. Karras and the plight of his mother. There was a load of relief once Regan was herself again. It provoked me. I was disgusted with the crucifix scene. I was appalled when the possessed Regan insulted Fr. Karras' recently departed mother. I was grossed out when the vomit was projectiled. I was unnerved when Regan first spoke in the possessed voice. When it was all over, I reflected. It would be so easy if evil were manifested so blatantly. Truly, this film put us to thinking like no other film before it.

There were some interesting side notes regarding this movie. Its released the day after Christmas 1973 was an interesting choice to say the least. Mercedes McCambridge had to sue Warner Bros. for credit for her work as the voice of the demon. Director William Friedkin revealed that the entirety of McCambridge's contribution to the film amounted to about eight seconds if you timed it with a stopwatch. On the other side of the coin, Linda Blair's brief appearance in *The Sporting Club* is credited. *The Exorcist* was filmed at twenty-three locations. (Visit IMDB on the Internet for details.) Evangelist Billy Graham claims that the devil lives in the celluloid reels of the movie.

The creation of the story is a story within itself. William Peter Blatty wrote both the novel and the screenplay. It all started when he was a contestant on the TV show *You Bet Your Life* which was hosted by the immortal Groucho Marx. Blatty tried to convince Marx that he was a wealthy Arabian sheik and had more wives than you could count. When Blatty was exposed as an imposter, he said that he did it because George Fenneman said, (that), "Groucho Marx was an ace at spotting a phony. George served as the announcer on the *You Bet Your Life* series for over a decade." Marx shot back, "That is incorrect because I've had Fenneman in my employ for fourteen years." When the host quizzed Blatty as to how he planned on spending the handsome winning sum of $10,000 William Peter Blatty responded that he was going to take a year off of work and write a novel. The novel was *The Exorcist* (g). Elinore Blair (Linda's mother) appears as a nurse in this film. According to Father William O'Malley, this film is 80% true regarding the actual exorcism performed in 1949. (The sex of the victim was male and it took place in another location (h).)

When the Academy Awards for films of 1973 were presented the next year, Groucho Marx won an Honorary Award recognizing him for brilliant creativity and for the unequaled achievements of the Marx Brothers in the art of motion picture comedy. It was strange that he would be awarded this distinguished trophy the same year that the plot that he inadvertently help bankroll would receive two Academy Awards: one for Best Writing Screenplay Based on Material From Another Medium which was given to William Peter Blatty and for the Best Soundtrack which went to Robert Knudson and Christopher Newman. 1973 was a monumental segment for motion picture classics. *The Sting* won Best Picture. Glenda Jackson got the Best Actress in a Leading Role for her part in *A Touch of Class*. Ellen Burstyn was nominated for that award. The distinguished John Hausman received the Best Supporting Actor Academy for his part in *The Paper Chase*, where Jason Miller was nominated. Linda Blair lost out to Tatum O'Neal for the Best Actress in a Supporting Role, for her bit in *Paper Moon*. Tatum was the youngest actress to receive such an award in a competitive category. You cannot argue with an Academy Award, but how often does Tatum's part in *Paper Moon* come up in a conversation? How many times does Linda Blair's devilishly dynamic dramatic role come up in a conversation? Blair played the part of two characters in *The Exorcist*; the innocent young girl and the devil's diva. These roles were most challenging and especially so for a girl who wasn't old enough to get a driver's permit in most states.

This was Linda Blair's third movie. *The Sporting Club* and

The Way We Live Now precede it. Her acting was intensely convincing. It was so much so that it was necessary for Warner Brothers to provide the teenage actress with bodyguards. Many people made serious threats on her well being because they believed her to be evil and or possessed. The Connecticut cutey had arrived on the silver screen in a big way and there was no turning back.

In an interview written by Christina Savvas on 21 March 2009 in the *Birmingham (England) Mail*, Linda spoke of *The Exorcist* on her third trip to the city in the land that once had this film banned. She believes that the driving forces for the enduring success of *The Exorcist* are the quality, craftsmanship and professional perfectionism of the cast and crew. She said that it was perfect, intelligent and mistake free. She referred to it not as a horror film, but a theological thriller. She thought that the intelligent religious aspect and the fear of the unknown are what emotionally impacted us.

She made many TV commercials and did modeling prior to her movie career. *The Exorcist* was her first major role. If you saw her in the *Kerry* doll commercial, you would appreciate what a cute little lassie this was. When I first viewed this old tidbit, it brought back a million memories of my two oldest daughters and the hours that they played with Barbie dolls. Blair was adorable in this commercial. She was Shirley Temple-esque. I have pondered more than once what would have become of Linda Blair had she been cast in a role similar to Elizabeth Taylor in *Lassie Come Home* or *National Velvet* instead of Regan in *The Exorcist* early in her career. Linda's love for horses is unrivaled and she probably would have been a media darling instead of The Scream Queen had she been cast in one of Taylor's roles.

I have also found it interesting that the patented "Linda Blair Head Spin" in *The Exorcist* is still a popular topic on talk shows the world over. She was seen on a Los Angeles 11 O'clock news show in 2000. This segment was been shot in Britain. The head spinning of a doll was the lighter moment on her first Mexican television appearance. *The Exorcist* is available through the Internet on E-bay and Amazon but was not available in the United Kingdom for fifteen years (i). This cinematic classic rates at number nine on the all time Box Office grossing list, bringing in over $232,000,000 during its tenure, beating out then current Box Office favorite, *The Sting* from the same year. Her hair-raising portrayal of Regan McNeil earned her the number nine spot on the American Film Institute's Villain's list for movies made in the last hundred years according to CelebrityNews.

1973 was a marked year indeed. It was the year that the Supreme Court ruled on the famous Roe vs. Wade. On January 28, a ceasefire was signed and American ground forces would no longer be involved in the Viet Nam War. Spiro T. Agnew resigns as Vice-President of the United States, and the Watergate Scandal began to unfold. Skylab was launched in 1973. The Miami Dolphins doubled up the Washington Redskins (14-7) in Super Bowl VII. It was seen live by over 90,000 fans at the Coliseum in Los Angeles, California. Miami Dolphin free safety Jake Scott was named the game's MVP. The Oakland A's decisioned the New York Mets, 4 games to 3, in the World Series. Yogi Berra became the first man to manage the New York Met and Yankee teams to the World Series. He guided the Yankees to the 1964 Fall Classic. The presentation of media awards occurs the year after the event took place. A good example of this was the Oscar that Marlin Brando earned in his role in *The Godfather*. The movie was released in 1972, so Brando was to have been awarded his Oscar at the 1973 Academy Awards. He sent Sacheen Littlefeather in his place to receive the award. It was his way of protesting the American government's treatment of Native Americans. *The Godfather* was awarded the Oscar for Best Picture of 1972 at the awards in 1973.

Film star and "Leg Lady" Betty Grable passed away in 1973. Former President Lyndon Johnson finished his final chapter in 1973 and Picasso would paint no more in this life as the books were closed on these great personalities this year.

Born Innocent
1974

This is a made for TV movie that had enormous impact on the public. It features Linda Blair as a troubled young teenager during the 1970s. This film merely scratches the surface of the tribulations that an adolescent female might have faced through the decade of transformation. Pop music dropped the roll from rock and roll. Nashville abandoned the western swing from country and western. Disco slipped into the Top 40. On the front page of the newspapers, we discovered that our government was not squeaky clean as the Watergate scandal woke up a trusting client, the American public. History took a strange turn, as an upstart nation that rumbled with the international giant and won. The United States was the international giant who was kicked out of Viet Nam by a determined gorilla army. We traded in our invincibility for vulnerability. Mega movie hits included *The Godfather*. We finally came to grips with the fact that there were families in the business of crime. *The Exorcist* shattered any past expectations of horror movies. In a decade, television changed dramatically. During the 1960s Mr. and Mrs. Don Petrie (Dick Van Dyke and Mary Tyler Moore) slept in separate beds on the *Dick Van Dyke Show*. It wasn't until the 1970s that the sound of a toilet flushing would be permitted on television, as it was on the series *All In the Family*. As her previous performance (*The Exorcist*) had done, this flick would set precedence and cross over the line that censorship would permit.

I had three sisters that experienced their teenage years during these times. This movie brought back some reality and memories that tug at the very strings of my heart. Linda Blair is institutionalized for being a chronic runaway. These things weren't figments of the writer's imagination. One of my sisters amassed many runaway miles and had the option of staying in a state run school for troubled girls or moving out of the country.

At age fifteen, she opted to move to Canada where she lived with my aunt and uncle. The only time that the police were of any assistance whatsoever regarding her running away was the time she was found skinny-dipping. It seems strange that they couldn't find her in the clothes that she left home in, but they noticed her but naked. It must have been a popular place for young ladies to skinny dip. Born Innocent nailed the legal system right to the cross. The system did all that it had to do so that it could move onto the next case. Chris Parker, played by Linda Blair, wasn't a rotten kid. She was confused. She loved her mom and dad, but found circumstances at home unlivable. Blair played the part masterfully. She wasn't the criminal type, but was put in with young, hardened criminals, as well as other victims of circumstances. Among them was a teenage hooker who was the daughter of a prostitute and a Native American lass who was with expecting a child.

Born Innocent has a grim beginning. Chris Parker (Linda Blair) is shown being processed as a prisoner. There is the slamming of the jail doors. There are the usual unfelt phrases: "Turn key. Watch the door" "Catch the end of the line for me. Come on." It is interrupted by, "We've got a juvenile over her." "How old is she?" "Fourteen", is the response. There is the echo of the background sound that isn't clear, as any visitor or resident of a penal institution would immediately recognize. You'll notice the inmate that watches Parker's entrance through a mail slot on the lower half of her cell door. It goes to the next series of bland verbiage, "Do you have any jewelry? Take off your belt. Come with me, please. Take any bunk that is empty". Linda Blair is fabulous in this role without saying a word. Her body language tells it all. She is ashamed. She is apprehensive and she is doing her all to suppress her fear. The female jailer is a great study as well. Her face displays the tension of the prison worker, whose job entails a career of waiting and preparing for something bad to happen. She doesn't look cold nor cruel, but distant and all business. Chris seeks the corner to survey her new surroundings. She speaks to no one. In all of the time that she spends in jail, she speaks to no one. Yet, her body language delivers the message that words cannot tell. She is sent to the juvenile detention center after spending the night in jail.

Chris receives a rude awakening as she enters the juvenile detention center. Her parents have turned her over to the authorities. She isn't allowed to get in touch with her folks and this greatly confuses her. She is already in trouble. She just left jail and now her mom and dad have given up on her. The desperateness of this disappointing situation is obvious. Despair and doom are now her constant companions. Hope is just another four-letter word. The first thing that is noticed in the juvenile center is the absence of the echoing background noise that permeates the walls of a prison.

Her parents are absent when she makes her first court appearance. You can tell that Chris needs them if for nothing else but for someone to lean on. Just a familiar face could give such a huge boost in that situation. If you were a fourteen year-old girl and just spent the last two days in jail and a juvenile detention center, wouldn't a face from the family make you feel that at least somebody cared? Even parents yelling in rebuke would make you feel like a person of worth. It seems as though Chris has just dialed the wrong number in the game of life and there isn't even a stranger at the other end of the line. It is in this court that Chris is ordered to the state's girls' home. It seems that this young woman with talent and promise is being sent to the end of the line.

The cast of supporting actresses is well done. There are girls representing every background. There is the pregnant girl and the chubby lassie with glasses. Some of the girls don't wear glasses. Some are blonde and many are not. Some are Black and some are Hispanic and some are White. There is a Native American. The point that is being attempted is that there is no stereotypical student in a girls' facility.

The director does some dandy work in his effort to bring

about the innocence of young Chris. One of the more impressive images is that of the institutionalized teenager on the swing. She looks so young as she pumps the playground equipment. For some reason, the mindset is that if there is a girl on a swing, she must be free and innocent. It brings a feeling of exhilaration to both the girl on the swing and the person watching her. I doubt that there is a person alive who can say that they never felt that joy, innocence and freedom when they swung this timeless playground piece.

The next scene deliberately swings the other way. It is the first of the Linda Blair shower scenes and it is by far the most unnerving. She is showering and is attacked by her companions and raped with the handle of a plunger. It is one of the most upsetting film clips of all time. She is no longer free. She is no longer innocent. The girls in her environment no longer deserve to be called human beings, as human beings shouldn't dare act in such a cruel and revolting manner. It is the most convincing cry that Blair has ever stained the screen with.

Life travels in circles. Chris attempts to run away from the facility. Running away was her ticket into the same awful place. Chris Parker has an horrible dilemma. If she runs away from home, she is institutionalized. When she is institutionalized, she needs to run away from the girls that raped her. We know what she is running from in both instances, but what is she running to? No one understands her at home. Her mother is battling the bottle and the booze that oozes from it. Chris is treated in a brutal and inhumane manner at the facility. It is even more disturbing to the student, because it isn't the establishment that has brutalized her. It is her peers. They are the very people that she should be identifying with. They are the ones that should share the common bond. She may be running because that is all that she can do. There is no prize at the end of the race. There is no feeling of conquest upon completion. There is only the knowledge that those people that have hurt you cannot touch you as long as they can't catch you. Maybe if you keep running they won't be able to catch you.

She is finally run down by a couple of guards in two different trucks. One is an old Chevrolet Apache and the other is a 1960s model Ford F-100 pick up.

After being captured, Chris is put into isolation. You wonder if this may be a blessing in disguise. Joanna Miles is brilliant in her role as the gifted and caring councilor. Councilor Clark is finally able to get through to Chris. Chris says that she is ready to go home. She will never run away from home again if it means she will be returning to the school for girls. Chris tells Clark that she will try harder to be understood by her mother. She promises to stay out of her dad's way. She says that she will help her mother. After being raped by your peers and finding nowhere else to turn, even a home where the parents don't understand you is an upgrade. The kind councilor has dialogue with Chris while she is in isolation and in the classroom. She knows that Chris was an above average student and that she wants to be a stewardess. (The occupation of stewardess has been re-titled to flight attendant.) It isn't a window-dressing. You can feel the love. Chris tells her of the atrocities that befell her in the shower room.

Councilor Barbara Clark filled the rest of the staff in on the shower activity as they consider furloughing Chris for a few days back to her home. One of the staff members denies that any kind of abusive gang raping activity could possibly have taken place. A startling statistic comes forth in the staff meeting. One out of every five girls that is released from the facility returns. Chris can see where she went wrong and wants to return to her parents. Chris gets her furlough.

On the way home, her dad asks her if "It wasn't too bad a place? Was it?" He hears no reply. They make the trek in a 1961 Ford Falcon 2-door sedan.

Her father (Richard Jaekel) is the textbook answer to "Why did God invent Preparation H?" The young lady isn't home but a few hours and he is blaming his wife for picking on him. He is blaming Chris and her brother for ganging up on him and making him feel like third string dirt. He is very forceful and authoritave. He not only fails to listen, he fails to give the other party an opportunity to speak. Mr. Parker brings the most sadness into the movie. He thinks only of himself and plays the victim. You might think that he would be thrilled that his daughter was coming home. There should be delight in his demeanor and dance in his step. Chris gets the grump from the stump instead. The self-centered boy that failed to grow up stifles her mother's sweet happiness for her daughter's homecoming. The same self-centered boy is the one that Chris and her brother call Dad. He is physically and emotionally abusive. He makes Chris feel anything but welcome at home.

Mom doesn't offer much help either. The television is preferred company to Chris. She even tells her that things aren't so bad since she left. Do her parents really want her at all?

Parker's home life didn't improve when she returned after her first stint in the state run facility. Mr. Parker could not have been more realistic. He loved his daughter, but was brought up in another generation and the values that went with it. He wanted his daughter to stay with the family, but he wasn't ready to deal with the needs of a teenager who was of another gender. Although none of Chris' desires at home seemed unreasonable, the father insisted on maintaining control. Little girls don't become women overnight. It is a gradual process and the teenage years are part of the saga. He wasn't up to dealing with this reality. Chris had high hopes of living with her brother, but that was another hopeful expectation that went up in hopeless smoke. The conclusion of the film brings the reality to the hopelessness of these situations.

It was a very touching, relevant movie. I not only have four sisters, but three daughters. There were scenes that were particularly disturbing. There is no way to explain or compare the feelings of a home that loses one of the family to circumstances that might not have been so devastating if change had been forthcoming. Empathy is felt as Blair's character meets unintentional rejection again, and again. The rape scene in the shower is awful. Parker was raped with a plunger. You shudder to think of one of your family enduring such a cold-hearted act. The fifteen-year-old starlet spent 5 hours naked on the soaking wet tile floor before this scene was satisfactorily done (a). So much for the glamorous life in the limelight of Hollywood.

Blair had difficulty dealing with the baggage of abuse that went with the movie Born Innocent. She said that as difficult as it was for her she felt that it was worth it because "it made a difference to a lot of young people at the time (a)."

The movie is dated and it was difficult to get in playing condition, but it was worth watching again. It was the highest rated made for television movie of 1974.

Even the vehicles bring a sense of relevance to Born Innocent. I connected with the young woman on her trip home. Often was the time that our family of nine would pile into the 1961 Ford Falcon that was my father's pride and joy for the Sunday ride to church. It got about 27 miles per gallon and came with a manual three-speed transmission on the column. Its only option was the heater. Dad wrongly claimed that a radio would run down the battery.

One of the pick up trucks used to coral the escaping Chris was a late 1950s model Chevrolet Apache. It was a popular truck during the late 1950s and into the mid 1970s. The one used in this movie is from around 1959. They were dependable workhorses that were often seen down on the farm. They rolled off the assembly line with the basics; six-cylinder engines that were geared more towards power than speed. You could get them with V-8s, whitewalls and wheel covers. There is also a mid 1960s Ford truck in this scene. They were tough and well received, especially as truck prices began holding their value better than cars did. Many options were added as the popularity of the truck outgrew the farm. You could get them with power steering and power brakes as well as automatic transmission.

Most self-respecting farmers would turn up their noses at these bells and whistles twenty years before this film was made.

Even though *Born Innocent* was released in 1974, the theme is current. Hopefully the methods of treatment for the girls in these schools have more options than the farm trucks of old. Maybe if Mr. and Mrs. Parker had spent some time in the Falcon going to church or camping or some other family function, bringing her home from the girls' school wouldn't have been their final option.

It is interesting to note that this movie is what prompted the television networks to implement the family viewing hour which was a short lived agreement in which the networks would be free of sex and violence during the eight o'clock hour (b). (If I am not mistaken, the rape scene was deleted for television.) It was a short-lived practice.

Born Innocent is available on E-Bay and Amazon. The book is also readily available.

Airport 1975

Linda Blair was surrounded with legendary giants of the silver screen in this film. Her role turned out to be less than what was expected. She played the part of Janice Abbott, a teenager in dire need of a kidney transplant. Charlton Heston, of Moses fame in *The Ten Commandments*, has the top billing as the boyfriend of Nancy Pryor and is the brilliant pilot/designer of the featured 747 airplane. The beautiful Karen Black plays Nancy Pryor. (She would appear with Linda again in the 1990 spoof *Zapped Again*.)

George Kennedy is younger than what we're used to seeing him in this movie and brings compassionate machismo. His wife and child are aboard the seemingly doomed airship. (Kennedy would share the credits with Linda Blair 30 years later in *The Monster Makers*.) He is a veteran of six airplane tragedy movies. He brings credits from the film *Earthquake* and three of the Naked Gun flicks to his resume as well.

Gloria Swanson plays herself in this edge of your aisle seat drama. It would be her last role in Hollywood. The seventy-four year old film legend brought some class and spunk to this movie. Efrem Zimbalist Jr. plays the part of Captain Stacy. It wasn't all that much of a challenge, as there weren't that many lines to deliver but he did a fine job just the same. It was as minor a role, as was Blair's. It was neat to note that he (Zimbalist) won the Golden Globe Award for the Most Promising Newcomer-Male in 1959, the year that Blair was born. She won the Golden Globe for Best Supporting Actress-Motion Pictures in and was nominated for Most Promising Newcomer-Female in 1974 for her work in The Exorcist. Speaking of Most Promising Newcomers-Female, singer Helen Reddy was nominated for said award for her part in this film. She played the role of the optimistic singing nun. Dana Andrews was in this movie and he was up to the task. A couple of his other memorable roles were that of Fred Derry in *The Best Years of Our Lives* and Donald Martin in *The Ox Bow Incident.* Television pioneer and the coach from the movie *Grease*, Sid Ceasar is great in Airport 1975. His character is one who has a bit role in the featured film on the flight (*American Graffiti*) and he wants to impress Gloria Swanson with his triumph. His outgoing persona keeps the plot fluid in places that could otherwise be dull and dragging. Another twist of fate involved is that Linda Blair would play the part of Rizzo in the Broadway production of *Grease.* (Ceasar played the role of Coach Calhoun in the 1982 movie classic.)

Susan Olson from Little House On the Prairie plays the role of Janice Abbott's mother. Myrna Loy plays the drinking Mrs. Devaney in this production. She is a guzzler of boilermakers and loves every drop of it. Loy is a veteran of seven decades of acting and she is bright and entertaining in this role. Erik Estrada (*Chips*), Conrad Janis (*Mork and Mindy*), Norman Fell (*Three is Company*) and Larry Storch (*F-Troop*) also make appearances in this drama. Beverly Garland appears as Mrs. Freeman in *Airport 1975* and would play Linda's mother in *Roller Boogie* in 1979.

Dana Andrews is featured as the pilot of the small aircraft. He played a fighter pilot returning home at the end of WWII in the Academy Award Winning 1946 release, *The Best Years of Our Lives.* This classic is the trivia question that stumps the experts: What movie beat out *It's A Wonderful Life* for Best Picture in 1946? Andrews brings a breath of reality to all of the roles that I have had the pleasure to see him in. He is the master of attempting to hide his nervousness. If you saw him in The *Ox Bow Incident* you would appreciate this comment. In the *Ox Bow Incident* he is about to be hung for a crime whose guilt no one is certain of and he as the nerve to ask permission to write his wife a letter. In *The Best Years of Our Lives*, he doggedly perceivers in his quest to find suitable employment after returning from a war that left his married life shattered and his dreams shell-shocked. They are interrupted by the eternal shrapnel spattered sounds of his crewmate meeting The Good Shepard.

Andrews was born the son of a Baptist minister New Year's Day 1909 in Covington County Mississippi. It was a time when sharecropping was a way of life in much of rural America. Andrews attended Sam Houston University and hitch hiked to California. Dana dreamed of becoming an actor and worked live on stage with Robert Preston (of the original *Music Man* movie and the Broadway production) in a play that focused on the lives of composers Gilbert and Sullivan. Andrews' career zenithed when he was featured in *The Best Years of Our Lives*. He starred as Dr. Norberg in the 1966 less than classic *The Frozen Dead*. Perhaps this flick laid the groundwork for *The Chilling* that featured Linda Blair as the leading lady in 1989. Another common thread of the life of Dana Andrews that weaves its way into Blair's collection of common curiosities is his relationship to the movie *Sara T.: Portrait of a Teenage Alcoholic*. Dana Andrews was hexed by this disease and was one of the first of the Hollywood set to open up and speak out about it. He was an outspoken member of the National Council on Alcoholism, and was adamant about the nation's refusal to address the problem. Linda Blair's next movie made bold statements and revealing truths about one of the world's leading problems and the lives that it destroys. Dana's birth name was Carver Dana Andrews and the fine actor turned to real estate later on in life, claiming to have made much more money in that field of endeavor than he ever made as an actor. Another actor by the name of Ronald Reagan made a similar move. Andrews suffered from Alzheimer's disease in life's declining seasons and ultimately gave up the ghost 17 December 1992 as a result of congestive heart failure and pneumonia. (a.)

In Airport 1975 Dana Andrews is piloting a small aircraft through stormy weather and apparently suffers a heart attack, crashing his plane into the 747 piloted by Captain Stacy

(Zimbalist Jr.) The Jumbo Jet survives without a qualified pilot and one of the flight crew must bring the flight to a safe conclusion. It is a thrilling drama of the highest degree.

I saw *Airport 1975* at the drive in theater when it first released. It was a blockbuster at the time and was discussed by the masses. The leading roles were done to perfection by professionals whose credit resumes would roll from Hollywood to Broadway with awards along the way. Everyone is convincing and the supporting cast was a delight to watch. Myrna Loy was especially entertaining. One of the reasons that this film was a success was that the audience could at least like or identify with one of the characters. Arnie (played by Conrad Janis) is the only one of the cast who is not all that likable. This is a thrilling drama that was a classic during its time.

I won't give away the whole story. An L.A. bound 747 is hit by a smaller aircraft and the pilots' pit and its occupants are either killed or incapacitated. One of the flight attendants is thrust into the role of pilot and the course of events will keep you on the edge of your seat.

There are logical questions that the layman doesn't offer while viewing Airport 1975. These are questions that you might ask regarding the logistics in the plot after you've caught your breath at the conclusion. How is it that one of the crew is sucked out of the cockpit by the vacuum created when the lighter craft collides with the 747, and the other is not? Why isn't the pilot placed near the controls during the dilemma? He does regain some coherence at one point and would have been vitally valuable in saving his ship. How could all of the crew who flew to save the sailing air vessel be rounded up and reach the same spot on such short notice and set in the same location in such a short time? It's funny that you don't think of these things when you are glued to your seat and agonizing with the cast as to the outcome of the movie.

Lovely Linda was about sixteen years old when Airport 1975 hit the screen. She was a popular cult topic at the time.

Her relationship with Rick Springfield was highly publicized. She was climbing up from the child model/actress that was so adorable in the Tubsy and Kerry Doll ads as well as the Ivory soap commercial. She was able to do what the immortal Shirley Temple couldn't. Blair was becoming an adult actress. Her physical persona struck a similar resemblance to Liz Taylor. Her blossoming bosom was more interesting than the 52 curls in Shirley Temple's hair. The scandal sheets surrounded Blair as they did Brittany Spears a generation later. They pried, peered, peeked, meddled, and distorted many activities that teenagers naturally experience.

Rumors are left out of this composition if there is no foundation to them. So, when I found an October 1974 issue of Spec magazine that had "Linda Blair Sex-Hex! The Drive She Can't Control!" splattered on the top of its cover, I invested in a copy of the magazine and investigated the article. The headline hooked me. I bought it and found out that the teenager was very enlightened and had an unbelievable grasp of her circumstances. Quite frankly, there was nothing earth shattering revealed in this tabloid, although its headline would leave you to think otherwise. Other than she is a very attractive, well-grounded teenage actress, there isn't much revealed in regards to her so-called scandalous behavior. She wants to have control of her career and image and that's her desire at age 15 as well at age 50(b).

This was the time that she began seeing actor/singer Rick Springfield. He was one of the performers at the famous Hollywood nightclub "The Whiskey A Go Go" where Linda Blair and her chaperoning older sister, Debbie frequented. It was during this time that Springfield and Blair hooked up for a lunch and dinner date. Springfield describes her as bright, with a good sense of humor and hot in a teenage heartthrob sort of way. He was invited to the Blair home for the Christmas Holiday and arose that day with an unbridled vigor. He was so excited that he fell down the stairs in his exuberant haste to wake the family. He broke his foot in the process(c). From what I've read, seen and heard in interviews, the giggling girl dining with the rock superstar was quite taken in by the mysterious performer from Down Under (d). She was advancing from an infatuated schoolgirl to the dinner date of another established star.

They were the consummate Hollywood couple. He was a young musician. She was the hottest young actress in Tinsletown. He was obviously smitten by the young kitten, as he claims to have spent many hours on the phone with her when she was away. She spent her work time on the West Coast at his apartment. During his time between record labels, Linda fitted his apartment with a TEAC 3340 four-track tape machine so that he could cut his own demos. Linda later reclaimed the tape machine and gave it to her new boyfriend, Neil Giraldo, who played guitar with Pat Benatar (e). I am sure that both musicians were delighted with the gift. Thirty-some years later, Linda sent Rick a Christmas card wishing him a good holiday and warning him of the impending danger of the stairs (f).

Airport 1975 was filmed at Dulles International Airport serving Washington, D.C., Salt Lake City International Airport, Edwards Air Force Base and LAX Airport that serve the Los Angeles area. The helicopter transfer took place in Heber Valley, Utah. Part of the filming took place at the Old Van Nuys Airport, which was also host to the *Casablanca* movie that featured Humphrey Bogart and Ingrid Bergman (g).

Sara T. Portrait of a Teenage Alcoholic
1975

Linda Blair celebrated her sweet 16ᵗʰ birthday the month before this movie was released. It is a tale that needs telling. Her character is one that could be your cousin, your brother, your mother, or yourself. It is a chilling scenario that is real and it happens everyday, every year in every city to people that everybody knows. In stark contrast to *The Exorcist*, this film doesn't explore the realms of possibilities, walking the fringes of reality and fantasy. *Sara T.* tells it like it is. It throws a cold glass of reality in your face.

The story starts with the charming girl down the street helping her parents host a celebration for the newly promoted patriarch. There are many happy people enjoying the drink as they party. It has all the aura of a beer commercial. No one there is suffering any ill effects of the booze that night. One of the reasons to drink says the executive who promotes Matt Hodges, played by William Daniels (Sara's stepfather and the man who was just promoted to Vice-President in some company) is, "I made your father Vice-President." He offers the youthful Sara a drink. She declines in the presence of her mother, but guzzles it down once she is alone with it in the kitchen. You drink if supper is early. You drink if supper is late. You drink to celebrate supper being on time.

Although this film was released in 1975, the message is there for the ages. Sara's battle with the bottle has many innocent victims, as any war has. The person that Sara feels closest to at home in the movie (the maid) loses her job because of Sara and her passion for the poison. (Sara drinks the booze and then cuts what remains with water. Her parents blame the maid.) Her self-respect is trashed when she gives herself to a carload of boys for a bottle of booze. She bungles a babysitting job because she leans on a bottle of wine for support when she has an argument with her boyfriend (played by Mark Hamil). A sad and tragic scene occurs when Sara steals her beau's old hag and rides her into night traffic while she is under the influence. (This would have been a heartbreaker of a scene for Blair, as she loves horses with a passion that few personalities could approach.)

After being shoved into counseling the face that Sara sees in the mirror isn't just Sara, but Sara the alcoholic. It is a difficult thing not only to see, but a challenge to accept and confront. Dr. Kittredge (Michael Lerner) confronts Sara's family with the prospects of the teenager being an alcoholic. Some painful truths are brought to the forefronts of our lives. Dr. Kittredge states, "(Being) Troubled, lonely and frightened....Booze helps them get through the day. Because it works... for a while. It giveth and it taketh away and one day, it's going to kill you." No truer words on the subject of alcohol and alcoholism were ever spoken. During his dialogue the psychiatrist makes some pointed remarks that cut the family to the quick. "You'd sooner see her as crazy" is one that comes to mind. One of the saddest truths about alcoholism is that many people can support the recovering alcoholic, but the only person who can help the drinking junkie is the alcoholic herself (himself).

I was impressed that the teenager was able to come to grips with her disease of alcoholism. Her family was in denial. Their little darling was lead astray by the wayward boyfriend. The maid must have added water to the scotch and consumed the rest. She is a teenage girl and is subject to mood swings. When Sara said that she had been drinking every day for the past two years, it went over everyone's head. It seems that her drinking escapades are all somebody else's fault. It is difficult for her to deal with the absence of her real father (Larry Hagman) and his ultimate rejection of Sara.

She is introduced to a boy (Bobby is played by Eric Olson) at an Alcoholics Anonymous meeting. Bobby appears to be ten years old at best. Eric Olson is perfect in this flick. How could a little boy be an alcoholic? The facts, figures and faces in this film are all too familiar. It is scary. It is far more frightening than *The Exorcist.* I don't remember ever seeing a girl turn her head around in real life. I do remember people throwing up from over consumption. I also remember sneaking lemon extract (7% alcohol). I drank some of my Dad's Christmas gift (Sunny Brook) from one of his customers and he thought that my mother was consuming his gift. I didn't realize that I drank about ½ bottle of at various sittings. My dad looked at me in disbelief, thinking that I was protecting Mom. Mom looked at me in shock. She knew that she didn't drink the stuff, (The only time I ever saw my mother hoist a drink was the one Tom & Jerry during the Holiday Season.) but it bothered her that I would. I'm glad that she didn't bake too many lemon pies. I must have been about 13 when I pulled these shenanigans. When Sara said that she would drink rubbing alcohol if nothing else was available, I couldn't help but think of the lemon extract.

Another subliminal fact to watch for in the movie is how many of the people that surround Sara drink. It is as though it is something that is ingrained in her culture. It took great courage for Sara to admit to her disease. In some cases, a full recovery from dependency includes relocation. All too often, the victim is enticed into old settings and old habits by old friends and the whole scene starts over again.

Mark Hamil, who played Luke Skywalker in *Star Wars*, played Linda's boyfriend in this movie. He is eight years Linda Blair's senior. He received the Saturn Award for the Best Actor in 1984 for his part in *Star Wars VI Return of the Jedi* and in 1984 for his role as Luke Skywalker in *The Empire Strikes Back*. His first Saturn was in 1977, two years after his bit in *Sara T*, for his role as Luke Skywalker in the original *Star Wars*. If you were wondering what Larry Hagman was doing between his gig as Jeannie's husband in *I Dream of Jeannie* and the cold hearted heavy J.R. in the TV series *Dallas*, he was playing the part of Linda Blair's real dad in *Sara T: Portrait of a Teenage Alcoholic*. Of the three roles, this is the one that is most believable.

If you know anyone who drinks a little more than a little bit, this movie will make things seem a bit more believable. *Sara T* proves that history repeats itself. It starred Linda Blair and was the highest rated made for TV movie, just like *Born Innocent* the year before. This is one of the most difficult Linda Blair movies to find. (On 12 June 2009 it was listed at brutallo.com. for sale. I also saw it listed once with Finnish subtitles.) I have never seen it on television rerun circuit. I also have to confess that I didn't watch too much television from 1972 through 1979. For a time I didn't own one. When I finally did own one, I was never able to get in more than one channel, and I also didn't spend a ton of time at home during these years. So, I was deprived of some of Linda Blair's best work when it was a contemporary art. Yet, the themes that *Sara T.* and *Born Innocent* grapple with are timeless. This movie is one of the most accurate appraisals of the demonic dilemma that disguises itself as alcoholism. I am somewhat bewildered that it hasn't been implemented as a teaching tool. From what I have witnessed, it would be far more effective than the money that has been used on "D.A.R.E." and if the props could be updated, the timeless message could hit the target identified as the teenage alcoholic.

One wonders if Linda Blair volunteered her services for some of these roles because of a community spirit or these roles were just another acting gig. The answer to the question can be found in an interview in Femme Fatales where she claims that her agents landed these (*Born Innocent* and *Sara T.*) gigs for her. She said that they were doing all that they could to benefit her career. She reminisces proudly about these roles and the positive affect they had on people's lives (a).

Sweet Hostage
1975

This is Linda Blair's crowning jewel as an actress. She plays the role of Doris Withers, a young rancher's daughter in New Mexico. She is kidnapped by an escapee from a mental institution in Massachusetts. Martin Sheen is the nut case on the loose. It is a challenging role. Doris is introduced to us shooting a rattlesnake and is upset with her mother for chopping it up. Doris wanted it as a trophy. She did keep the rattle from the snake for a good luck charm and to prove that she did indeed slay the reptile. Young Doris is known and liked by all when she drives into town. She is not endeared at home at the same level as she is in the small New Mexico town where she gets gas. She is the only child of two crusty middle-aged roughnecks of local origin. Bert Remsen plays her father masterfully. He is nearly paranoid about the possible sexual exploitations of his rough little girl who is built like a young woman and turning into one as well. Dad is working day-to-day and living paycheck to paycheck. He doesn't cut the figure of John Wayne perched upon a fine stallion as he gazes at the enormous expanse of his possessions. He has a few chickens and not much more. Her mother reminisces about her past and whiles about the great opportunities missed because she married Doris' father. It looks like the classic tale of opportunities missed because of choices made that weren't the ones that led to the path of rubies and riches.

Linda's father's truck blows a hose and breaks down on her way home from town. It is there where she is offered a ride home by Leonard Hatch (Martin Sheen). He escaped from an insane asylum in Massachusetts. The contrast in characters is captivating. He fancies himself as a liberating dreamer and seems well schooled in English literature and the fine arts. His English is impeccable. He insists on the same from his young companion. She is cocky, stocky and speaks like one of the hicks from the sticks. When Leonard observes her disabled pickup he inquires as to if she ran out of gas. Her response is most memorable. "I ain't that stupid." As the conversation continues, she admits to being kicked out of high school for punching a teacher. When you watch the spirit that she displays when she kicks the broken down truck, you don't doubt it for a minute.

It is an intriguing tale of two people who meet under the strangest of circumstances. She is the kidnapping victim. He is the heavy villain who robs a store and steals a truck. She is held captive in an abandoned cabin in a remote area of rural New Mexico. As their days together grow longer, they grow together. She is no longer held captive, but becomes his companion. In their time together, she is transformed from the tough little dropout into a young lady. As they share their time and space, he isn't as crazy as he appeared in the beginning.

It is refreshing to see a love story without all of the graphic sex that comes to the silver screen in the early 21st century.

Everyone from the shopkeepers to the sheriff to the boy with a crush on Blair and the parents all play their parts perfectly. You might think of them as the people in your neighborhood.

This movie was released on 10 October 1975 and was filmed in Taos, New Mexico. It is rugged terrain and it can be as beautiful as it is tough, just like the leading lady. Linda Blair is tops in this flick. She has to play the role of the country girl who is short on good grammar and long on country smarts and common sense. She also plays the role of a young woman in love for the first time. She plays the part of a kidnap victim and a refined young lassie that pens poetry for her man. She plays a lot of different characters in the same film and does so convincingly well. Linda also handles that pickup truck impressively for a kid who just got her license. Very few actors work their eyes as well as Linda Blair does in this fine performance. The transformation from Doris the Farmer's Daughter to Crystabelle the cultured young lady is remarkable. All of this is done by a sixteen-year old girl who would be just another high school sophomore if she were anyone other than Linda Blair.

Martin Sheen's portrayal of Leonard Hatch is one of the reasons for the richness of this production. He is graceful, yet masculine. He is forceful, yet gentle. Sheen was born Antonio Gerard Estevez in Dayton, Ohio in 1940. He is 19 years older than Blair. His children (Charlie Sheen, Emilio Estevez, Renee Estevez and Ramon Estevez) are recognized in the entertainment industry. Martin Sheen's other notable work on the set includes his role as President Josh Bartlett on television's *West Wing*. He played Vince Walker in *Gandhi*. Sheen has 213 television and film credits to his name to date (a). His early work in *The Incident* (1967) was most memorable. It was a black and white film and used a New York subway car as the set. It is one of the best black and white dramas filmed after 1960 that you'll ever see.

Originally, Linda Blair had expectations of being cast along side of then boyfriend, Rick Springfield. Blair admitted to falling madly in love with Sheen, but no real life love affair followed. In an interview in 2003, she stated that working with Martin Sheen in this film was "probably the biggest highlight of my life (c)". There was some talk of the two as a budding romantic couple, but in an interview with *Tiger Beat* magazine, Blair mentioned that they were usually the only two on the set, so they ultimately ended up eating together, as would only be natural. We are often found in the company of our workmates even after the 5 o'clock whistle blows.

There is a dance number that is performed by Blair and Sheen that will not have them spoken of in the same breath as Rogers and Astaire. Nor will their rhythmic number be remembered in the same vain as Abbott and Costello. Yet, it was powerfully effective as seen. It is the first time that the two of them (Withers and Hatch) reach out to each other and do something together that is not necessarily a life supporting activity. They touch. They twirl into one being for the duration of the song. She is elevated from captive to woman. He is no longer her keeper but her partner. They didn't have the perfect rhythm at the start of the dance, but it did finally come to them. They were stiff as they started to feel each other out, but as they became comfortable with each other, they relaxed and the rhythm from each of them began to flow. It was the first time in the movie that the cast and audience felt that our two stars lit up the night with a mutually trusted bliss. Dance is the tonic that invigorates the soul.

Only the Native American owner of the gas station owner, Harry Fox, comprehends Doris' feelings when she is finally freed and is about to be returned to the uncultured existence she knew before being abducted. He understands as she takes the snake's rattle and caresses it.

The vehicle that Leonard Hatch eventually keeps is the forgotten four wheel drive sport utility vehicle that emerged off the assembly line before its time. It was the International Harvester Scout II. The Scout was introduced in early 1961, just two years after its conception. It was originally designed and marketed to compete with the American Motors' Jeep. (Which was originally built by Willys.) The first Scouts were equipped with four-cylinder engine that turned out 93 horsepower. The earliest Scouts were the Scout 80s and they were produced from 1961 through mid 1965. The Scout outsold the more famous Jeep during the 1960s. Scouts were offered in both two-wheel and four-wheel drive packages. It was followed by the Scout 800, which offered a more robust 195 hp four-cylinder engine as well as a 232 cubic inch inline six-cylinder and a V8. In 1969 International offered a 304 cubic inch V8 power plant. The Scout II (as seen in Sweet Hostage) was introduced in 1971. They had fancier bucket seats and a more conventional windshield than the earliest version. The last International Harvester Scout (or Scout II) completed manufacturing 21 October 1980 (c). This uniquely styled sport utility vehicle was retired before its time.

Sweet Hostage was nominated for a Golden Globe as Best Motion Picture Made for Television. It is Linda Blair's favorite film (d).

Another noteworthy tidbit is the theme song (*Strangers on a Carousel*). It is beautiful. You will discover that most of the music in Linda Blair films is superior albeit dated. *Sweet Hostage* is surely one of Blair's best-kept acting secrets.

Victory at Entebbe
1976

The movies are a splendid spot to escape reality. It is o.k. if you are scared at the theater even if it isn't all right to display your fear at home. *The Exorcist* scared the devil out of **us.** History can be as frightening as any movie. History is especially horrifying because it keeps repeating itself. During the 1972 Munich Olympics, the Israeli Olympic team was slaughtered on sight by Muslim terrorists. Four summers later, an Air France plane was hijacked and flown to Uganda by terrorists from Germany that had sympathies with Palestinian terrorists. If you were around 25 years later, you might remember another aerial terrorist act. It is ingrained in our brain as 911. History repeated itself once more. We wonder what despicable acts the bloodthirsty Middle East terrorists will commit in the next 25 years.

Considering *Victory at Entebbe* was released less that six months after the fateful hijacking that inspired its creation, you have to be impressed with the movie. The script is based on recent history. The cast reads like a Who's Who in Hollywood. Anthony Hopkins (who later gained fame as the diabolical Hannibal Lecter) plays Israeli Prime Minister Yitzhak Rabin. Burt Lancaster plays Defense Minister Shimon Peres. He is steadfast in his objection to negotiating with terrorists.

Helen Hayes lends spunk and perspective to the character Etta Grossman-Wise. Without her, this movie would lack the life that keeps your interest during the lull of internment of the hostages. In reality, hostages probably spend most of their time in a dull lull awaiting someone else's next move. The 76 year-old (at the time) two-time Oscar winner (Best Actress in a Leading Role back in 1932 in *The Sin of Madelon Claudette*) was the tonic that kept *Victory at Entebbe* rolling. It is interesting that her other Oscar was for the Best Supporting Actress in *Airport 1970*. Isn't it ironic that Linda Blair would star in the sequel to this film

51

(*Airport 1975*) and the two of them would be paired up in another airplane drama?

The name Etta Grossman-Wise was fictitious. The real name of the victim was Dora Bloch. According to the account given by Henry Kyemba (who spent five years as the top cabinet minister in Idi Amin's Uganda) the plane was reported hijacked about 9 a.m. on June 28th 1976. His office was notified by General Idi Amin and Kyemba was told to dispatch a doctor that the Palestinians would approve. The Ugandan leader also specified a Nubian nurse for the crisis. The hostages were held in an old airport building that was being used as a warehouse. The plumbing facilities were antiquated and inadequate. Most of them huddled in fixed chairs in the embarkation hall, while others lied on piles of clothing. They were twelve- hour hostages before they were fed a meat stew with rice. Three elderly French women were taken from the warehouse to the hospital in order to maintain calm after one of them urinated at the side of the hall. An elderly French man was also taken to the Entebbe hospital with a heart problem. He was released and Amin proclaimed to the world that this old fellow had searched the world over for a remedy to his ailing heart and found the curing medicine within the beautiful borders of Uganda. These four individuals were released and turned over to the French embassy (a). On the evening of July 3rd, 106 of the 300 some passengers remained hostages as the others, who were not of Jewish dissent, were released.

The dilemma continued on July 2nd when Dora Bloch choked on a piece of meat, which became imbedded in her throat. Dora held dual citizenship with Great Britain and Israel and her son had accompanied her on this traveling excursion, as far as the warehouse where the hostages were kept (c). She was permitted to bring her cane and handbag with her to the hospital. Henry Kyemba, who was the minister in charge of the hospitals, health etc. met with Dora personally and thought that it would be best if the aged specimen of spunk be given a good bed and the comforts of safe plumbing for the night, and would be best served to be released in the morning. Kyemba didn't feel that it was Amin's desire to bring death to any of the hostages. However, Amin failed to have a back-up plan in case the original failed. Dora Bloch was ultimately forced out of her hospital bed by a couple of Amin's henchmen and dragged screaming down the hospital halls until she was whisked away to her certain death. This was done in full public view. By this time, the public had witnessed so many such abductions that it became a part of the everyday culture in Idi Amin's Uganda. Certainly, the witnesses were not happy about the abduction, but what could they do? If they called the police, they would be calling the same government that was hauling the poor old woman away. If they interfered, they would probably join her in a tragic death. Amin would later call Kyemba to inform him that Bloch was killed. Her body was dumped on the side of the road to Jinja. Government officials made an attempt to burn the corpse, but the old girl's white hair stayed put and she was identifiable. Freelance Uganda photographer Jimmy Parma took pictures of this abandoned mother. He was later found with bullet holes and knife wounds to his inquisitive body (d).

This movie did hold true to such minor details as the blue skirt worn by the hijacker's leader. The blankets and mattresses were only provided for the hostages after they had been in hostile hands and they were beginning to complain of back pain. There is little doubt that Amin was involved in the hijacking, as he saw it as an opportunity to humiliate the Israelis and thus boost his stock in the eyes of the region's Islamic leaders.

Kirk Douglas and Liz Taylor appear as the married couple that were the parents of Hannah Vinofsky (Linda Blair). They petition the reigning rulers of Israel to negotiate in order to save their daughter. It has been long-standing Israeli policy not to negotiate with terrorists. Mrs. Vinofsky agonizes over her decision to let Hannah wear the red ribbon that would make her look older. The chances of a child escaping the wrath of the terrorist are better than the chances of release of a young Jewish woman. The Vinofskys even go to government headquarters as part of group of sign carrying protesters.

Richard Dreyfus is the Lt. Colonel Yoni Netanyahu who spearheads the rescue at Entebbe. The smirking scholar from the film *American Graffiti* is the Prince of Pudge in this role. I don't know if he was asked to put on weight for this movie or if he was eating the fruits of success. He appeared much thinner in *Mr. Holland's Opus* (1995). Dreyfus played the role of future Israeli Prime Minister Benjamin Netanyahu's older brother. Ironically, he (Yoni) is the only Israeli casualty of the military unit during the raid. Dreyfus does a good job in this role. Dreyfus plays two other historical heavyweights on the silver screen. One of them is that of American Vice-President Dick Cheney in the movie *W.* I had to do a double take, because at first glance, Dreyfus was decked out as a dead ringer for the former VP in *W.* He is also the star that shined as Meyer Lansky in the 1999 HBO production of *Lansky.* Meyer Lansky is the Jewish man that was the banking brains of the Mafia during the days of Lucky Luciano. The successful raid that saved most of the hostages was ironically done the same day that the United States of America celebrated its bicentennial, July 4th 1976.

Cambridge Godfrey was originally slated to play the role of the unpredictable General Idi Amin Dada. He died on the set. Godfrey's replacement was Julius Harris. You will not appreciate the fine job that Harris did until you see The Last King of Scotland, which was released in 2006. (It was about the reign of terror that Idi Amin imposed on the people of Uganda.) The dreaded Amin was as gregarious as he was charming. I heard rumors of him using cadavers created by his bloodthirsty hands as fuel to generate Uganda's power plants. I do not know this for a fact, but I do know that Amin murdered hundreds of people and disposed of their bodies at the Owen Falls Dam near Jinja, Karuma Falls and Bujagali Falls. These places were used as dumping grounds in hopes that the crocodiles would eat the bodies and thus the evidence of the slaughter would disappear (e). There were more bodies than the crocodiles could eat and many of them bloated and were viewed by the local citizens. He publicly humiliated his allies and brutally eliminated his enemies.

A major salute goes to the set director, Charles Rutherford, who was challenged with a minimal time constraint. He was also put to task as to keeping things historically accurate. The entire film was a major undertaking, as it was written, cast, filmed and hit the screen within six months from the event. Associate producer, Albert Simon, production designer Edward Stephenson and production manager Phillips Wylly deserve thumbs up and a pat on the back for rolling this film out in timely fashion.

There was a lot of positive emotion that came out of this movie. Etta Grossman-Wise is the witty philosopher that is capable of derailing the eccentric hostage that is faced with a new dilemma. The pilot of the hijacked Air France plane showed enormous courage when he lined up with the Jewish hostages when he could have walked away with the freed Gentiles. His crew demonstrated equal courageous determination as they also lined up with the other victims. There was a lot of camaraderie demonstrated by the cast. Hannah Vinofsky oozes with kindness as she teeters on the brink of womanhood. Her transition from the child to woman (the teenage years) is brought to the forefront when her mother (played by Liz Taylor) agonizes over attire worn by Blair and how it makes her look like a woman. Hannah's generous spirit is uplifting. The politicians in Israel demonstrate more heart than we might have expected. It has always been the policy of the nation of Israel not to negotiate with terrorists. Defense Minister Shimon Peres is adamant about this and he noticeably agonizes over the loss of life of the hostages because he knows that their lives will not be spared if imprisoned terrorists are not turned loose to commit murder again.

It is interesting to note that there was an Israeli film on the same courageous rescue that came out in 1977. It was called *Mivtsa Yonatan*. The scenes are filmed twice in *Mivtsa Yonatan*. One was shot in Hebrew for the natives and connoisseurs of Israeli action flicks. The other was shot with the players speaking English, for those of us who enjoy Jewish cuisine but don't speak the language. The only review of *Mivtsa Yonatan* that I read was favorable, but claimed that the historical integrity of the movie was somewhat lacking. It was said to be an exciting, albeit dated movie.

History repeating itself is a common theme. The Holocaust is mentioned several times in the context of this film. It should never be forgotten. It is mentioned during the separation of the Jews from the Gentiles. The prisoners on the right at Auschwitz go to the gas chambers and the ones on the left are left to live. The hostages who go to the right are the Jews and they will continue to be hostages. In Victory at Entebbe, the ones on the left are free to leave and they left. During a candid conversation between the Air France pilot (Christian Marquand) and Hannah (Linda Blair) some serious reflective contemplation occurs. She poses questions that many Holocaust students frequently consider. "I was thinking. My father came from Poland and he was in one of the camps. I used to argue with him all of the time. How can you just walk into one of those camps, you know, without doing something? And he used to say to me, "You don't know. You'll never know. Thank God. It's funny, isn't it?"

I found it interesting that Linda Blair was able to work with both Mr. & Mrs. Richard Burton (Liz Taylor) during her ongoing film career. In this riveting rendition, Liz Taylor played the role of Linda's mother. In *The Exorcist II,* Richard Burton is the priest that Blair seduces. This is a strange twist of fate, even for Hollywood. Liz Taylor had an impressive film career. Liz and Linda were both successful child actresses. Blair came bursting into the limelight of stardom in *The Exorcist* at age of 14. Liz Taylor first gained great recognition for her role in *National*

Velvet at the age ten in 1944. Taylor had already been seen in *There's One Born Every Minute* (1942), *Lassie Come Home* (1943), and also in 1944 starred in *The White Cliffs of Dover* and *Jane Eyre*. Taylor started her career as an emotional bomb, filled with explosive energy and spent a great deal of her career as a sizzling bombshell, whose face was splashed on the covers of many magazines. In 1960 she was rightfully awarded the Oscar for The Best Actress in a Leading Role for her bit as Gloria Wandrous in *Butterfield 8*. She earned the Award again in 1967 as Martha in the classic *Who's Afraid of Virginia Wolf?* She won a BAFTA award as the Best British Actress for the same movie that year as well as a Golden Laurel Award. She won the Silver Berlin Bear Award at the Berlin International Film Festival as Best Actress for acting in *Hammersmith Is Out* in 1972. It was the same year that she was awarded the David di Donetello Award for Best Actress in a Foreign Film in *Zee and Co.* She was nominated for the same Best Actress in a Leading Role in *Suddenly Last Summer* (in which she did receive a Golden Globe Award for Best Motion Picture Actress), *Cat On a Hot Tin Roof* and *Raintree County* These nominations took place from 1957-59.In 1998 She has also proudly received The Life Achievement Award by the Screen Actors Guild.

She was one of the many to appear with Linda Blair on the silver screen that also appeared on the daytime soap opera *General Hospital*. Taylor played the role of Helena Cassidine during November of 1981(f.)

Taylor was born in London on 27 February 1932, but her parents were Americans. Her parents were art dealers from Linda Blair's hometown of St. Louis, Mo. At age seven, with the ominous clouds of war hovering over all of Europe, the girls of the Taylor troop headed back to America, while the patriarch tied up the loose ends of the art gallery business. In her breakthrough film, *National Velvet*, Liz starred alongside another movie legend, Mickey Rooney.

Another of Taylor's claims to fame is her frequent walk down the aisle of the wedding chapel. Her first husband was Conrad Hilton of the Hilton Hotel name. One of his relatives by marriage (Kimberly Beck) starred alongside Blair in *Roller Boogie*. As previously mentioned, Liz was twice wed to the great Richard Burton, who she met while filming "Cleopatra" in 1963. Between 1974 and 1976 she would divorce, re-marry and divorce Burton, whose description of Liz's physical features is dead on the mark to match Blair's (see *The Exorcist II*). Incidentally, both are five foot-two.

More than twenty-five years have passed since the *Victory at Entebbe*, and more than 60 since the burning of the Reichstag in Germany, we were faced with the dilemma of 911. Those responsible for the burning of the Reichstag were never apprehended with any certainty. The culprits of the dastardly deeds done to the USA at the Twin Towers and the Pentagon were never apprehended with any certainty either. It is great comfort to think of them as dead, but the gutless acts of the terrorist live on. Logic looses out in the contrast of our fears of the fanciful illusions portrayed in *The Exorcist*. Yet, when compared to Entebbe we seem to treat the acts of kidnapping and murder of innocents in the name of political righteousness as just another news event on another day. Which plot was more realistic? This was one movie that needed to be made as quickly as it was and it should be viewed not only for our appreciation of the art and the artists involved but for our own good. History isn't going to go away. Up to a point, we will keep making it.

Linda had some worthy competition in the awards department for her performance in 1976. Faye Dunaway won the Oscar for Best Actress in a Leading role for her outstanding effort in *Network* and Beatrice Straight received an Oscar for Best Supporting Actress in the same fine film. It was a competitive year, as she edged out Jodi Foster who was featured in *Taxi* that year. *Rocky* won the Oscar for Best Picture that year while Ford Motor Company appeared to be imitating Mercedes styling with their Granada model at that time.

The Exorcist II
The Heretic
1977

History repeats itself just like blockbuster movies. This was one with great expectations. The lovely Linda was nominated for a Saturn Award for the Best Actress in a Horror Movie. The sequel was released in June of 1977, when Blair would have been graduating from high school had she been most anything but an actress. There are few things that can satisfactorily compete with the first time; whether it is your first love, your first vacation or your first day away from home at college. After viewing the Pyramids, how can your look at a life size replica with the same awe? After seeing *The Exorcist*, how can you view its sequel with the same appreciation and captivity? Although this is a good movie, it can't stack up to the original. Maybe the reason is because it was not the first Exorcist.

It surely wasn't because the acting was sub par. Richard Burton co-stars as the priest and friend of Father Merrin in this epic. Father Merrin was the priest that gave his life in the original Exorcist. It becomes Father Phillip Lamont's (played by Richard Burton) personal mission to prove that Father Merrin was truly a dedicated priest and not a heretic. Richard Burton was a Shakespearean actor and uses his voice flawlessly. Linda Blair said, "The best part of *The Exorcist II* was working with Richard Burton." (a.) She is also quoted as saying that they got along beautifully. He often walked around quoting Shakespeare.

This wasn't the first time that Burton played a role in a religious related film. He played Marcellus Gallio in the 1953 mega movie *The Robe*. Burton was awarded the BAFTA as the best British Actor. In two 1967 movies; *The Spy Who Came In From the Cold* and *Who's Afraid of Virginia Wolf?* which he shared leading credits with his wife, Elizabeth Taylor. He won a Laurel Award for the Best Male Dramatic Actor in the same two movies that year. He also won a Laurel for Best Male Dramatic Performance in *Becket* in 1965. The man whose career spans five decades also received the Valladolid International Film Festival Award in 1964 for his role in "1984".

George Orwell's *1984* is much more conceivable than *The Exorcist II*. Burton did a fine job in a role that was most difficult to excel in. Richard Burton amassed more fame off the set than he did on it. His marriages to actress Elizabeth Taylor, as well as his drinking escapades brought us headlines for a long time. He will always be remembered as a master craftsman in the acting profession.

Louise Fletcher does a good job playing the shrink in this film. She is pleasant to the eye and fits the part well. Her concern for her patients comes across as genuine and her character adds some credence to the movie. She won an Oscar in 1976 as Best Actress in a Leading Role in *One Flew Over the Cuckoo's Nest*. She received a Saturn Award in 1984 as Best Actress in the production of *Brainstorm*.

James Earl Jones can be seen in this horror wannabe. His resume reads like a king's grocery list. He is credited with many voices in animation. He is best remembered by me for his role as writer Terrence "Terry" Mann in *Field of Dreams*. He is not only recognized by sight, but his rich, deep, clear and succinct voice makes him identifiable by sound. In this sequel he plays the part of a professor and the role of some tribal guru dressed up like a locust. When you think about the other roles of James Earl Jones, you get a feeling of how this movie goes.

Ned and Belinda Beatty show up in *The Exorcist II*. Can you have a movie between 1970 and 1985 that Ned isn't featured in? He was in the original *Deliverance*. In *The Exorcist II* Ned is the pilot that takes Father Lamont to the area of Africa that features the locust.

This lowly regarded sequel also featured Ted Nash, an aspiring young saxophone player. Ted can be seen playing his horn in the early part of the film. *The Lullaby of Broadway* is the music used for Linda's tap dancing selection in the rehearsal for a live presentation that shows up later in the film. Nash dubbed *The Exorcist II* as "The worst movie ever made... and was proud to be a part of it." He also confesses of his fruitless attempt to date the leading lady. You must love what he claims her response is when he asked her on a date. "Unfortunatly, I'm from Connecticut," same old line he says on his web page. (b) Young Ted also played with the Benny Goodman Band the final year of Benny's life. (b)

Believe it or not, this picture features one of the surviving holdovers from the classic film, *Casa Blanca*. Paul Henreid is featured as the Cardinal from the Catholic Church in *The Exorcist II*. He played Ilsa Lund's (Ingrid Bergman's) lover/husband Victor Laslo. His effort thirty-five years later didn't do as much for *The Exorcist*'s sequel as his labors did for *Casa Blanca*. Of course, he didn't have to deal with a six-foot locust in his bit with Bogey and Bergman. *The Exorcist II* features the late Dana Plato, who unsuccessfully auditioned for the role of Regan in the original *Exorcist*.

Linda Blair (the possessed one) attempts to seduce the priest. The other Linda Blair watches in shock. Blair has looked hotter and more seductive in later roles as Lonnie Stevens in *Fatal Bond* and as Sophie Stevens in *Bedroom Eyes II*, but she looks flawlessly youthful and sensual in this sequel. It seems that Linda has difficulty trying to be sexy in the seduction scene. It's strange that she would have a difficult time of this, as she obviously possesses all of the right parts in all of the right places and a face that has graced more than one dozen magazine covers. Perhaps she was trying too hard. It is coincidental that Burton describes his twice bride, Elizabeth Taylor, nearly identical to the blossoming Blair. About Liz he said, "...She is an extremely beautiful woman, lavishly endowed by nature, with a few flaws in the masterpiece. She has an insipid double chin, her legs are too short and she has a slight potbelly. She has a wonderful bosom, though. (c)" With the exception of the double chin, Linda Blair of eighteen fills the bill of Burrton's reference to Liz Taylor whom he had just divorced the second time the year before The Exorcist II was released. There is little doubt in my mind that he could have found her sexually attractive in this scene. Most men would warm up to her, but wouldn't boil over with excitement during Regan's attempt to seduce Father Lamont.

You will also see some weird scientific concoction (synchronizer) that plays a role here. It looks like some sort of lighting device that may well have earned an 8th grader an A in shop class.

If you start gathering the data for this film you'll see why it is hard to follow. You have a Catholic Priest, a psychiatrist, a girl possessed, a large Black professor/ locust. It features planes, buses and a black Checker Cab. There are filming locations in Utah, Arizona, Washington D.C. and Warner Brothers studios in Burbank, where Bugs Bunny has been known to be filmed.

The special effects aren't as convincing as they were in The Exorcist. Everything was done lavishly and to a tee, except one thing. That one thing was the giant locust. It looked like an art room project. If the locust were just used in a flash in one scene its image's lack of conviction could be forgiven. However, this larger than life, full colored bug keeps showing up like a telemarketer on your phone. It was unwelcome and just would not go away. Couldn't they have zoomed in a locust, magnified it and then superimposed it in the film? They did import several thousand specially bred British locusts for the film (d).

There are many things that contribute to this film's lack of success. The original script is what won over the award-winning cast, hooking them to the gig. That script was then rewritten five times before the rehearsals began (e). It was continually rewritten throughout the filming (e).

Despite a good filming crew and some decent special effects, in spite of fine acting performances, the plot is devilishly doomed. *The Exorcist II* was one of Blair's cinematic regrets.

In case you were wondering what was enormously popular at the theaters in 1977, *Star Wars* was the top gate getter. It was also the year that we returned the Panama Canal to the Panamanians. New York City endured a major electrical black out. The average annual income was $15,000 and the incomparable Elvis Presley died.

1977

After working a dozen years as a model and actress, an eighteen year-old girl decided to take a sabbatical from the lights, the camera and turn to her choice of action. Linda Blair was an accomplished equestrian at the age of eighteen and it would be the last year that she would be eligible to compete in the junior ranks. She stood to receive up to one million dollars for her part in *The Exorcist II- The Heretic* (a). She took the booty and put it into hoofs and a 33-foot Apollo camper. She was enjoying her life on the Connecticut farm. Her horse was there to be cared for. She also had three Jack Russell dogs that were champion hunters. Although she really loved acting and wanted to do more work, a year off should not have turned into the off year that it did.

In the article featured in People Magazine (July of 1977) all seems to be going well. She is dating aspiring Connecticut musician (keyboard player) Ted Hartlett. She had been romantically involved, (co-habituating) with Rick Springfield when she was 15 and he was 24. At this time, Rick was known as a headliner at the famous Whiskey A-Go-Go in Los Angeles. The aspiring actor broke into the top 40 scene with *Speak to the Sky* in 1972 on Capitol Records and wouldn't make the popular list with a hit again until signature hit *Jesse's Girl* nine years later. According to Blair, she and Springfield "Just grew out of each other (c)". According to Circus Magazine (Oct. 1976) Linda was also letting Deep Purple guitarist Tommy Bolin live in her house. She also dated bassist Glenn Hughes of Deep Purple prior to the July issue of *People Magazine.* (Deep Purple's signature song is *Smoke On the Water.*)

She explains her fixation with musicians thusly, "They are sensitive, and though their heads might be all messed up, they are more screwed on than other people" She was rumored to a thing with Jim Dandy, one of the members of the band Black Oak Arkansas (d). Throughout all of these affairs, she seemed to maintain a closeness to her mother. I found it interesting that they designed and made stage costumes for Southern Rock Bands Molly Hatchet and Lynyrd Skynyrd. Elinore Blair helped create some of the gowns that her daughter wore to various awards shows. Elinore said that nothing should stand in the way of love. Linda's connection with Lynyrd Skynyrd could be said to have caused bad luck. Some of the band members were killed in a plane accident in late 1977. In December of that she was arrested for possession of drugs with the intent to sell (e). She flew to Florida for the funerals of the band members who were killed in an airplane crash. An acquaintance suggested that Linda accompany her to a friend's house to see some dogs that she was selling. It was at that time the acquaintance convinced her to buy some cocaine. She continued to keep in touch with these individuals after she returned to Connecticut and to her dismay, discovered that her phone was tapped. There were about thirty other people involved in this shakedown whose phones were tapped. She was charged with buying the cocaine in Florida and selling it in her home state of Connecticut. Police found amphetamines in her purse and she was charged with conspiring to purchase and distribute cocaine and possession of amphetamines (f). The conspiracy charge was reduced and she ended up getting three years probation (g). Linda claimed that the dogs she was speaking about in the phone conversations were the canine puppies that she wanted to buy. The authorities thought otherwise. They claimed that "dog" was the code word for cocaine. Her legal counsel decided to plead guilty and she was made to do several anti-drug commercials and do a stint in a nine-month drug rehab program (g). As an added note, I have disc jockeyed in taverns for 25 years and never heard cocaine referred to as dog.

According to Michelle Lee, she and Blair did snort cocaine one night with the band at a party after a Lynyrd Skynyrd concert (h) during the fall of 1977. Glenn Hughes (bass player for the bands Deep Purple and Trapeze) claims that he and Blair lived together in Los Angeles and that one of the reasons for their break up was her cocaine problem. He also states in his autobiography that a few weeks after the break-up she was busted in the infamous Lynyrd Skynyrd drug deal. Rick Springfield also strongly infers that Blair smoked pot (i). To her credit, Linda did not need to return to the rehab center, as so many Hollywood celebrities tend to do. Her legal woes were mentioned on an October 1999 episode of *E! True Hollywood Story*. In the interview, she claimed that her cocaine arrest ruined her Hollywood career. There was a little more revealing irony arriving on film in 1979.

There is a feeling that all of the accusations that were made regarding Linda's involvement during this time, a few things are overlooked. She is a teenage girl with an enviable and (so far) successful career. So much is learned from failure. We gain knowledge from the struggle and rejection, but what kind of knowledge could this 18 year-old girl glean from her stunning successes? This is 2012 and one million dollars is still a lot of money. What would you do with a million bucks at the age of 18? There is also one other aspect that is overlooked by the critics and naysayers. Linda was close to the members of the Lynyrd Skynyrd band. It must have been a personal loss to her.

I don't know if her career was ruined by this drug accusation or not. It has been nearly impossible to achieve the success she aspired to in The Exorcist a second time. For an aspiring actress in her early teens the expectations were grand indeed. I don't know if anyone's encore performances could match the success of that film. The drug charges surely were detrimental to her career, but there were other factors that figured in. Most leading men are six-foot tall or taller and she quit growing at five-foot-two. How do you pair up a female that short with a man that tall on the screen? It was successfully accomplished with has as the leading lady in Fatal Bond, where she teamed up with Jerome Ehlers. She shined in that cinematic drama that has been a well-kept secret from Down Under. She was said to have an uncontrollable weight problem in the years after The Exorcist II (j). Although, I have never seen a picture of her where you could say that she was fat, there are some photos that depict her on the heavy side, but not fat. The media has been embracing the bleach-blonde-bobble headed girls with silicone breasts the size of Mexico located on a frame resembling a broomstick since the 1970s. She didn't fit the image of what Hollywood thought a woman should look like, and it may be that did her more harm than the embarrassing drug charges. Frankly, she looked (and looks like) someone who might live in your neighborhood. She appears like one of the girls that you might encounter at a rodeo. Her's is a common look accented by the penetrating brown eyes, the charming, yet disarming smile, and the short body that she has portrayed in an attractive fashion over the past forty some years. Even at the age of fifty, she is still turning heads. Another part that factors in the mix, is that with all of these attributes, she is perfect for almost any role as a supporting actress, and I'm sure that she has turned down a number of offers for such, going for the big fish. There is one commodity that Linda Blair has no matter her age, weight, and bra size or make up artist. She is a most accomplished actress whose work has stood the test of time.

Another item that factors into the mix of Blair's failure to capture the big box office hit is that she is seldom seen in a leading role as an adult with a high profile leading male co-star.

The closest that I can remember her coming to that blessing was when she auditioned for the role of Emmeline in the movie *The Blue Lagoon*. The role went to Brooke Shields. I feel that Linda could have done a superior job to the taller starlet. Blair always demonstrated a serious passion for the men that she was romantically cast with. She also was involved in talks to play the role of Iris in *Taxi Driver*, which was a role that went to Jodie Foster (1976). Had she been awarded that role and performed up to her capabilities, I feel that her career would have spring boarded to superstardom, and the starship would have yet to land.

It is strange that Linda hasn't taken off work for a full year since 1977.

Summer of Fear
aka
Stranger in Our House
1978

Summer of Fear is directed by one the movie industry's top thriller/suspense directors, Wes Craven. This is his first made for TV movie. Some of his more celebrated works include *The Hills Have Eyes* (1977), and *A Nightmare On Elm Street* (1984). He is also the brainchild behind the making of all of the "Scream" movies to date. He is very detail oriented and his fussiness is apparent in his work. All of the action and lines delivered in this film are purposeful. The action is real. You can feel the tension between the characters in *Summer of Fear*. You can also feel the love that the family has for each other and how it is undermined and in the end, how it is resurrected. This is more than just another brain twister. There is as much on screen excitement as there is intrigue. His direction seems to bring out the best and the most of the abilities of the properties crew, the filming crew and the acting crew. His research on the topics presented in *Summer of Fear*, also known as *Stranger in Our House*, is apparent and helps the viewer feel more a part of the movie. Everything seems so very authentic.

The prolific (Linda Blair) actress stars in another out of this world production in her only acting effort in 1979. She plays Rachel Bryant, a vibrant horse-riding woman in her late teens. She is blest with two brothers, no sisters and two loving parents. She is cursed by the untimely death of her mother's sister and her husband. It is thought that their maid is also killed in the automobile accident.

Her cousin, Julia Trent (Lee Purcell) moves in with the Bryants, as they are the only family that she has left. Things around the Bryant house slowly change once Julia moves in.

Rachel is dating the boy across the street. His name is Mike Gallagher, (played by Jeff McCracken) and he happens to be her riding instructor. Rachel's horse takes an immediate dislike to Julia and attacks her. It isn't long before Rachel's brother takes a liking to Julia. Rachel comes down with an unusual case of the hives the night of the big community dance. Mike is supposed to take Julia to the dance that Peter's band is performing at, and Peter is supposed to bring her home. Mike and Julia leave the dance early and their chemistry is blossoming, to put it mildly. Rachel and Julia share the same bedroom, so you can imagine what kind of stress this brings into the young women's lives.

Rachel's episode with the hives subsides sufficiently for her to participate in the horse riding competition. In this movie the type she participates in is called the trail competition. Sundance, her dear horse, does magnificently until the gate routine. It is here where the bronco goes bonkers. It is an emotionally powerful scene. Rachel is thrown from the horse and if you watch carefully, it appears that the animal rolls over on her on its way to a stop. (I wonder if Linda Blair is the soul that is rolled on by the horse or if a stunt double is used. I really don't know how this person avoided injury.) The poor horse breaks its leg. It is there where it is determined that the pride and joy of Rachel Bryant must be put to sleep.

Rachel introduces Julia to her best friend, Carolyn Baker, (Fran Drescher). Carolyn is a nurse at the local hospital and she takes a shine to Julia as well. Julia is also warming up to Mr. Bryant. She plays chess with him and is schooled well enough in the game to beat him more often than not. Rachel has lost her friend, her horse, and her beau to the charms of the newcomer. Her reaction is predictable, but she discovers a picture of herself in a bikini that is covered with markings that would indicate a type of voodoo or some other type of witchcraft.

She lives in a higher upper class neighborhood. Her father is a stockbroker and her mother is a freelance photographer. So it isn't surprising that one of her other neighbors from across the street is a professor, whose expertise is the occult. The jilted young Rachel approaches Professor Jarvis (MacDonald Carey).

Carey is a 46-year film veteran. In "Summer of Fear" he dons those ridiculous looking, oversized eyeglasses for his role as the professor. He is best remembered as Tom Horton from the TV soap opera Days of Our Lives. Born 15 March 1913 in Sioux City, Iowa, Carey began his acting career in 1942 as Jonathon Caldwell in "Take A Letter Darling.' He was featured in two movies that year, "Dr. Broadway" and "Wake Island". Perhaps his most memorable role was that of Fred Gaily in "Miracle on 34th Street." That film also starred the legendary Natalie Wood as the little girl who would help prove that Santa Claus was indeed real. MacDonald Carey was also a fixture on the television as well. He was featured in many other roles beside the one on Days of Our Lives. I'll give you an idea of how the early days of television was brought to us. He was featured on the Lux Video Theater from 1952-54. In 1950 he was seen on The Christophers and Your Show of Shows. From 1953-56 he starred on GE Theater and the metal bands of TV land even featured the University of Iowa alumni. The Kaiser Aluminum hour did so in 1957 after he left the Alcoa Hour. His acting added depth and intrigue to Summer of Fear. He passed away in 1994.

He gives her a few books on the subject. She pours into them and makes some interesting observations. For instance she finds out that the horse has the keenest sense of witch detection among animals. Was it any wonder that her horse began acting in a strange and violent manner when Julia arrived? Is this why the stranger insulted the horse? Maybe the marks made on Rachel's photo weren't just some doodles applied by a bored prospective art student? Perhaps they were an applied curse that would bring about the hives.

The rest of the Bryant family thinks that Rachel is just feeling jilted and frustrated by the cousin that lived in Massachusetts but spent extensive vacationing time in the Ozarks. They disregard her accusations and just want to go on with their lives, figuring that the young woman will get over the hurt and discomfort of the dilemma.

Carolyn gets Rachel into the hospital to visit Professor Jarvis after he is admitted with a sudden circulatory condition. It is there that he informs the quizzing Rachel that the one sure way to find out if someone is a witch is to photograph them. He claims that a witch can control many people and events, but they cannot appear in a photograph, as they have no control over what the camera lens sees, because the camera is an inanimate object. After Mrs. Bryant discovers her husband and Julia flirting by the refrigerator she sides in with her only daughter and agrees to photograph the stranger in their house.

Mrs. Bryant is called out of town on business before she has time to develop the film. Rachel realizes that it is on the route to the job that Julia has planned a perilous end to her dear mother's life. She commandeers her old beau to intercept the matriarch. Julia witnesses their abrupt road trip and follows the two of them. There is a whale of a high-speed chase that ensues involving three cars. Two of them are of car coinsurer's note.

Rachel's old boyfriend, Mike Gallagher, is seen driving an orange 1969 Dodge Charger R/T during this realistic chase scene. This era Dodge came with an available 440 cu. in. V8 engine and a Torqueflite automatic transmission. Both three and four speed manual transmissions were available. This is a similar car to the famous General Lee that was used on the Dukes of Hazard television show. On a side note, the props manager for the Dukes of Hazard owned one of these cars before he went to Hollywood and joined the Universal Studios. He is Dan Stoltenberg and I worked with him in 1970. They were one of the quickest hot rods off of the line in their time and could reach ridiculously high top end speeds as well.

The classic driven by the witch Julia is a 1962 Ford Thunderbird. They were seldom called Ford Thunderbirds, or Thunderbirds for that matter. Those of us who owned them affectionately referred to them as T-Birds. They were originally intended to be sporty and quick two-door coupes. The Ford Motor Company introduced them in an effort to compete in the marketplace with GM's Corvette. In 1958 they were redesigned and their theme was changed to a classy but sporty two-door personal luxury car. They came with a 352 cu. in. V8 engine, fueled by a four-barrel carburetor, automatic transmission and duel exhaust as standard equipment. You could option out a more powerful 390 cu. in. engine and some of the real street racing nuts would install a rear end from a Ford pick up truck to give it that extra oomph off of the line. The 1962 model came similarly equipped and also featured a tilt steering wheel and power windows as well. They were very heavy cars and they all came with posh, sporty bucket seats. I doubt if they were as fast off of the line as the Mopar that you see in Summer of Fear, but the first T-Bird I had sported a speedometer that went up to 140 mph and mine was known to reach that speed. I can't say that I enjoyed seeing them wrecked at the conclusion of the chase, but the show must go on.

The cars aren't the only hot items to enjoy in this (Linda's last made for network TV) movie. 1978 was a big year for big hair for women, and Blair's hair is as big as it gets. She surely has one of the thickest heads of hair in Hollywood. She fits her clothes in a subtly teasing fashion. It is western wear and it flatters a fine little figure that doesn't need much more flattery. Linda currently owns her own line of western wear for women. Fran Drescher (most known for her part as the Nanny on TV) appears as nurse Carolyn Baker in Summer of Fear. She sports short shorts here and rivals Catherine Bach for the Greatest Legs of All Time. Men's eyes will enjoy the Blair bottom jeans and Dresher in Daisy Dukes nearly as much as they will the story.

What a lot of people don't know is that Linda was hospitalized for health problems due to stress and bad food that year. She had an ulcerated intestine (b). The doctor told her that if she didn't change her eating habits and stress level she would die (c). The frightening thing about this diagnosis is that Blair looked healthy on film (except for her episode with the hives).

This made for TV film is one of Linda Blair's better efforts. It keeps you guessing. The only downfall to this twisted tale is that it moves slower than most movies of this genre. The Summer of Fear has a strange, unpredictable ending, which is not at all unusual for a Linda Blair movie.

Wild Horse Hank
1979

I really enjoyed watching this film. Linda Blair stars in her first role as something other than a victim. She played the part of a girl that was possessed by Satan in *The Exorcist*. She was the victim of the system in *Born Innocent*. She was a sick young lady in desperate need of a kidney transplant in *Airport 1975*. She fell prey to the Demon Rum in *Sara T. Diary of a Teenage Alcoholic*. She was a kidnap victim in *Sweet Hostage*. Once again, she went flame over heels with the devil in *Exorcist II, The Heretic*, playing the role of an older Ragan from *The Exorcist*. This movie provides a different genre for Linda and it is based on the novel *The Wild Horse Killers*.

In *Wild Horse Hank* she sheds the garb of the victim and dons the plaid flannels of the horseback superhero. The college co-ed (Hank played by Linda Blair) is home for the summer and discovers that one of the neighbors plans to round up a herd of wild mustangs and send them to market for 37 cents a pound. The feisty female must confront her father before she attempts to rescue the wild horses that are destined to doom. It isn't the usual Hollywood daddy-daughter confrontation. It is one of the classiest parenting lessons on film. It's about a father letting his daughter go and pursue her dream, even if it isn't exactly what he had in store for her. You might expect dramatic yelling and sermonizing. You might expect the rebellious young lass and the rugged old dad to go nose-to-nose, toe-to-toe. They do yell a little bit, but it's more out of excitement than it is out of anger. What you get is a father reasoning with his daughter. He implements one of life's best lessons in reasoning. He listens. She doesn't yell and scream and insult. She reasons. You and I like these two characters from the start. There is love, respect and concern for each other by each other and it makes the plot richer.

Al Waxman plays the role of Jay Connors, the nasty neighbor who is plotting to round up the herd of wild horses and haul them to market. Hank arrives at his place after she captures her bolting stallion. She finds it on his land. In her first face-to-face reference with him, she refers to him as a "ballooned bellied ape." Needless to say, this confrontation leads to fisticuffs. Fortunately, her father has pursued her and is able to rescue her from the drunken clenches of Jay Connors. He gets banged up a bit.

In order to rescue the herd for good, they must be placed on federal land. The Ran Tan Reservation is the nearest place and it is over 150 miles away. It would entail going through the Badlands desert, crossing a river and going over mountains. They would have to cross a pass that is the only way to get there. That pass cuts through an Interstate and even the most optimistic soul knows the outcome of a herd of horses and a convoy of traffic colliding together is one last death dance.

Hank is determined to take the herd there. Jay Connors is just as determined to stop her. She is a good-hearted soul. He is a drunken lush. She treats her herd and family with love and respect. He treats his property, wife and child as after thoughts.

Connors has a little brother, Charlie (Michael Wincott) that isn't like Pace. Charlie falls for the heroine. It puts some romance in the movie and this adds to the plot because it is more of a personal attraction than it is a sexual attraction. It gives more substance to the characters and plot. Blair looks right at home on a horse.

The character typecasts are very marked in Wild Horse Hank. The good guys are always the good guys and the bad guys are always nasty and mean. Jay Connors and his helpers may let up a little bit, but they never have a change of heart.

Before the movie ends, everyone is rooting for the rugged

lady and her quest to set the mustangs free. Many truck drivers; bartenders, ranchers and clerks do whatever they can to aid Hank and her cause.

This is a great tale with a happy ending. There are many things that this movie accomplishes besides revealing a great story. It demonstrates that women can do things that men can do. It was produced during the heyday of the women's movement. It did a nice job of bringing women's talents to the forefront without bashing men. It also reminded us of how well men and women can work together to bring about a good deed. There was a time or two when Charlie Connors came to the aid of Hank.

It ends with Hank Bradford and her dad and Charlie riding home in the Bradford pick up truck. It also the first time that we get to hear Linda Blair's patented giggle. It is a healthy laugh and it is as unmistakable a trademark as her head spin.

This is the eighteen year-old Blair's eleventh movie. It is her first to be filmed outside of the United States. It was filmed in Alberta, Canada and Nevada. Fatal Bond and Dead Sleep were filmed down under in Australia. Red Heat was filmed in Hungary and Austria. I wonder if this may have been Linda's favorite movie to do to date. She has a deep love of horses and this is apparent as you watch Wild Horse Hank. Although she is slightly short of brilliant in her role as Henrietta "Hank" Bradford, I cannot imagine anybody else playing the part and playing it as well.

Richard Crenna plays Hank's dad, Pace, and does a pretty good job. You can tell that he loves his daughter and their relationship is exposed early in the film. He is just like a good luck charm, as he seems to show up just at the right time in order to aid his daughter. If you could imagine what a 1970s rancher would look like and act like, it would be just like Richard Crenna's character, Pace Bradford.

Can you imagine anyone acting as mean and nasty as Al Waxman in the role of Jay Connors? He plays the consummate redneck of the pre-eighties era. He drinks to excess. He drinks before he provides for his family. His priorities are out of kilter. Teaching Hank a lesson is more important than feeding his family. Crenna played the role of Bruce Cutler in the made for television movie *Gotti*. He received a Gemini Award for Best Performance by an actor featured in a supporting role in 1997 for his role as Adams in the made for TV movie *Net Worth*. Waxman was born in Toronto, Canada in 1935 and also was awarded The Member of the Order of Canada for his services to the performing arts of Canada in 1996. He died 18 January 2001 during heart surgery.

We are introduced to Michael Wincott in this movie. Wincott is best known as Rochefort in *The Three Musketeers* and as Gary Soneji in *Along Came a Spider*.

Here, he is Charlie, the younger brother of the steel hearted Jay Connors. They are deliberately contrasting in appearance. Jay is rotund and Charlie is tall and thin. Jay is mean and vindictive and Charlie is easy going and good-hearted. He does a great job of not over-acting. He is calm and also provides one of the more comic parts of the show. You can tell that he is trying to impress Hank the evening that she is putting up for the night in an abandoned farmhouse. During the conversation, he leans up against a door and lights a cigarette. The door breaks open and Charlie, who is trying so hard to look cool, tumbles out the door and onto his back. Like Richard Crenna, Wincott is a native Canadian.

Richard Crenna was also seen in *Dr. Goldfarb, Won't You Please Come Home* and in *Rambo, First Blood*. He is a veteran of many movies and early television. He was seen in the early 1950s series *The Millionaire* and as Luke McCoy in the 1960s series, *The Real McCoys*. His lean, rugged appearance makes him a natural for parts in westerns and farm productions. Richard won an Emmy in 1985 for The Best Performance By An Actor in a Lead Role in a Limited Series or Special for his role as Richard Beck in the movie *The Rape of Richard Beck*. He passed away 17

January 2003 in Los Angeles.

You'll appreciate the scenery in this movie. The mountains in the background and the golden grasses that speckle the desert are seen on camera and come to us from the Dinosaur Province and Waterton Lakes National Parks in Alberta Canada.

This is family entertainment at its best. It epitomizes Marnie Pehrson's attitude and quote, "Faith Precedes the Miracle." Hank Bradford didn't know how she was going to rescue the mustangs, but she knew that if they were to be saved, she would have to do something. She sacrificed her time and talents to bring them to safety. She worked hard and took risks to get them to their destination. Some mini-miracles occur on the path to their salvation. Who could have envisioned the girl that played the possessed child in *The Exorcist* would star in such a Gospel based theme of a film like *Wild Horse Hank*? We begin to grasp the scope of the ability and talent of Linda Blair. Just as a side note, Linda once commented that she would have loved to play the role that Liz Taylor played in *National Velvet*.

Up until now (Oct. 2008)* it has been a difficult movie to get a hold of. It occasionally shows up on E-bay and is a bit pricey. I was unable to find it in any video stores. Can you imagine what would have happened if Disney had turned this gem out? I just can't see Lindsay Lohan mounting a horse. I think that if Brittany Spears played the part, she would be on and off of the horse as often as she is on and off of drugs.

And should I die before I finish this work, I think that I'll see John Wayne and Linda Blair riding together into a Utah sunset just prior to my introduction to St. Peter.

Roller Boogie
1979

In the Official Razzie Movie Guide, this movie is rated as one of "The Most Enjoyable Bad Movies Ever Made." It is most enjoyable and has been viewed no less than a dozen times in our home the past year. It has a fluid plot. If you like funky boogie music, this roller disco dolly has it in heaps and leaps. If you like mob movies, this one qualifies as one of the strangest. If you like gorgeous girls in leotards, this one pulsates in polyester. It is the quintessential villain verses victim film and is uniquely done on ball bearings. It had the tagline "Love On Wheels." The romance is typical, but it is this cheesy in real life for people of this age. The child verses parent misunderstanding plays into the plot. In this 1979 (the last film released in the 1970s/IMBd has its release day as 21 December 1979) flick, there are roller skates everywhere. One liners pop up like a room full of jack-in-the boxes. Guys with washboard bellies and girls with classy chassis roll on and off the stage at every turn.

Linda Blair plays the role of a well-to-do musical prodigy who is making the move from high school in L.A. to the Julliard School of Arts. She tires of the life of material excess and demanding practice and rehearsals and yearns to be the winner of, of all things, a roller boogie contest. She does all of her own stunts in Roller Boogie. In an interview with Rusty White (a), she says, "Everything that you can tell is me, is me. I could not, obviously do the flying camels or some of the moves like a figure skater...I never really skated back then. So they had professionals for the more difficult stuff in the movie." Despite training for six weeks, she took a tumble on the set and suffers bursitis in her hip as a result.

Playing across from Blair is the 18 year-old Jim Bray. He is the very polished sultan of skate, earning 275 roller skating trophies at the time of the making of Roller Boogie (b). The wiry red head is not the next coming of Elvis Presley, however. Bray landed the role as the result of some unusual circumstances. Canadian actor David Kennedy was originally slated for the role as Bobby James. Kennedy was also Blair's beau just before the movie was to be shot. He and Blair parted company and as a result it was felt that someone else would be needed for the part. Bray was to be Kennedy's stunt double for the film and ended up being the co-star (c). It is Jim Bray's only movie and I don't know if it is because he did not care for the experience or if he was hopelessly void of acting talent.

Roller Boogie borrows some ideas from some other classic American movies. In one scene Blair is on top of Bray on the beach. They are both wearing swimsuits. It is reminiscent of Burt Lancaster in "On the Waterfront". The Roller Boogie rendition lacks passion. If you were on the beach and someone of the opposite sex was on top of you and kissing you, wouldn't you be doing something with your hands? Bray appeared as if he didn't know whether to squeeze the tease or build a sand castle.

In the scene at the pool for the party of the ensemble another movie classic is borrowed. All of the formally attired guests end up in the pool, just like they did in *It's A Wonderful Life*.

Roller Boogie was rich with contemporary music. There is a soundtrack available for this film. It also offers a rock song "Good Girls" by Johnny Coolrock that should have been a big hit during the 1980s and possibly beyond that. The tune "Boogie Wonderland" performed by Earth, Wind and Fire is featured in this musical. It spent 12 weeks on the Top 40 charts, peaking at #6. (2) It is the consummate disco-boogie song. It is a great dance number. The phenomenal rock diva, Cher, sings the opening track in this film, but is somehow omitted from the rest of the movie. She would have, could have very easily been part of the cast in this cinematic endeavor. Mavis Vegas Davis sings *All For One, One For All* and *Evil Man* on the soundtrack. Ron Green chimes in with *We Got the Power* as well as *Takin' My Life in My Own Hands*. Cheeks belts out the tune *Top Jammer* and accompanies Bob Esty in *Electronix* a.k.a. *Roller Dancing*. Michelle Alllis delves into *Love Fire;* a duet with Esty   Bob Esty is responsible for the rest of this musical mother lode. Cher and the band Earth, Wind and Fire are the only musical contributors from this movie that show up in the Billboard Top 40 book with any other significant accomplishments.

The choreography in *Roller Boogie* never gets the credit that it so richly deserves. It took 52 takes to get the song and dance number *Good Morning* in *Singing in the Rain* right (e). If you look at the dance in Roller Boogie you must wonder how many takes on skates it took to achieve that beautiful blend of fancy, fun and function that this movie does deliver. The great David Winters deserves much of the credit for this wonderment of waltz on wheels that keeps the movie rolling. Ry Hay also deserves kudos as the skate coordinator. Jim Bray compensates for his acting inexperience with his outstanding skating ability.

The production also features another eye-catching gem on wheels. It is a 1969 Excalibur. There were 44 of these sleek retro rods built in 1969. I saw one in an ad at Camelot Classic Cars in Milwaukee.(f) Linda Blair and Kimberly Beck looked classy on wheels in this Hollywood reel as well. There is also a car wax with the same name and there is a picture of the Excalibur on the can. My car caressing brother swears by this stuff.

One other technological advance is showcased in this dandy disco ditty. You'll notice the car phone in the Excalibur. It has a cord and only the elite of our society would have such fancy gadgetry. Inline skates were a thing of the future in '79 and polyester was the rage of the fashion rack. It was the constant companion of disco music. Like a good couple, they seemed to have come in and gone out together. Although Terry Barkley and Bobby James didn't arrive in this film together, they did share the final scene.

There are many things that are enjoyable in *Roller Boogie*. The contrasting costumes are the first things that come to mind. Terry Barkley is attired in the latest fashion of the highest quality. The lacey top that she sports in the roller boogie contest is breathtaking. It accentuates her highlights. It is lavishly extravagant, yet simply white. It gives her the appearance of being graceful and fluid. The skates give her another three inches in height. Her smile would melt the ice had they been filming on skates of ice instead of the rolling variety. The dress that is worn by Blair when she is playing the flute early in the movie is cut nice and of high quality. Terry Barkley's friend wears the finest and refers to her new Gucci carrying bag for her skates. Bobby James, on the other hand, wears off the rack pants and a T-shirt. His friends wear ordinary colored shorts and T-shirts. Terry is driving an Excalibur and has two Rolls Royces in the garage. Bobby is riding in his friend's pick up truck. Bobby's hair is nicely feathered, as was the style in 1979. Terry's hair is seen in some very fancy braids when she emerges from her green automobile. Bobby's buddy works as a fruit vendor and Terry's dad is a high priced attorney. The contrast makes the movie more interesting.

The music reaches both spheres of the musical world. There is the disco-funk that is featured in the roller rink. Meanwhile, back at the Barkley estate, you are indulged in the classics. Terry is the accomplished young flutist. The credits bring to life the efforts of the producer to make this flick authentic. You'll even find that Potch Halligan is listed in the credits as the flute instructor.

While Terry lives in a pillared house with a pool, Bobby James lives in an upstairs apartment. His phone is the pay phone on the corner and the greatest contrast of social class is greatly displayed in the scene where Terry calls him from her car phone. She seems to be making an attempt to live like the roller culture as she runs away from home and spends the night in her car in the parking lot across the street from Bobby's apartment. You'll notice a poster of the Bee Gees on the right hand side of Terry's bedroom in the scene where she changes her attire from fancy flutist to Roller Boogie Diva. Bobby James may have had a poster like it in his room. If you were a child of the '70s you may have had one just like it hiding the hole in your wall as a teenager.

The final whammy of contrasting cultures is what happens to two of the cast after this movie was released. Kimberly Beck was married to William Barron Hilton of the Hilton Hotel Hiltons (g) and Jimmy Bray gets to do a few interviews about roller-skating. Beck plays the unapproachable sizzling soul sister of Terry Barkley. She plays the role of Trisha Jarvis in the 1984 *Friday the 13th: The Final Chapter*. She was in the cast of *General Hospital* in 1975 as Samantha Livingston.

This may have been the movie in which Blair was seeking to evolve from child prodigy to screen queen. Her parents don't understand her in the movie. As the film begins, her current boyfriend is a hormonally challenged young buck and she is preparing for the final stages of summer vacation. She and her father team up to do a string/flute ensemble and then it should be off to Julliard. She plays the role of most teenagers who tire of training in the pursuit of their dreams and is distracted by the new challenge of a roller boogie disco contest. It is there she meets someone more interesting than her old pre-arranged flame. It is Bobby James (played by acting rookie Jim Bray). He is the regal rogue of the roller rink. Some seedy characters attempt to take over the roller rink and their leader has retained Terry

Barkley's (Linda Blair's) father as his attorney. There is plenty of action and good-hearted musical comedy. Linda Blair works her hips in a telegraphic matter in this fun filled film as she struts her way back to the mansion after the first pool scene. Blair also works her eyes like a pro in Roller Boogie and the romance is a lot better than some of the critics give it credit for. It's good, clean fun and one of those movies that will never be enshrined as a classic, but if you own it, you'll watch it many times with or without your children.

Linda Blair is an aristocratic urbanite in Roller Boogie. She played the country girl in Wild Horse Hank. I think that the reason she was so convincing in both roles is due to her love of animals and riding experience and her current environment in Hollywood. I think that her heart was with the horses and her curiosity was with the Hollywood scene. Hollywood was a lot to handle for the 20 year-old. Would it affect her in the same way that it did Brittany Spears, Lindsay Lohan, Maureen McCormick and so many others?

There is a scene where Terry (Linda Blair) and her mother are having a mother-daughter moment on the family staircase. Beverly Garland does put in a fine performance as Lillian Barkley (Terry's mother). There are two things during this dialogue that I found striking. The first is Mrs. Barkley's quest for the correct drug for the current situation that she has found herself in. I counted five prescription drugs that she pulled from her purse. I don't know if this was done to intentionally bring the problem of the flood of prescribed drugs into our lives to the forefront or if it was just done to poke a little comedy at us during what would be a tense moment. The second is when Ma Barkley told Terry that she could accomplish whatever she put her mind to. This statement exceeds the acting realms of Roller Boogie. Linda Blair has proven that she could indeed do anything that she put her mind to.

As a side note, Beverly Garland's daughter, Carrington, makes an unaccredited appearance in this movie.

Linda Blair was interviewed at an after-concert party for the band Cheap Trick in Japan. She mentioned that she was filming Roller Boogie and that she hoped that it did well at the box office. She said that the only payment she would receive from the movie was a percentage of the ticket sales. She may have been dating band member Robin Zander at this time (h). It was a most revealing bit of You-Tube film. Her youthful vibrancy was sincere as she spoke of being an entertainer. The young lady had been in front of a camera as a professional for 14 years and she still has that look in her eyes that tell you, "I just can't believe that I am a movie star!" Even doing an impromptu interview Linda masters the mood with her eyes. She seemed to be enjoying the party and do I dare say behaving herself?

Cheap Trick was a phenomenal rock and roll band from 1972 through the early 1990s. Their only #1 song was *The Flame* which anchored the top of the charts for 2 of the fourteen weeks that it spent there. Their first charted hit was *I Want You to Want Me* from the spring of 1979. It was their only million selling single. The lad linked to Linda was Robin Zander, who was the vocalist. Rick Nielsen played guitar and Tom Peterson was featured on bass while Brad "Bun E" Carlos sat in on drums. I was fortunate to see Cheap Trick twice in the mid '70s. The first time was at Smitty's, a two-lane bowling alley in Waunakee, Wisconsin. (At the time of this writing it has been updated and renovated and is dubbed "The Attic Angel".) If I recollect correctly they played in the basement. The other time was at a swankier spot in Portage, Wisconsin called "The Godfather's II." They put on a real show in Portage, with Nielsen removing one of the ceiling tiles and spinning it on the top of the neck of his guitar as he played. I can still hear the owner of the bar yelling, "You guys will never play here again!" He was right as rain. Cheap Trick signed a lucrative contract with Epic Records and was playing in Japan before you could say, "Who was that man in the baseball cap with the guitar?" I played music at an Elk's Club Party around 2002 in Portage and many of the patrons vividly recalled Cheap Trick and their one night stand at the Godfather's II.

Did you know Elvis Presley used to rent out the local skating rink in Memphis when he had time off and did some skating? He passed away in 1977, two years before this film was released. He, too, experienced phenomenal success at an early age.

Although *Roller Boogie* didn't finish in the top ten for the Academy Awards, it must be said that the winner for Best Picture (*Kramer vs. Kramer*) may have been the better movie. Sally Field won Best Actress that year for her role as Norma Rae in the movie entitled the same.

This was 1979. It was the year that the Shah was chased out of Iran and found refuge in Egypt. Billy Joel's *Just the Way You Are"* grabs a Grammy and *Roots* was seen on everyone's TV screen. *Deer Hunter* won an Academy Award. Uganda's reigning government official, Idi Amin (see *Victory at Entebbe*) was overthrown. Two Iowan girls' high school basketball teams play four scoreless quarters. A 4-2 victory was the final outcome in the 4ht overtime period. Was it possible that they were playing on roller skates?

Ruckus
1982

Dirk Benidict plays Kyle Hanson in *Ruckus*. The movie begins as Hanson emerges from a flatbed truck reminiscent of Tom Joad returning home from prison in *The Grapes of Wrath*. Kyle doesn't speak intelligibly in the opening scenes. The set seems to be somewhere in the South and the cast seems to be a bunch of stereotypical Southern rednecks. Kyle is a returning member of Special Forces from the Viet Nam War. Jenny Bellows (Linda Blair) is the woman in waiting for her husband who has been missing in action for some time. Her father-in-law, Sam Bellows, (played by Ben Johnson) notices the uniform that Hanson is wearing and asks if Kyle was in the same unit as his son and if he has seen him. From there the movie takes off in many directions.

Dirk Benidict is an interesting choice to star alongside Blair in 1982. He played Officer Gil Foley in *Chopper One* in 1974, so he may have had some experience with the type of warfare waged in the Viet Nam Conflict. He also starred as Lt. Starbuck on *Battlestar Galactica* from 1978 to 1980. The veteran actor was featured as Templeton "Faceman" Peck on the TV series that introduced us to Mr. T. (*The A Team*) from 1983-'87. His was a familiar face on the screens of our lives, although the name seldom is brought to mind. He really loved his role in *The A Team*, as it lent his pent up silliness outside of the box. He stated that Mr. T and Dwight Schultz made the job of acting on the set for *The A Team* an enjoyable experience and that the two actors were funny behind the scenes, adding laughter to the task of acting.

In *Ruckus* he and Linda share another interesting common thread. Linda has authored the fine book *Going Vegan*. The true Vegan eats nothing that comes from animals and wears no clothing made from animals. Rattlesnake stew and possum pie don't whet my appetite, but spaghetti without meatballs or sausage would haunt me longer than a Blair horror movie. Benidict subscribes to the Macrobiotic diet. This diet encourages the digesting of whole grains, vegetables, and legumes and beans. It also permits gently processed foods, such as fish. It frowns on some vegetables, such as peppers and tomatoes. Macrobiotics isn't just a diet, but like Veganism, it is a way of life. Benidict refused medical treatment for his prostate cancer in 1974. Instead, he chose the Macrobiotic diet, fasting and exercise and has a clean bill of health to this date, 2009. Like Linda, he appeared on a cover of *People Magazine*. Dirk was born in Montana in 1945 and has also authored *Confessions of a Kamikaze Cowboy* and *And Then We Went Fishing*.

In *Ruckus* Hanson is questioned by some taunting locals and throws one of them into the river from a bridge. He is then pursued by a posse and shoots one the pursuers in the leg with a homemade arrow.

Hanson meets Jenny Bellows as he runs and hides from the posse and a sweet romance evolves, but not until she is given the news about her husband's whereabouts. What sounds like a romantic drama resembles a futile attempt of the director to make a movie based on the television series "The Dukes of Hazard" which was very popular at the time that Ruckus was out. It is laced with the banjo picking, truck crashing, madcap chases and good guys that don't shoot guns but shoot arrows, just like the Dukes. It even makes a lame attempt to cast Blair in a role similar to Catherine Bach as the hot lady in the boy's show. Bach's greatest visual assets were her legs and Blair limbs weren't her strongest suit. (You may be thinking that it would be difficult to make a movie displaying Linda Blair's most impressive screen assets.) To be blunt, Jenny Bellows did use her eyes well, but they could have been utilized more. Jenny even drove a Jeep, as did Daisy Duke.

There is plenty of action in *Ruckus*. You'll see a number of fights and crashes. Vehicles get blown up. People get locked up. A ferry even gets blown to itty-bitty bits.

Despite the difficulty caused by attempting to make a romantic action drama into a slapstick comedy, the players faired better than you might think. Dirk Benedict did all that could be done in for the part that he was awarded. Ben Johnson played the role of Jenny's father-in-law very well. This is one of the two movies that Blair gets to play the role of a mother in. (The other was the made for T.V. movie *Monster Makers*.) Linda Blair never married and never had children. She indicated in an interview that it would be difficult for her children because of her role in The Exorcist. In another interview, she claims that the reason is that the world is dealing with overpopulation. As mothers go, I think that she would have been a good one, as she is compassionate, good hearted, has a unique sense of humor and puts her heart and soul into whatever is the task at hand.

Linda snuck a reference to her classic *The Exorcist* in *Ruckus*. As she gives herself the quick once over in front of the mirror, she quips, "You devil you", feeling satisfied with her appearance, and who wouldn't be? The film has an unexpectedly nice conclusion.

One of the best-kept secrets in Hollywood for six decades had to be the acting ability of Richard Farnsworth, who played the role of Sheriff Jethroe Pough. Farnsworth made his first appearance on the silver screen as a stuntman in the 1939 film *A Day At the Races*. He worked mostly as a stuntman in movies like *This is the Army* and *The Mighty Joe Young*. He worked with John Wayne as a stuntman in *Fort Apache* and *Angel and the Badman*. His countenance lends some credence to the movie, as there isn't much else in Ruckus that borders on reality. He is deliberate in his speech and practical in his thinking. Farnsworth would have made a great sidekick for some of Hollywood's giant good guys. He didn't cut the image of a leading male, but his talent helped keep this film from sinking.

Bobby Hughes appears in *Ruckus* as Jenny Bellows' young son, who is about to embark on a career in kindergarten. He is one the businesses' cutest kids. He plays a small role in another film with Linda Blair, *Up Your Alley.*

Again, the music in this Blair movie was very good. *The Dukes of Hazard* had Waylon Jennings. *Ruckus* had his sidekick, Willie Nelson. There is a heartfelt country tune titled *One Day At A Time* featured in *Ruckus* that is pertinent to the lead character. Kyle Hanson is a survivor who liked living in the jungle and could have been the inspiration to the Hank Williams Jr. song *Country Boy Can Survive.*

Ruckus was made in 1981 when Linda would have been 22 years old. She wanted to lose her image as the teenage girl and play a role as a blossoming woman. One of the reviews that I read compared this film to *Rambo.* Maybe the enemy was as bad at shooting as the hunters in Ruckus, but other than that, there is little similarity. Linda was injured when one of the motorcycles that she was riding took a spill. This was one of the priciest movies of Linda Blair to find on E-Bay. I think that the reason for it is that most people threw the cassette away.

Rumor had it that she was putting on weight due to a hormonal malfunction that was successfully treated with medicine. (a) Linda has never commented on this. She appears to be heavier in this movie than she did in *Roller Boogie* from two years past, but the view was great from where I was sitting.

The Viet Nam War was recent history when *Ruckus* was shot. I have shared the same employer with a disabled veteran of that war for 35 years. It was a topic as hot as some of the pictures in a Linda Blair photo shoot. Voices were raised and tempers flared over the war. Many good men gave up years of their lives for the cause of ending the conflict. Many good men gave up their lives. My respect and gratitude go out to these groups as well as the disabled ones who have been getting on with life the best they can.

When I was 9 years old my father and I had a discussion about the war. I told him we had to fight it because if the Communists were victorious in Viet Nam they would take Korea next, and then Japan and then Hawaii and the continental United States would be their final prize. His immediate and serious response was that if we were truly concerned about the domino affect of conquered Communist states, we would be waging war with Cuba. This conversation took place in 1964 and my dad served in the US Army Corp of Engineers in thee European Theatre during the mid 1940s. We didn't win the war in Viet Nam and this is 2012 and the Vietnamese Communists have yet to invade us.

This seems to be Blair's first attempt to be cast as something other than a teenager or child. Liz Taylor was successful in the transition from childhood star to adult actress, but a couple of sawed-off super starlets faded into the dark in their similar attempts. We didn't see too much of Shirley Temple after she passed puberty and Judy Garland seemed to spend an eternity with Mickey Rooney on film after *The Wizard of Oz*. Although Garland did have a successful singing career and success on Broadway. Natalie Wood is one of the only other childhood superstars of film to graduate successfully into a grown up in Hollywood films. Despite a good showing in *Roller Boogie*, Linda needed a vehicle to get her recognition as an adult star. She took her father's advice and took the work that was offered her. Mr. Blair said that every job would offer its opportunity (b). It was interesting the Robert Redford asked for Linda to star with him in *Ordinary People* in 1980 (It was filmed in 1979 and released in 1980.) (c). Mary Tyler More was awarded the job and the movie won four Oscars.

The 1980 Academy Award for Best Motion Picture went to

Ordinary People. Former Screen Actor's Guild President, Ronald Reagan, was elected as the President of the United States of America. It was also the first year that the Kansas City Royals appeared in a World Series, losing to the Philadelphia Phillies. It was the first trip to the big dance for the Phillies since they were dubbed "The Whiz Kids" in 1950. The Pittsburgh Steelers won in their 4th Super Bowl appearance in 6 years, soundly drumming the Los Angeles Rams 39-19 in front of over 103,000 fans. It was the last time that the storied Rams of LA would stroll to the Super Bowl.

Hell Night
1981

This was the second movie that featured Linda Blair in 1981. It is obvious that she is taking on more serious acting roles. She is returning to the genre that catapulted the little leading lady into the sky as a bright and shining star seven years ago, horror. At age 22 she was a veteran of the movie business and Hollywood scene.

The movie was filmed in Hollywood and the Garth Mansion in Redlands, California. I found it every bit as frightening as *The Exorcist.* Linda plays the role of Marti Gaines, a young collegiate who is aspiring to gain entrance into a sorority. She and Denise Dunsmore, played by the well-proportioned Suki Goodman, must stay Halloween night in the old Garth Mansion. In order to gain admittance into Alpha Sigma Rho fraternity, Jeff Reed and super surfer Seth are to join in the challenge. The supposed haunted mansion has a bizarre history. Patriarch Garth was unable to have any normal children and all but one of them was murdered by the father. It is said that the surviving family member still lives there, but no one is sure. To add a strange twist to the spookiness of the overnight experience, a couple of Alpha Sigma Rhos and their young female friend combine to sabotage the mansion. As the plot unfolds, we're left with the cast wondering what is real and what is prank.

Everyone is attired in Halloween holiday costume. This is an interesting marketing tool for the film and I'm sure that it wasn't considered at the time. As long as everyone is attired in a costume, the movie could actually take place during any era. The clothing wouldn't be dated. Marti is in a medieval gown. Her roommate assignment for the spooky rendezvous is Jeff Reed

(Peter Barton) and he is dressed in similar suit. Surfer Seth (Vincent Van Patten) looks like maybe he was one of Zorro's accomplices, and his roommate, Denise is dressed like a saloon girl from an old western movie. She has the garter and nylons and the revealing bra and looks the part of the tramp that she is. A little humor is interjected as she continually refers to Seth as Wes.

There is a budding romance between Marti and Jeff, but nothing that would warrant the R rating that is stamped on the movie. The conversations are believable and it is interesting that Marti was a mechanic in her father's garage before going onto college. Jeff is from a wealthy family and admits it in a humble sort of way. You will like both of these characters. You will hope that they will both emerge from Garth Mansion with their level heads on their shoulders. You will have to see the movie to find out if they do.

You may not feel the same way about the two guys from Alpha Sigma Rho. Scott and Peter go to great lengths to scare the nightlights out of the prospective personnel. They have booby trapped the mansion with enough special effects to earn *Hell Night* the award for The Best Special Effects in the 1981 Catalonian Film Festival.

There is also a scene at the local police station that reeks of reality. Seth is able to escape the mansion and runs back into town in those hideous boots for help. Everyone is in the festive Halloween mood and ignores him. He heads to the police station and they put him off as a hoax as well. It reminds me of any time that I have called the police to inform them of a dangerous situation. Just like in real life, in the reel life the city's finest fail to respond and threaten to lock up Seth.

Most horror movies are excessively graphic. This one is successful in scaring you to the edge of your seat without extended body piercing knives, chainsaws or fangs. It will keep you guessing. You will be surprised who the victims will be.

You'll recognize Vincent Van Patten who plays Seth in this

film. Seth is the guy who wears the loud boxer shorts in most of his scenes. He was also featured in *Roller Boogie*, playing the part of Gordo. If you are a *Baywatch* fan, you'll recognize him as Dr. Morella. He is the son of Eight Is Enough's patriarch, Dick Van Patten.

Another *Baywatch* connection is featured in *Hell Night*. Peter Barton (Jeff Reed in *Hell Night*) was cast as Damon Luke in a 1999 episode of *Baywatch*. Prospective employers would put Barton in the injury prone pile of applicants that would get secondary attention. He was badly burned in a stunt in *The Powers of Matthew Star* and the seriousness of the burns delayed filming for about a year. You'll also notice that he limps in *Hell Night* after he is thrown down the stairs. I wonder if Marti's sweet question, "Are you all right?" was scripted or sincere ad lib. His limp during the remainder of the horror flick is real and it was due to his forced dissension down those stairs. Barton considered hanging up his career as an actor until Linda Blair convinced him to do *Hell Night*. They made a lovely couple in the film.

Jenny Nueman plays May West in this film. She is part of the prank patrol, and it was thoughtful of the writers to include the name, although not of the same spelling, of the great departed Hollywood legend, Mae West.

If you're looking for a new Halloween movie at your house that you haven't seen before, this should be the one!

Just for fun in '81: The winner for Best Movie was *Chariots of Fire*. *On Golden Pond* featured the winners for Best Actor (Henry Fonda) and Best Actress (Katherine Hepburn) for the year.

Chained Heat
1983

Of all of the movies in all of the theaters in all of the cities and towns that a Linda Blair film could be seen, this is one of the few that shouldn't. Linda even confessed that had she known that this movie was going to be such a foul fix of film; she may have balked at the beckoning to be cast in it. She was dating Rick James shortly before this film was being made and I'll bet that she didn't know that the relationship would turn out to be as misleading and disappointing as *Chained Heat.*

She played the role of Carol Henderson, a late teen who is doing 18 months for vehicular manslaughter. It is her first trip to a state penitentiary and it would surely be an enlightening experience. It would be her only movie between 1981 and 1984. Some people say that she was blacklisted in Tinseltown for her alleged involvement in the drug deal involving the funeral of the late rock group Lynyrd Skynyrd. After seeing this bomb, I think a little time off wouldn't have hurt her. This film has everything that a perverted 14 year-old boy could hope for. There is some nudity. There is some lesbianism, although more suggestive than graphic. There are more boobs in this film than we have had in the White House in the last two centuries. Somewhere between them lies a plot, maybe.

As you review the cast of *Chained Heat*, you'll notice one common thread. Linda Blair, who plays Carol Henderson, recently graced the cover of *Oui Magazine*. Stella Stevens, who plays the role of the hardhearted Captain Taylor, was a centerfold for *Playboy*. Greta Blackburn plays Lulu and was a *Victoria's Secret* model. Louisa Moritz played a whore in the 1981 movie *True Confessions*. Sybil Danning played the prostitute in the 1972 classic, *Bluebeard* that also starred the Heretic sidekick, Richard Burton. The cast doesn't look like the crew for a *Leave It To Beaver* sequel.

Blair did the photo shoot for *Oui Magazine* for their October 1982 edition. She would have been 23 at the time. One of the contributing reasons for this was her hope that she would be seen as a serious adult actress instead of the victimized teenage cutie with an attitude. Although Linda confesses that the shoot didn't do all that much to improve her career, (Hollywood was using older actresses at the time.) she has no problem with the pictures (a). She appears on the cover of the magazine, lying on the beach, donning sunglasses, topless with her arms folded over her chest. It is a shame that the photographer covered her captivating brown eyes as I have always felt that they were two of her greatest assets through the years. It was disappointing that the interview/article never appears on the internet, as it is said to be one of her best, and she gives as good an interview as anyone. After reading the interview, I found this to be true.

I wasn't the only one to find the photo shoot of Linda Blair in *Oui Magazine*. Musical Guru Rick James found the article interesting as well as her opinion that he was the sexiest man on planet Earth at the time. He sent her some roses and they arranged a meeting in New York. Mark Fleishman asked if he could get a photograph of them and they promptly removed their tops for a quick click of the camera and the picture seemed to show up everywhere. They went sailing in the (Caribbean) islands for about two weeks. Rick said that she was one of the sweetest ladies that he had ever known and that they saw each other off and on remaining good friends (f). He even took her to his recording studio and showed her how to compose music on the keyboard. It was here that his tune *Cold Blooded* was composed. It seemed that Linda had a keen sense of expanding her horizons at this stage of her life. Although her affair with James was highly publicized at the time, I don't feel that it was an exclusive relationship to either of them. Yet, I still wonder if

Blair ever put lyrics to a tune.

There were two rape scenes in *Chained Heat* that disturbed me.

Poor John Vernon has to play the part of the disgustingly perverted prison warden with a Jacuzzi. It is one of his favorite places to interview the inmates. John will show up as an authority figure in numerous Linda Blair films. He isn't a very likable lush in this one.

His daughter, Katherine Vernon plays a minor part as one of Carol Henderson's (Blair's) cellmates. It is her first credited role and prolific, albeit unspectacular, career keeps rolling along with 64 acting credits to date, most notably the role of Ellen Tigh in the TV series *Battlestar Galactica*.

Sharon Hughes is Carol's friend to the end compadre in *Chained Heat*. Her name is simply Val and she is a returning veteran to the prison system that is corrupt and dangerous. She plays the role of one of Linda's best friends in the 1988 Blair movie *Grotesque*. She is perfect for the part. She has enough connections with the guards to get her and Carol invitations to one of the parties that the prison staff throws. What I found remarkable was the method of escape that was implemented. The girls snuck out of the laundry room into a limousine. She does a respectable strip tease at a private party for some of the select inmates off premises. Her dancing saved Carol from being the victim of a sexual assault. She and Carol work well together in their attempt to avoid the corrupting factors that are ever-present in jails. Together, they devise a daring plan to uncover the corruption with hopes of improving their lot. Hughes' acting resume is rather short.

What is amazingly ironic is that Lawrencia Bembenek used the laundry room at the Taycheedah Correctional Institution in Wisconsin to stage her escape in 1990. She crawled out a laundry room window. A bio-pic of sorts was made of Bembenek (*The Heart of the Lie*) and Linda Blair plays the part of one of Bembeneks' friends and classmates at Milwaukee's Police

Academy. I wonder if the escape to the little tryst with the prison help may have inspired Bembenek's escape from Taycheedah.

Tamara Dobson's resume, on the other hand, isn't short. She plays the role of Duchess, the Vassar alumni of dark race. According to the Guinness Book of World Records, she is "The Tallest Leading Lady in Film." Duchess was the leader of the Black prison population and was wise to the manipulations of the prison leaders to keep tension and trouble between the races. She cut a most imposing figure and from behind my eyeglasses had the most impressive figure of the eye candy dished out in this bungling blunder of a film. Her forceful movements and speech made her character come to life and gave some credence to *Chained Heat*. The 6 foot 2 Dobson was released from the prison that her body kept her in on October 2, 2006, dying of pneumonia and multiple sclerosis.

Louisa Moritz plays the part of the buxomly Bubbles. The Cuban immigrant changed her name from Castro to the name of the hotel where she stayed in the 1950s. Her reel claim to fame came as Rose in *One Flew Over the Cuckoo's Nest*. There is some irony here, because Moritz is a Yale alumnus and is a practicing attorney in Southern California. She must be very convincing in court, because there have been very few who could play the role of the dumb blonde as well as she does in *Chained Heat*.

The role of Captain Taylor was an unusual one for Stella Stevens. Although she had played the role of Lt. Janet Alexander in *The Women of San Quentin*, (another women's prison move released in 1983) Stevens usually appears as the hot female. In *Chained Heat*, she comes across as a bi-sexual tough girl with the women's version of a butch hairdo to match. She is listed a five foot-five, which makes her about three inches taller than Blair. She seems to be shorter in *Chained Heat*. She started life in Yazoo, Mississippi 1 October 1936 and was first noticed by a United Artists agent in the tearoom of Goldsmith's Department Store in Memphis. (She was born the year after Memphis' number one son (Elvis Presley) was.) Some sources list her as a native of Hot Coffee, Mississippi. She was wed at age 15, bore a child at 16 and was divorced at an age when most of us were starting our senior year in high school, 17. She was attending Memphis State University when she was discovered waitressing at Goldsmith's. Her career took off in 1959 when she played the part of Appassionata Von Climax in *Lil' Abner* (a). She won the Golden Glove Award in 1960 as the Most Promising Newcomer-Female thirteen years prior to Blair winning the same award for her part in *The Exorcist*. Little Linda would have been completing her first year of life when Stevens was receiving this award.

Stella appeared as *Playboy's* Playmate of the Month in June of 1960. She was voted the 27th sexiest woman of the century according to the Internet Movie Data Base. Her figure is a greater asset than the books at Enron. She is listed as a 36C-24-36 (a), although she didn't' come off as particularly alluring in *Chained Heat*. She has been seen on TV standards such as *General Hospital* and *Ben Casey*. She teamed up with Elvis Presley to steam up the screen in *Girls! Girls! Girls!* in 1962 and was cast alongside another vocal legend, Bobby Darin, in *Too Late Blues*. I best remember her as Linda Rogo, the wife of Detective Lieutenant Mike Rogo (played by Hollywood legend Ernest Borgnine) in *The Poseidon Adventure*. She was in the original *Nutty Professor* in 1963 in which Jerry Lewis starred (b). The little bombshell even played the part of a nun (Sister George) in *Where Angels Go Trouble Follows!* The unforgettable Rosalind Russell was awarded the lead role of Mother Superior in that comedy that tells the tale a group of an old school religious order nun traveling across the US in a bus with a nun from the now generation (c). (I was surprised to find this gem abundantly available on DVD.) It has to be on the other end of the acting sphere than the role Stevens played in *Chained Heat*.

Chained Heat had some redeeming qualities. The good girls won in the end. Yet, it seems sac religious to call hookers, crack dealers, thieves and murderers good girls. The victim of a prison guard rape refuses to exact vengeance on her perpetrator.

Blair says that the film bore little resemblance to the script that she read when she signed on for the part. She was supposed to play the part of a college girl that has never done drugs. This co-ed then goes to a party and has her drink spiked with drugs and is subsequently jailed. There is no mention of any of this in the movie (a). In *Chained Heat* she is thrown into the slammer for vehicular manslaughter and the movie is centered on the bizarre prison activities.

This movie was listed by Giesen/Hahn as one of the worst films of all time (e). If you find a movie featuring Linda Blair in it and the title has "Heat" or "Savage" in it, you might wish you had spent your time at the concession stand or your money on another rental instead, unless you are a warped, frustrated 14 year-old boy and your parents aren't home.

Savage Streets
1984

Outside of *The Exorcist*, this tough talking, law busting boiler blower of a movie has the largest following of all of the Blair movies to date.

It was released in October of 1984 (1) and was filmed in sunny Los Angeles, California. A quartet of nasties called the Scars hit Brenda's (Linda Blair's) deaf, mute sister (Linnea Quigley) with their car. Trash talking takes place and an insincere apology is offered and followed up with gang leader Jake (Robert Dryer) offering Brenda a chance to ride around with the boys and have some fun.

The girls, in turn, steal the car later that night and trash it. It might be called an act of vengeance, but to trash a 1957 champagne pink Chevrolet convertible with a continental kit isn't an act of vengeance, it is a crime against Americana. The producer should have found a more criminal car for the villains. I think that a black 1957 De Soto with slotted dish chromies would have made them look much more menacing than a pink convertible. (What self-respecting band of hooligans would cruse in a pink convertible anyway?)

The gang of four takes revenge out on Brenda's sister, Heather. They brutalize and rape her. Brenda and one of the school's very attractive cheerleaders, Cindy Clark, are having fisticuffs in the shower while Heather is being victimized. She is discovered by Brenda and the friends that were with her when they stole the Chevy. Heather is a near lifeless heap in the boy's room at the school.

There are some strong, convincing characters in *Savage Streets*. Robert Dryer is the Scars' leader and he is strong and imposing. His word is your command. Sal Lindi plays the part of Scars' member Fargo. He is easily seen as the number two man and washboard makers the world over have used his stomach as a model. Scott Mayer plays Red, the gang's most unstable member. Johnny Venocur borders brilliance in his film debut as Vincey. He is the Scars' newcomer and hasn't a clue as to what he is in for. His indecisiveness left me unnerved. He lacked the courage to stand up for what was right when he knew the difference. He objected to the wrongs, but ended up being sucked into the horrors of bad company in his desire to be accepted as something more than just another kid in the crowd at school. At some time in most of our lives, we could have been playing the person that lacked the courage to turn our back on the status quo and set course in a better direction. Of the entire cast of male characters, his is the one that we might most easily identify with. On the stronger side of the male route we have John Vernon. He is in a number of Linda Blair films. In *Savage Streets*, Vernon is the principal. His forked tongue can match anyone's in the obscene language department at this school. He is stern and his word isn't to be questioned. He also generates about as much warmth and compassion as a frozen fish.

Seeing Linda Blair decked out in leather was an appealing thought. Even that was a disappointment. In one of her lines at the bar, she states that she has given up on God since her father died. I can't argue with her character's feelings, but given the circumstances, she might have voiced it with a little more passion. Some of her friends (Debra Blee as Rachel, Marcie Karr as Stevie and Ina Romeo as Stella) do all right in the sputtering *Savage Streets*. Brenda's best friend, Francine (played by Lisa Freeman) does bring some color and heart to The Streets. She is engaged and lets Brenda in on a little secret. She also sticks a knife into the face of Jake in a bar brawl at the MX tavern.

I don't live in the Golden State, so some of the movie didn't make sense to me. Do students in California really smoke in the principal's office? Do high school girls really go the bars and drink in LA. How in the wide, wide world of sports could any self-respecting man let anyone step on the top of his car door to enter a classic convertible? Wouldn't you seek cover after someone shot an arrow into you leg? Wouldn't you seek cover after they shot you the second time? Do California schoolgirls really shower at school with their bras and panties on? Wouldn't it make the rest of their clothes look funny when they got dressed after showering? These questions were never answered in this movie. Another notable tidbit is the cheerleading squad in this cult film. The squads that would later appear in *Bring It On* (2000) would not have much to worry about in a form of a challenge from this school's crew of rhythm lacking wannabes. There are the famous Rockettes and then there's the Clutzettes. You can ascertain the difference immediately.

I would like to say that I didn't like *Savage Streets*. I have daughters so rape scenes bother me. You can see the boom microphone in one of the earlier scenes at the top of the screen, just like you can in *Chained Heat*. I am one of millions of Americans who is trying to clean up my language one word at a time, and even the ladies in this cult classic should be blowing bubbles for the soap that should have been used to wash out their mouths. I have found that when you go to teach someone a lesson, you're usually the one who learns it. I don't like to dwell on revenge. Yet, I was rooting for Brenda to give these rapists and murderers a taste of the sour milk that they dished out. She does so in a most creative way. If you don't like the rest of the movie, you'll at least like the way it ends up. Imagine, a Linda Blair film ending up in a cemetery.

As for the 1957 Chevy, it was the last year that GM used that body style. It was completely changed in 1958 and was completely changed again in 1959, making the '58 even more rare than the 1957 is classic. This one most likely came with the

283 cubic inch V-8 engine that put out 220 horsepower at 4800 rpm (1). This is one of the few that I have ever seen with a continental kit and I think that the paint used on the Chevrolet in *Savage Streets* was the original color. You'll appreciate how small Linda Blair really is when you see her perched behind the wheel of this gem. In addition to the visible boom mike seen earlier, you'll also see that the shifting lever is either in second gear (if it is a standard shift transmission) or Park if it is an automatic transmission. Either the car shouldn't have been moving or Brenda should have been ready to shift that savage beast into third.

The soundtrack for *Savage Streets* is typical 1980s. It has the loud backbeat bass and the distorted sound accompanied by the piercing vocals. The International Movie Data Base states that "with the exception of a rare independent edition by Turbo Productions in 2005, there was never a sound track released." The film's credits say that MCA records distributed the soundtrack, and the date on the jacket is 2003. At any rate, this would be a fine addition to an '80s music connoisseur.

Francine (played by Lisa Freeman) had a couple of classic lines. She refers to the young jock competing for Brenda's affection thusly, "He's harmless. Even his own hand turns him down." She imparts this advice for a line to use when it is the bathroom you can't refuse, "I have to go to the bathroom so bad that I'm going to have to wring out my socks."

Linnea Quigley, "The Queen of the B Movies" plays Heather, Brenda's deaf, mute sister. Heather is the rape victim. She is 5 foot 2 just like Linda Blair. She is listed as 33-23-33 and weighs in at a whopping 98 pounds. She is about a half-year-older than Blair. A native of Davenport, Iowa, Quigley headed out west where she belonged and was featured in several films. The most notable are *The Return of the Living Dead* (1985) and *Corpses Are Forever* (2003). She lists her role in *Savage Streets* as one of her three favorite movie roles. From the standpoint of learning your lines, what could be easier than playing a deaf-mute? She is also listed as *Maxim* magazine's 9th Hottest Woman of the Horror Movies. She is not ugly by any means, but she certainly didn't inspire a pool of drool in *Savage Streets*. Amazingly, Linda Blair isn't listed in *Maxim's* Top Ten list of Horror Hotties. Linda is a 34 D-cup- 24-34 cutie with the deep, expressive brown eyes and flawless face and tips the scale appealingly just to the right of Quigley. Blair is possessed with the stuff men dream of. The plot reminded me of a coffee cup. It was pointless. There were no real winners and I doubt that any of the characters live happily ever after. Perhaps the shame of it all is that you really won't like any of the characters enough to care if they did live happily ever after.

It remains, however, one of the more popular Linda Blair cult films and is readily available and is readily available on E-bay and Amazon.

Night Patrol
1984

When you see that dwarf Billy Barty, deadpanned *Smother's Brothers* **regular Pat Paulsen and the Unknown Comic are together with Linda Blair and Jaye P. Morgan great things of comedy should be in order.** Muary Langston (usually) plays the Unknown Comic and he is a riot in a policeman's uniform as the show starts rolling. He accompanies the plot in going out of control thereafter.

Some funny moments compensate for a weak story in *Night Patrol*. Officers Sue Perman (Linda Blair), and Kent Lane (Pat Paulsen) and Officer Melvin White (Murray Langston) team up with Billy Barty (the horizontally challenged Captain Lewis) in a *Superman* shtick.

Officers Lane and White provide one of the funniest scenes in a roach infested diner. The "Cream of Washroom Soup" line is one of the silver screen's best.

Night Patrol has many one-liners. It features some very funny skits. The trailer is pact with most of the best. If only the skits would be the formula for a good movie. This is a classic case of silliness run amuck.

A day cop is put on the night shift where he is paired up with a womanizing stud. Pat Paulsen plays the part of the stud and that in itself is laughable. The desk clerk (Officer Sue Perman played by Linda Blair) finds Officer White (Muary Langston) irresistible and he is clueless as to her sentiments. White moonlights as a comedian in a nightclub and has to conceal his identity because the precinct captain (Billy Barty) has a no moonlighting policy. White alters his true identity on stage by wearing a paper bag over his head. He is also seeing a psychiatrist to overcome phobia. To add some twists to a wreck of a plot there is a man wearing an identical brown paper bag holding up businesses in the area of the nightclub.

White's comic career takes off and an agent (Jaye P. Morgan) books him in Las Vegas. White fancies a foxy looking frequenter of the club and she only wants him for his potential earnings.

If you are watching *Night Patrol* and expecting to see a movie, forget about it. The plot is so lame that you may need a professional to walk you through the scenes. It would be best that you readjust your expectations. I don't think that this should be classified as a movie, but should be considered as a non-stop comedy gag.

Initially we see Officer White on a small motor scooter in pursuit of a Cadillac. The Cadillac driver is in a straight jacket. He is a non-English speaking pervert and White is clueless regarding this fact during his conversation with the suspect, who also has a body in the trunk.

A bicyclist crashes his bike into a loaded garbage can and that spills into a busy walkway. Officer White approaches the accident and stumbles over a man who is experiencing an apparent heart attack. Two men steal the man's wallet and drop it when they see White. He dutifully picks it up and gives the wallet to one of the thieves after he trips over the victim.

White feeds some pigeons and they demonstrate their appreciation by dumping on the good-hearted officer. He responds by firing his pistol into the flying flock of poop plopping pigeons.

His next step is into a pile of dog dung. As he attempts to deal with the criminal canine at hand, he is watered on by mans' best friend. All of this happens in the first five minutes of the movie.

The master of the twirling police baton racks himself with his nightstick. He discovers a passed out vagrant and attempts to revive him. You can only guess the outcome of his most valiant efforts.

Officer White is in crossing guard's elite class. He ushers a bunch of youngsters across the street, right into traffic. No one gets hurt. One little girl chooses to stay behind. White is no match for the little lady in the white dress. A little boy utters a laugh line as he crosses the street and says to the cop, "Mister, I found this gun." Can you imagine whose gun it was?

A vagrant is soon seen soliciting a hooker. An exchange of words between the two is funny, very funny.

I don't know if the scene where White and Kent are undercover cops was meant to be funny or if it was a comment on our racist society. Our representatives of LAPD's finest are called to check out a Black nightclub. They naturally figure that they should dress like a couple of pimped out gigolos. They discover that it is a very classy place. Suits and ties are required and they are the only guys there not wearing them and, coincidentally, they're the only white guys in the place.

White America's view of our brothers of another color is brought out by this skit. The stereotypical Black still seems to be viewed as brilliant, smooth talking conversationalists, dancing dynamos, and astounding athletes or masterful musicians. The fact of the matter is that women, Blacks and even aging White guys like myself can accomplish any task that we are capable of if we are granted the opportunity. I would like to add that my physician of 15 years was a fine doctor and a man of color. He would still be my doctor had he not retired. To send a second witness to out society's mistaken perception of the Black can be found in the foundries during the early, successful years at the Ford Motor Company. All of the employment at this facility right up to its superintendent was Black. Mr. Ford boasted that the foundry was its most efficient unit in the entire Rouge manufacturing complex (a). It seems sad that after a quarter of a century many Americans still stereotype Blacks as irresponsible criminals. Of course, the Black nightclub is robbed while the one undercover cop is in the bar's bathroom. Langston takes a poke at White America's foolish notions about Blacks and laughter may be the best medicine to promote the healing.

The music in *Night Court* was top notch. It was '80s music at it's best. It flowed with a good beat. I don't how so many of Blair's movies got such great opening songs and such a fine score of tunes thereafter, but it is one of her cinematic benchmarks.

When the police close in on the real bag bandit this film borrows some of the choreography concept from the *Blues Brothers*. It is a tune that strikes a sound familiar to the Ray Charles classic *What'd I Say?* It also implements the Clint Eastwood classic draw in which the unforgettable line, "Make my day" is appropriately altered to, "Make my night". There is further tribute paid to Eastwood when the title track from the movie *The Good, The Bad and The Ugly* is used in a chase scene.

It is rapid fire, non-stop skits, gags and laughter. There are more one-liners than you can shake a police baton at in *Night Patrol*. Unlike *Savage Streets*, this film is deliberately pointless. There are so many things that are intentionally ridiculous, that it causes laughter. It isn't tasteful, but it is funny. I wouldn't recommend this film to the Bible thumping straight-laced public or children, but if you can stomach the raw edges of humor, it is funny.

Night Patrol features a very cherry early 1950s red orange Ford truck that is parked in front of a fire hydrant. It is occupied by a couple of engaging lovebirds. It is the only vehicle of note in this film featuring both pooping pigeons and lovebirds.

The strangest cast in the crew is Pat Morita. This is the same Pat Morita that starred as Mr. Kesuke Myagi in *The Karate Kid*, which incidentally was released in June of 1984. In *Night Patrol*, he is the rape victim. He was forced to commit acts by homosexual women. The humor in *Night Patrol* isn't always in the best of taste, and Pat usually played the part of credible characters. He has 158 TV and movie acting credits to his name. He was the first American born Asian to be nominated for an Oscar Award. This was for his role in *The Karate Kid*. He was diagnosed with spinal tuberculosis as a youngster and told that he would never walk. His skit in *Night Patrol* isn't what you would expect from the actor who put the heart, head and soul in *The Karate Kid* to do as his next gig.

Night Patrol was a ragged attempt to outdo *Police Academy* at the box office. They were both funny movies. It is ironic that

Night Patrol was written before *Police Academy*. I think that *Police Academy* had a better plot and I think that *Night Patrol* would have been just as funny without all of the nudity and off color sexual innuendo it offered.

Part of the blame for this film gone awry lay at the feet of director Jackie Kong. She reportedly wanted the affections that she sent Langston's way returned and it didn't happen. She had Murray do numerous retakes for no apparent reason and hurled insults at the crew. Some of the crew walked off and Langston eventually left the project that he gave birth to (b). His voice was ultimately dubbed in. They had to use jokes that were not Langston's. They added unlimited farts to Billy Barty's character and the excess gas really stunk up the movie. The gas did nothing to enhance the plot or his character. Why would a dwarf who was serving as a police chief need anything more than his appearance and title to bring attention to his character? According to Blair, the film was never completed (c). It was the only film that Jackie Kong has directed to date (d.)

This was Blair's first attempt at comedy. She fit the bill well. She did the ditsy dingbat bit beautifully. It seemed that she enjoyed making people laugh more than she liked scaring the devil out of us. She was 25 when this movie was put together. In the scene at the Las Vegas party for The Unknown Comic, she struts her stuff. She was decked in an open cut beige dress. It was a cleavage concealing concoction, but it gave credence to her claim of possessing a pair of "D"ixie cups. There is a more revealing shot of one of them near the close of the never to be classic. There is one other thing of a personal nature revealed in the closing bedroom scene and it is one of Linda's most pleasant and patented attributes. Listen to her laugh.

Night Patrol is also abundantly available to seekers of silliness of all genres

1984 was a year of many newsworthy events. There was the fierce famine in Ethiopia. More than 70 banks failed in the United State, proving that Reagonomics was more *illus ional* than functional. It was one of Hollywood's best years for moviegoers. The patrons of the arts could see *Ghostbusters, Indiana Jones and the Temple of Doom, The Karate Kid, Terms of Endearment* or *Police Academy.* The movies had to be superb in 1984. They had to compete with the Olympics, which were being held in Los Angeles.

Red Heat
1985

One of the most familiar lines associated with the performing arts is, "Break a leg." In this forgettable Linda Blair prison movie it was more than just the old shout from a director at the commencement of the production. Linda did break her leg while filming *Red Heat*. In the scenes that feature her negotiating through the underground streets of Maflim, Budapest, Hungary where Red Heat was filmed in 1985, she is hobbling and being assisted in flight because of the broken leg. She was pictured at the reopening of Studio 54 with a cane in a national magazine.

This is the second and hopefully last of Linda Blair's prison movies. It has a more exciting and meaningful plot than *Chained Heat*. *Chained Heat* is more for the 14 year-old boys looking for some quick gratuitous girly shots. Yet there is more of a plot than was featured in *Chained Heat*.

Christine Carlson (played by Linda Blair) is reunited with her fiancé (played by William Ostrander) in a nation bordering a Communist state. They have a spat because Mike (her fiancé) decided to re-enlist in the US Armed Forces and failed to discuss the decision with Christine.

She goes out for a walk and witnesses the arrest of a political prisoner (Hedda who is played by Sue Kiel). Christine is also arrested so that there are no witnesses to Hedda's arrest. A confession is coerced where Christine states "of her own free will" that she was an agent working with Hedda and was a member of the CIA.

They are taken to a remote prison where nothing gets to the outside world without being screened first. There is a total lack of justice. There is no legal representation for the accused, who ultimately become prisoners. Subtle means of torture are used in the interrogation of Carlson. The bright spotlight is constantly in her face. She is denied food and offered coffee. She is wise enough to refuse the coffee. She is denied sleep and isn't permitted to rest her elbows on the table. *Red Heat* was released in May of 1985, when Ronald Reagan first took office. We would applaud the Berlin Wall coming down during his administration. As this is being written, there are scores of political prisoners being held in Guantanamo Bay by our government. Our prisoners have been denied legal council, and there are allegations of inhumane interrogation proceedings. Some of them have been locked up for years with no trial. It is sad to see our country become the type of government that we perceived to be the enemy's.

Before hope is given up, there is someone to the rescue. Mike has connections with the military and they have connections with Intelligence. Can there be any doubt that our Intelligence is more than eager to save an American citizen from the despicable clutches of the Communist captor?

Like most Americans, Mike's country ignores his needs and he is left to fend for himself and the woman he loves. He proves to be a resourceful man of means in *Red Heat*. He finds a way and a band of professionals who are keen to the call of freedom.

Meanwhile, Christine is abused in the prison. She is harangued and required to obtain information from the other political prisoner (Hedda). She refuses and her resolve is intensified as the film rolls. She has a confrontation with the leader of the corrupt inmates and witnesses the death of another woman who dared challenge the cold-hearted Sofie, played by Silvia Kristel. Sofie is a hardened murderer, a bully, a ringleader and is well connected with the prison staff.

After Hedda and Christine create a rather spontaneous lunchroom protest, the other girls begin to side with the two new political prisoners. It marks the beginning of the end of Sofie's reign of terror. Sofie cannot tolerate this and plans to terminate Carlson. It is a very deliberate process and you must wonder why she didn't plan a simpler and more definite means to eliminate the opposition.

The film was shot in Maflim Budapest, Hungary and it is the first work that the 26 year-old Blair would do in Europe. Six other movies (to date) share this filming site. Among them is the *Boy in the Striped Pajamas*. That is a film about a Jewish boy in a concentration camp. The filming facility is obviously great for prison movies. It has the cold, sterile, intimidating atmosphere that only a prison can bring to life. It is the only life that a prison has to offer.

There is some nudity in *Red Heat*. It is mostly shower room shots and it isn't all that arousing. Christine and Mike are intimate in one of the early scenes, but it is done as tastefully as possible. She is wearing an eye-enhancing nightgown, that isn't too revealing and you might see him shirtless.

There are also some sex scenes that aren't graphic, but are very suggestive. There is one lesbian rape scene. The victim of that horrific crime is later murdered by the rapist. There is also a scene where Christine is brought before Sofie in her office and "punished" for not spying on Hedda. Although it isn't revealing, it is unnerving. There is another scene where a young prisoner is attacked with a handle from either a plunger or broom. These scenes are disturbing if you are a woman, or have daughters or sisters. These scenes don't even register on the cheap thrill graph. The girls are donned in denim prison attire that is about as sexy as a burlap bag tied with twine around the waste.

There is a lot of action in *Red Heat*. Mike and his rescue workers become engaged in a heavy gun battle. There are a couple of fights between the prisoners. There is the arrest. The clandestine work of the underground workers is exciting.

Some of the film was interesting as it depicted the prisoners doing production work in a factory setting. There were some heavy presses being used to hammer out metal. I was surprised that hand pullout restraints weren't used during the filming as Blair worked at one of these large industrial machines. The pullouts are slipped around your wrists and pull your hands away from the press as its head comes down on the metal so that the press doesn't smash your hands. OSHA requires them. I have seen the stubs and missing fingertips of men who ran these types of presses before the restraints were required. Christine could have actually been sent to the prison hospital with a more serious injury than the one featured in the film. It may also be noted that the state prison facility in my neck of the woods is (or has been in the past) involved in production work.

As sad as Red Heat was, it does provoke questions. How many people in the prison system in our country are guilty of the crimes that they are charged with? Were the attorneys who represented their clients dedicated to them? How many prisoners are serving time in efforts to promote political careers? Why does is seem that poor people are more severely punished for the same crimes that rich people commit?

Another question that arises comes from over a half century of being an American. Does the United States Government care as much about its citizens as they did about Christine Carter? The question is not asked in flippant reference to the movie alone. A policeman had to have a valid reason to pull a driver over ten years before *Red Heat* was made. Law enforcement officials can now pull people over for no apparent reason and require the stupidest things of them. I have been pulled over on a four-lane highway with heavy traffic and given a field sobriety test. The cop was over a foot taller than I was. (I am only four inches taller than Linda Blair.) He asked me to look at his penlight while he held it in the air. I told him that I would need a stepladder to see a penlight at that height. I was asked if I had been drinking ten minutes after I offered to take a breathalyzer test. I asked why I had been pulled over and the fine officer of the law said that I cut him off when I turned. I watched him when I turned and his brake lights didn't come on and I brought this to his attention. Needless to say, he wasn't too happy with my attitude. He had some more insulting questions for me and said that he could write me up and make it stick. I was tempted to ask him to try it, but thought better of it. It is practice in De

Forest, Wisconsin to quander off a section of roadway and pull over all traffic for no reason, save it is to quiz the drivers of their drinking practices. It seems peculiar that the law doesn't practice this procedure on people that work the day shift, because if they did, there would be an overwhelming outcry due to the inconvenience of people's lives and the practice would be stopped. How often has a state facility been cooperative with you when a problem arises? *Born Innocent* and *Red Heat* dare ask if our government cares at all about those of us who fall out of mainstream America. Did it provide adequate counseling and placement for the runaway and her family in *Born Innocent?* Did they even acknowledge the possibility that Christine Carlson might have been abducted or that she may have fallen victim to foul play in *Red Heat?* Of course not. She didn't come from a family of prominence or influence. Leave it to Linda Blair to take on these roles like nobody else could. (Could you even imagine Brooke Shields playing the role of Christine!)?

Before *Red Heat* was released, we had to have a search warrant and reasonable cause before entering a dwelling to search for things that would be of an incriminating nature. If law enforcement thinks you have illegal drugs in your home, they can come over and come on in and there isn't a thing that you can do about it. Let's hope that they don't plant any incriminating evidence. A friend of mine had a roommate that was angry with him and called the police. He said that my buddy was about to make a major cocaine transaction and had the stuff on him in the car. The local police were on him with guns drawn before you could say, "Which way is up?" My pal didn't have a clue as to what was going on at the time. It wouldn't take much to get the headline hunting anti-drug squad into someone's home on false pretenses.

So, as cinematically challenged as *Red Heat* was, it did successfully rescue us from the hypnotism of apathy. It provoked questions.

Our supporting featured star in *Red Heat* is Sue Kiel, who

played the anti-government crusader, Hedda. Sue is the woman of interest that is arrested by the Secret Police of the old Iron Curtain nation. She is tall and provides the daring, sophisticated look that lends you to believe that she may indeed be an agent of a usurping faction. She fits the role well. She is resentful that Christine signed the confession that states that she (Christine) is an agent for a foreign nation and Hedda is implicated in a conspiracy. As time rolls on, Hedda grasps the reality of the situation. Christine had no other alternative. It takes a while. After Christine receives some "special" treatment, Hedda befriends her and the good karma begins to flow.

Sue Kiel has a short sheet of cinematic accomplishments. Her most recent work is the role that she played in the *Red Shoe Diaries,* (1992) which was a late night attraction on one of the premium channels offered by cable TV. Her other television credits include single appearances on *MacGyver,* (Blair also did a bit on the *MacGyver* series.) *Cagney and Lacey,* and *The A-Team.* She opened her screen career as Ms. Magruder in the 1984 hit *Repo Man.* She was a miner star in a film that featured Grace Jones, Courtney Love and Dennis Hopper back in 1986. The box office bust was appropriately dubbed *Straight From Hell.* She had a role in *Down and Out In Beverly Hills* and *Survivor.* All of Kiel's movie work was done between 1984 and 1987. Hollywood is a fiercely competitive place, as she seemed to possess the talent and persona and should have been awarded more work from the looks of *Red Heat.*

The feature automobile in *Red Heat* is a first generation Ford Mustang. This model of Mustang was made from 1965-68. Automobile designer Lee Iococca has his hands involved in the evolving of this classic car. It could be economically practical, as a small two-seater or it could double as the hottest car on the block, depending on the consumer's taste. The early ones came from the factory with a six cylinder as standard equipment with an optional small block (289 cubic inch displacement) V-8. By 1968 you could get a Mustang with a 390 cubic inch V-8 and a four speed manual transmission. It was as fast as it was sporty. If Linda Blair had seen one of these in *The Exorcist*, her head would surely be spinning.

Here are some reasons for seeing red after you've viewed this version of *Red Heat*. Arnold Schwarzenegger and James Belushi starred in a movie dubbed *Red Heat* in 1988. Sue Kiel was featured in four episodes of the spicy late night series *The Red Shoe Diaries*. She was also featured in an episode of *Mac Gyver* in 1985 entitled, *The Thief of Budapest*. It is near the same city of setting for *Red Heat*. Another interesting coincidence is that William Ostrander who played the role of Mike in the Linda Blair version of *Red Heat* played a part in the movie called *Mike's Murder* the same year that this film was released. The original Emmanuelle was played by the same Sylvia Kristel (who plays the wicked Sofie in *Red Heat*). Like Linda Blair, she also appeared in an *Airport* movie. She played the part of Isabelle in *The Concorde...Airport 1979*. William Ostrander played a role in the 1983 movie *Christine* and would play character Christine Carlson's fiancé two years later in *Red Heat*. Strangely enough, *Christine* was a movie about a car that was possessed.

Linda Blair said that *Chained Heat* and *Red Heat* nearly ruined her career (a). Anyone who sees these films might understand why. It isn't all that difficult to get your hands on this one, but ....

Savage Island
1985

There are B movies and there are movies that just shouldn't be. **Savage Island is one of the latter.** This movie could have been the inspiration for rock band Jethroe Tull's tune *Bungle In the Jungle.*

The 26 year-old Blair plays the part of Daly, a woman who spent time working in the slave sponsored emerald lands of the jungle. Daly enters a fancy metropolitan office seeking to speak with the mastermind of the operation. She opens in a scene that features a security guard who is impressed with Daly's appealing appearance. He informs her in a professional manner that she is required to sign in. She refuses and he requests her signing in one more time and then he insists in a forceful tone of voice that she must sign in before she may have access and conversation with the top dog. She responds by distributing a bullet into the unsuspecting guard. Daly gains access to the big shot. The story of the emerald mining is unfurled from this point.

She explains that a band of mercenaries have been dispatched by her to rescue the damsels in distress in that god forsaken jungle island. The plot is as predictable as a tornado after the whistle is blown. The good guys get to the prison facility after a deadly encounter with soldiers. Of course there is a struggle and the matter of timing necessary for the great escape. The girls are rescued from the degradation and indignities that a women's prison movie might offer. They struggle through the leech-infested terrain while the dogs and guards are hot on their trail. Of course some of them make it to the Promised Land. I'll spare the ultimate outcome of Mr. Luker (played by Leon Askin, more famous as General Burkhalter on the sit-com Hogan's Heroes), the mastermind behind the jewel-procuring project.

There is some action involved in the escape. Not all of the prisoners are successful in this endeavor. Not all of the good guys get to the golden gate on this side of the vale. There is a lot of shooting and stabbing. People are throwing dynamite everywhere in one of the scenes. The same guards are shot several times in Savage Island. I don't think they could squeeze out enough dough to hire another half dozen bodies to fake being shot. I find it hard to believe that trained guards would leave their cover to aim and take shots at the enemy, but when Hollywood trains the troops it's surprising that the bullets came out of the right end of the gun.

There is some torture in this farce of a film. A young woman is covered up to her neck in some sort of muddy goo. It is here where she hopelessly awaits her fate. A snake finally slithers up to her and relieves her anxiety. A prisoner is perched and stretched and tied and left for hours in the cruel, hot sun. Whips are employed. The torture wasn't always particularly suspenseful or creative.

There were scantily clad women in burlap prison garb throughout *Savage Island*. They were dirty and sweaty. The movie case depicts some real hotties. On the case, Linda Blair is sporting a pair of spiked stilettos and a V-shaped top. She reveals all of her legs on the cover and they appear to be world-class limbs. In the film, she is wearing a blue dress that is low cut, but not plunging and her legs are covered down to her knees. She looks nice, but isn't the feature creature on the jacket of the film. The reel hotties are displayed in more revealing shots, but to say that this trash basket on film is loaded with sizzling sweeties is more than an overstatement. Filthy women wearing something borrowed from Betty Flintstone's dirty laundry basket doesn't do much for me.

This film has some hidden mysteries. Some of it was filmed in Spain. Some of it was filmed in Los Angeles, but the Internet Movie Data Base doesn't tell where Savage Island was filmed. (The IMBD is one of the most reliable sources regarding movies from all ages.) Orin Okie is one of the leading characters in the film. The actor who played this part isn't listed at all on the IMBD page and it is uncertainable in the movie credits as to who played the part. The movie credits have the actresses that played the parts of Muriel and Maria mixed up. I wonder if there is a reason for this. Don S. Davis received a Fright-Fest Director's Award for Best Supporting Actor in Savage Island. I wonder if there is a reason for this as well.

Leon Askin stars as the corporate gangster in *Savage Island*. He is best remembered as the tough talking German General Burkhalter on the 1960s TV cult comedy, *Hogan's Heroes*. He fit both parts to a tee. Leon was born 18 September 1907 in Vienna, Austria-Hungary. As a nine-year old boy, he recited a 17-stanza eulogy for Emperor Franz Josef in front of the city hall in Vienna. He was a most polished actor. The imposing Austrian was featured in many German movies, and starred in several Broadway productions. The first American movie that I saw him in was the 1952 Bob Hope/Bing Crosby hit *Road to Bali.* In that fun filled song and dance show, he played King Ramayana. He was convincing as Mr. Luker in *Savage Island.* Of all the cast, he played his part the best. The bloody shot of him is the best fake blood that I witnessed on the silver screen. After returning to his native Austria, Leon was awarded the Austrian Cross of Honor for Science and Art in 1988. He was awarded the Silver Cross of Honor in 1994 and the Gold Cross of Honor for service to the city of Vienna in 2002. He also received the Austrian Cross of Honor for Science and Art First Class in 2002. Mr. Askin sums up his career thusly, "The journalists in Vienna, Austria and also in Germany call me a legend. I'm a man who lived through difficult times. I'm a man who survived the monster of all times, Adolph

Hitler, and I'm still at my high old age of 93, successful in my profession and that is the pride with which I survive." This true professional died of natural causes on 3 June 2005 at the ripe old age of 95.

I question the purpose of the making of *Savage Island*. Was it done to reveal the horrible conditions that are sponsored in order to bring us precious jewels? Was it to inform us of the terror, degradation and abuse of women held in prisons? Was it made to entertain 12 year-old boys with some female body shots?

This was one of the worst movies that I have ever seen. Blair's performance was wonting in Savage Island, despite the fact that she looked good brandishing a gun while wearing dress. From all that I can tell, this is where Linda Blair hit the bottom of the B movie barrel.

It is a movie that is available on the Internet, but doesn't show up as often as *Roller Boogie*.

Night Force
1987

In this 1987 action thriller we get to see Linda Blair as a liberator instead of a prisoner. There are two recurring themes from the recent Blair Box Office Offerings. There is the woman in a shower scene (*Red Heat, Chained Heat, Fatal Bond* and *Savage Island.*) Kidnapping is part of the plot as was scene in *Red Heat, Savage Island* and *Sweet Hostage.* There is still nudity and a steamy damsel in some sort of confining cage. *Night Force* introduces a new form of film eroticism. Christy Hansen (played very well by Claudia Udy) is shown putting clothes on while being held hostage by Central American terrorists. I must confess that she looks smashing in the process.

The featured car in this film was a 1968 Chevrolet Camero convertible. Just as the first generation Thunderbird was Ford's answer to Chevrolet's Corvette, the Camero was GM's answer to Ford's Mustang. In its first year of availability, the Camero was offered with a standard inline 6 cylinder engine. They also came with the big block 396 cu. in. V-8 that could clear the air and their tail lights were often their most distinguishing feature in street racing. Steve Worthington drives it in the first chase scene when terrorists whisk off his secret love.

In *Night Force*, United States Senator Adam Hansen's daughter Christy is engaged to a wealthy, aristocrat's son. The wedding isn't what she truly desires as she is in love with her fiancés younger brother, Steve (James Van Patten) and a provocative scene involving the two of them is part of *Night Force's* beginning. Linda Blair plays the role of Christy's best friend, Carla. Her performance in this role is a marked improvement over her bits in *Night Patrol, Chained Heat* and her savagely wonting roles in *Savage Streets* and *Savage Island*.

After a shooting scene at the sports arena where Senator Hansen is supposed to speak at an anti-terrorist rally, his daughter is kidnapped as she exits a gym. Her fiancé is less concerned about her abduction than his brother is. One of the recurring themes in Linda Blair movies is the (American) government's lack of concern and perseverance regarding victims. After a failed attempt to rescue the love of his life at the time of the abduction, Steve is determined to bring back his sweetheart. A few of his friends gather together and do some shooting practice. They decide to journey to Central America in order to snatch the damsel in distress from a fate worse than death, and perhaps death itself. Carla shows up at the target shoot and volunteers her help. She explains that they won't taste success south of the border without someone who speaks the native tongue. She rattles off some Spanish and the boys believe that she is learned in the language. Guys are so gullible when a pert, shapely, brown-eyed girl speaks. Together the fearless five pile into a Jeep, with a cache of weapons, including a bazooka, and a utility trailer in tow.

Their first stop is a smoke filled bar where Carla is the only woman and there appears to be no one there who speaks English. To everyone's surprise, Carla doesn't speak enough Spanish to carry on any kind of conversation. The amigos at the smokey watering hole want some of the wares that the rescuers have in their possession. It is here that we are introduced to Bishop. He looks like a spy cut from a comic book. He dons the spy type hat and the long trench coat. He is resourceful and helps rescue the rescuers.

Richard Lynch plays Bishop and his role is essential to the film. Lynch holds dual citizenship, American and Irish. Brooklyn,

New York's native son was born 12 February 1940. He was in the Middle East with the 6th Fleet while serving in the United States Marine Corp, having enlisted in 1958. He spent some time on Broadway until he landed the role of Riley in the fine film *Scarecrow* in 1973. He also played Principal Chambers in *Halloween*. The versatile actor has 159 film and movie credits to date.

He is a Viet Nam veteran and experienced in jungle warfare. He offers the troupe shelter and advises the best means to spring Christy. He is a weapons expert who plays the flute to relax. He gives the quote of the movie when asked why he plays the flute. "Music is like a prayer," is his reply. There is a sweet scene of kindness as he offers Carla his blanket. He tells her that she is the reason for his enlistment in the cause. You keep waiting for a loving relationship between the two of them to develop beyond this and it never does. A couple of the reasons that Richard Lynch comes off as the Special Forces expert are his overseas experience with the Marine Corp and he is also fluent in several languages, including Italian and German. He is a sure fit in his role as Bishop in *Night Force*.

Christy is kept captive in a cage of makeshift timber that is freshly cut. A short guard provides her with a means to clothe her nakedness. He also offers fruit. This little guard aids her in the prison break on the condition that she does all that she can to get him into her country. The vicious leader of the terrorist band, Estoben, (played perfectly by Bruce Fisher) shoots the little guy. Estoben bears a striking resemblance to Fidel Castro. He is often seen sporting a fat cigar and his demeanor is always stern and serious. Christy escapes on horseback. One of the guards tries to take advantage of her after she is thrown by the horse. Estoben reprimands the guard with a bullet and you'll have to see the movie to see what he attempts next.

Just as *SFX The Retaliator* gives us a chance to see Robert Mitchum's son Chris Mitchum, *Night Force* brings us action actor Steve McQueen's son Chad McQueen. Neither of the acting legend's sons is up to the difficult task of filling their father's shoes in either movie.

There is plenty of action in *Night Force.* Despite the needless nudity, this film has something of worth to offer. It demonstrates the true meaning of friendship. It speaks of the rewards of perseverance and determination. We are reminded of the folly in believing that the government will rescue us from our misfortune. A lesson of value is taught, as we find that with success comes sacrifice. We discover that we can overcome the greatest of odds with faith in our cause, teamwork and fellowship.

SFX The Retaliator
1987

This 1987 mix match of movie making and the Mafia is also known as *The Heroin Deal.* I don't recall if heroin is ever mentioned, but there is a lot of shooting and murder and a briefcase full of cash at the beginning of this flimsy film. The 28 year-old Blair plays the part of a mob prostitute dubbed Doris Morgan. The mobster (played by Gordon Mitchell) is the leading figure in the organized crime family that is most demanding in regards to possessing the prize in the brief case.

After the opening scene that displays a deluge of gunfire, the briefcase is in the hands of Morgan. His hooker for the evening is the buxomly Doris. She excuses herself, cracks a safe and takes off with the booty in the briefcase. She sneaks out of the compound in a late 1960s Mercury Comet. Linda Blair (Doris) looks a little heavier in this film. This is not necessarily a bad look, as her hips and breasts are accented and her waistline is not significantly larger than what we have been used to seeing. The car is another story. Apparently, women who serviced mobsters in the 1980s had very little ego. The only other car that would rival the prestige of her late 1960s Comet would be an AMC Gremlin. The Comet, as shown, would not have been the wisest of choices for a getaway car either. In eight short years, Linda Blair has gone from cruising the scene in a late model

Excalibur (in *Roller Boogie*) to fleeing the scene of a crime in a Mercury Comet. The downgrade of the car is indicative of the sliding quality of movies that Blair was featured in those days. *Night Force* was the other film from that year in the heart of the Reagan era. (*Night Force* was done better.) The lighting and stage work in *Night Force* was superior to *SFX*. It is ironic that the flick named after Special Effects was done with poorer effects than the one called *Night Force*. Even the stars seemed to shine brighter in *Night Force*.

I was amazed when I discovered that the Comet was originally planned as part of the Edsel division of Ford. They became the Mercury divisions' answer to the Ford Falcon. They had higher quality interiors than their brother cars and were on frames that were 5 inches longer. They were offered as 2-door coupes, 4-door sedans and as station wagons with either 2 or 4 doors. Station wagons were usually targeted at the family consumer, affording them room and convenience. I have always questioned the wisdom of the two-door wagon. Can you imagine a family with seven children climbing over the front seat of the 2-door wagon in a muddy driveway on their way to church? The one seen in the early scene of this film appears to be a second generation Comet. They came from the factory with a 200 cid 6 cylinder engine as standard equipment, replacing the punier 1964 model that boasted a 170 cid six. In the last year of the second generation Comet, you could choose between a 260 cid V-8 or the more robust 289 cid V-8. It also offered a choice of a three speed automatic transmission or a four speed manual shifter. Its styling looked like a cross between a Ford Fairlane and a Rambler Rebel. Even when the Comet emerged to a mid-sized car, it still looked like an economy model.

There were some economic shortcuts implemented in *SFX*. Baker used the same control panel to execute his special effects for the entire movie. Even my 1987 television's remote control was more sophisticated than the almond colored box with less than ten lights featured on it. Although the microphone and its boom weren't displayed in this movie, it appears that only one spotlight was used for lighting in most of the scenes. For a movie that stars a special effects guru more is expected.

Doris is successful in exiting the compound, but is run down by Morgan's pursuing henchmen. They catch up to her on a highway and she flags down a Chevy panel truck that is driven by Steve Baker (Chris Mitchum). He is a Hollywood special effects master.

Chris Mitchum is the son of movie mega star Robert Mitchum. He is a veteran of the film trade, although he has never been a featured headliner as far as I know. He was seen in some of the late John Wayne's films, *Rio Lobo* (1970) and *Big Jake* in 1971. In 1970 he had a miner role in the Wayne film *Chisum* where he was coincidentally Deputy Baker. Christopher Mitchum was born 16 October 1943 in Los Angeles. He has a BA from the University of Arizona and has starred in some foreign films. One of the reasons that he wasn't awarded more prestigious roles after his fine performances alongside John Wayne was due to the political nature of the Wayne films. This is according to the casting director of *Steelyard Blues*. America's film industry was attempting to be politically correct for the first time during this period, and John Wayne referred to Native Americans as "Indians" or "Redskins" and those of Japanese dissent were referred to as "Japs." I have seen the mentioned Wayne films that featured Mitchum and didn't find them much more political than reruns of Mighty Mouse. The younger Mitchum's performance as Steve Baker was not as strong in *SFX* as his showings the John Wayne movies that featured The Duke in his waning years.

Baker permits Doris to ride with him after he tosses a fake grenade at Morgan's hired gun hands. He and Doris take off. The movie features some dime store surveillance stuff and a nightclub shoot out.

Morgan's mischief-makers kidnap Baker's lovely wife, Kate (played by the eye popping, jaw dropping Christine Landson whose only other movie credit is in the obscure *Blood Hand* which was done in 1990). She also manages to escape the hands of Morgan's thugs. I cannot fathom so many amateurs escaping the grasp of professional hit men. Some of the scenes where Morgan's men enter Baker's house to fetch him and the information that he might have were just plain ridiculous. Trained killers don't run and hide from the Bogeyman. They should have seen and heard flashing lights and loud noises before. Surely, by the late 1980s these goodfellas must have seen a rock concert and not run back to their cars in a frenzied panic.

You must have surmised that after all of the threats and gunfire in this film that not everyone lives happily ever after. You'd have to endure or enjoy the movie to find out who else gets it.

The music is typical of the 1980s. It is a hard rock backdrop and is somewhat relevant to the script. It is good, but not on par with *Roller Boogie* and *Savage Streets*. It doesn't feature any of the heart tugging stuff that *Sweet Hostage* closed with.

I wonder if the movie would have been better served with Baker explaining picking up a hooker with a briefcase full of stolen loot to his gorgeous wife. There are many available plots and genre for this, and most of us would rather look at Landson and Blair than this bunch of bungling bozos. It may have made an acceptable erotic thriller, or high stakes drama. It could have turned into a comedy.

SFX The Retaliator wasn't laughable, and it wasn't the sort of cinema that Mitchum, Blair and Gordon Mitchell could have been proudest of.

It was filmed in the Philippines and according to Linda Blair the native filmmakers at the time were doing on the job training. In one interview, she said that they would shoot a scene, yell, "Cut!" and that was it. Not too many people are cutting into line at the video store to rent this Philippino flop.

Aretha Franklin was the first woman inducted into the Rock & Roll Hall of fame in 1987. President Ronald Reagan signed the secret order permitting the sale of arms to Iran in January. Whitney Houston, Alabama and Lionel Richie were some of pop music's superstars in 1987. *Platoon* won the Golden Globe for Best Movie. On February 2, the Philippines (host nation to the filming of *SFX*) adopted a constitution that went into effect 9 days later. Philippino Federal Troops murdered 17 civilians in the Lapao Massacre the day before the constitution went into effect. 1987 was the first time that a no smoking ban was instituted in Federal buildings. Bruce Hornsby would grab a Grammy. Mike Tyson successfully defended his heavyweight title when he defeated Tommy Tucker in 12 rounds and the Minnesota Twins defeated the St. Louis Cardinals to win the World Series.

Up Your Alley
1988

This is one of my Linda Blair family friendly favorites. It is a B film that deals with the plight of the homeless American. I considered using the plural of American, but when the plural is used, the plight of the homeless becomes less personal.

William Friedkin, director of *The Exorcist* said, "I've always thought that a film should be, first of all an emotional experience. It should make you laugh or cry or be scared. But it should also inspire and provoke you and make you reflect."(a) *Up Your Alley* has some good humor and might make an overly sensitive person cry during a scene or two. More importantly, it provokes your thoughts and causes reflection about the homeless and their plight.

This is a fun flick to watch. Vicky Adderly (Linda Blair) is an aspiring reporter who is being romantically pursued by an irritating boss. His strongest suit is his Jacuzzi. A couple of homeless people are murdered and the reporting of this news is bland. Adderly enlists her talents for the task while the managing editor (Glen Vincent) entertains her in his Jacuzzi.

She turns to the streets for a first hand experience of the plight of the homeless. She fails in an embarrassing first attempt when she meets a homeless nut case of a man named Nick. (Johnny Dark played this difficult character to perfection.) She invites him to lunch at an upscale restaurant where he orders corn flakes and bananas. *Up Your Alley* uses one of Nick's phrases frequently. "Where I come from, they hang people for that."

Adderly's second attempt looks like it will be more disastrous. She dresses down for the part of a homeless lady and is surrounded by a gang of tough young thugs. A homeless man, David, (Murray Langston), and his new and excessively loyal companion, Sonny Griffin (Don Zany) encounter the fiasco.

David speaks up and informs the thugs of their misbehavior. Clever vocal exchanges are made and the rude kids on the block aren't going to go away. David (could this be Biblically inspired?) resorts to pulling out a slingshot and shooting the perpetrators in the foot. They give it up and a bond is made between the homeless duo and the clever reporter. Some perceptive references are made by the truly homeless. "We're just like Boy Scouts. Trustworthy, friendly, courteous, kind, loyal...." And "We're like the Three Musketeers." I am parphrasing but you get the message.

Adderly gives some great ink on this experience. Sonny found himself on the streets when his mother died. All that the seamstress left her boy was some articles of clothing and he hasn't a clue about life on the streets. He has obviously led a sheltered life. David is showing him how to live life in the homeless shelter. They become friends despite David's reluctance to bond with anyone.

They introduce us to some of their homeless friends. Nick reappears as one of them. He is an urbanite who dresses like a Texas cowhand. He even rides that imaginary horse and pretends to whirl a lasso in his scenes. Marilyn (Ruth Buzzi from the TV show Laugh In) is a forty something woman who thinks of herself as irresistible. The fact that nobody else does adds to the comedy. Joe (John Hanrahan) is the beer-bellied gray hair whose life as a veteran drinker lands him happily on the streets. Fish (Kevin Benton) is a Viet Nam veteran who chooses the gutters that the streets of life offer him. He has some problems with flashbacks from the war. This is one of the earlier attempts by Hollywood to address or acknowledge that such things were part of the lives of the men that we revere as war heroes.

Paul Ventimiglia does the original musical scores. A rock/boogie tune, *Livin' On the Streets* is featured in *Up Your Alley* and I think that it had the potential to chart in 1988, when this was produced. A great bluesy *Hey Can You Spare A Little Something?* compliments their lives as beggars.

We felt a bond with the characters in this thoughtfully entertaining low budget movie. (*Up Your Alley* cost about $100,000 to make and it grossed $3 million at the box office (b).) The movie opens to a rough gritty rocker of a song. Sonny is the first actor we see and he is singing Mr. Roberts' *It's a Beautiful Day in the Neighborhood*. The director utilizes Zany's whiny nasal voice to the max. Despite this, Sonny is a very likable guy. After seeing this well kept secret of a movie, you'll never think of anything but Sonny Griffin pushing a grocery cart full of his life's belongings along when you hear the theme song to *Mr. Rogers' Neighborhood*. *Up Your Alley* lets us witness Sonny evolving from a nice, homeless kid into a caring young man. David befriends him early in this film. The two of them are magic together.

Murray Langston is best known as *The Unknown Comic*. Born in 1945 in Dartmouth, Nova Scotia Canada, he made a number of appearances on the *Gong Show* during the 1970s. He wrote the script and appeared in *Up Your Alley* and *Night Patrol*. He also produced *Up Your Alley*. He got a lot of mileage out of a small budget in this one.

His career has a number of coincidences with Blair's. He was featured in another 1979 roller-skating cinematic production. He was the notorious drunk in *Skatetown*, one of three 1979 screen gems centering on the roller skating culture. *Xanadu* was the other featuring the timely icon Olivia Newton John (playing the role of Sandy Olson), who is remembered as the object of John Travolta's affection in *Grease*. In another strange twist of fate, Linda Blair would play the part of Rizzo in the Broadway Production of *Grease* later on. Murray shows up as the man in the car in the spoof *Repossessed* and as the ticket taker in the 1994 martial arts' cinematic gift to children, *Double Blast*. Linda refers to Langston as a dear friend to this day.

In another strange but true note that is neat, Murray was a contestant of the TV game show *The Dating Game* in 1973, the same year that *The Exorcist* was released. He was picked by the lovely Louisa Moritz to accompany her on of those exotic destinations that *The Dating Game* was infamous for. Louisa Moritz played the part of Bubbles in Linda Blair's early prison film, *Chained Heat*.

David's character development is subtle but appreciated. An intelligent, sensitive man has turned to living on the streets and the only friend that life has taught him trust is the bottle. Sonny and Vicky help him discover his inner light.

Vicky is given a crash course on life. The sweetheart of the suburbs is introduced to the rough edges of the poor side of town. The babe in the woods gets a taste of the good life that the gutter has to offer. The party girl who pursues a profession turns into a woman that cares about a man before this cinematic closet classic concludes. She exits with more character than she started with.

In stark contrast to *Night Force*, there is a budding relationship between the character (Vicky Adderly) played by Blair and the leading man, David (Murray Langston) in this movie. There seems to be a genuine closeness between these two. They were sweethearts in *Night Patrol* and ended up in bed together in that laughter filled laugher. A bedroom scene was unnecessary in *Up Your Alley*. You could feel the mutual depth of concern in this one.

Just to prove that reality reigns in *Up Your Alley*, Lance never improves. He is still a self-centered jerk after all that happens. Another of the films' subtle lessons is that even with a Jacuzzi and a job with prestige, Lance doesn't have what it takes to be truly happy or land a desirable woman for more than a night or two.

I don't remember any movie since Steinbecks's *Grapes of Wrath* of 1940 vintage that takes on the plight of the homeless as effectively as this one does. *Up Your Alley* doesn't make as strong of a statement as *The Grapes of Wrath*, but it has a much happier ending. It provides a unique contrast between the two movies and the times in which they were made. The Joad family in *The Grapes of Wrath* was searching desperately for hope. The family of homeless but happy souls in *Up Your Alley* is just looking for enough to get them through another day. They also don't have any genetic families verses the extended clan in *The Grapes of Wrath* and that is an even subtle and stronger statement that perplexes the thoughts more profound. How the times have changed! Langston does an admirable job in showcasing the plight of the homeless, while keeping them lovable and their dignity intact. You wouldn't think of The Unknown Comic as a master craftsman as the writer and producer of Up Your Alley. Some of life's surprises are most delicious. That also includes seeing Linda Blair in a believable serious role again.

There are many scenes that are touching in this comic drama. The laughs are easy and frequent. It was refreshing to see a movie that the characters would dare even laugh at themselves when they were funny. The plot is believably good. Good deeds are rewarded and there are no scenes of anyone naked. You'll find that Linda Blair looks darn good in clothes by the way. Although not everyone lives happily ever after, *Up Your Alley* has a nice ending.

The only logical reason that this fine film hasn't found its way to television as a late-night filler or weekend matinee is the foul language that creeps up from time to time. It is somewhat of a documentary of life in the streets on the poor side of town. In the unlikely event you find *Up Your Alley* in you neighborhood video store, it would be wise to treat yourself and your family to it. It is available on the Internet.

Moving Target
aka
Bersaglio sull' autostrata
1988

Linda Blair is fast approaching 30 in 1988 when *Moving Target* is released. **Co-star Ernest Borgnine is in his 70s.** Linda is slowly surrendering her schoolgirl figure and no longer features the face of the adorable young lady that graced the *Roller Boogie* poster. However, there is no mistaking her for anything but the attractive young professional woman that she stars as.

The plot in *Moving Target* is original and brilliant. It features murder, suspense, romance, chases, intrigue, dogs and enough of Allison Spencer's (Janine Lindemulder's) exposed chest that a sculptor could watch this film and do a bust of it by memory. It seems that ever since Bo Derek whet our appetite in the 1979 film *10* that movie makers can't get enough of near naked, washboard bellied blondes on the beach. Unfortunately, the rest of the cast is short on talent, and *Moving Target* leaves us moving in the wrong direction due to the poor directing of Marius Mattei and talent lacking souls in leading roles stumbling through a script.

A young couple is engaging in bedroom whimsy and it is brought to an abrupt halt by a motorcyclist who brandishes a deadly weapon. The man is shot dead. Yet, there is no evidence of this in the movie, as the shooting takes place at close range and there is no blood coming out of his body. The police later find the corpse and some blood nearby. The woman, Allison Spencer (Janine Lindemulder) escapes on foot and is rescued by a van on the nearby highway. The shooter pursues the van and its passengers are involved in a fatal wreck.

Allison and the other survivor are taken to the hospital where Sally Tyler (Linda Blair) works as a doctor. Sally is dating tennis legend Ferry Spencer (Charles Pitt) who happens to have lost a daughter in an automobile accident in Monte Carlo. Allison claims to be the lost daughter and who survived the accident overseas. The woman playing Allison is not who she claims to be and is exposed (in more ways than one) early in the movie. When Ferry discovers that Allison isn't his daughter he is left vulnerable to the physical charms of the imposter and his relationship with Sally Tyler suffers for it.

A local television station from the Miami, Florida area (where this is filmed), is following the murder, as is the local Mafioso. Allison is unknowingly carrying a valuable bit of merchandise. The TV crew is relentless in its pursuit of the intriguing story of the tennis legend and the discovery that his daughter may not really be dead. As the only survivor of the deadly van crash, Allison has amnesia, or so she claims. Billie Cody (Gabriella Georgelli) is the reporter dutifully determined to bring some undiscovered revelation to the world. Her producer is linked to the mob.

The media and mob aren't the only ones who are interested in what Allison Spencer has to offer. The police want to know what happened to the murder victim back at the villa where this whole fiasco starts. They are also curious as to the murder of the van wrecks' other survivor, which took place in the hospital. Ernest Borgnine plays Police Captain Morrison. His (and Blair's) performance exceeds the rest of the cast by a mile.

Ernest Borgnine was born (Ermes Effron Borgnine) 24 June 1917 in Hamden, Connecticut, a little northeast of Westport, where Linda grew up. His professional acting resume began in 1951 where he played Hu Chang in the movie *China Corsair*. He justly earned an Academy Award for his part as the shy butcher Marty Pilleti in a great film from 1955, *Marty*. His was a masterful performance. It is an outstanding example of what a character acting should be. To date, he has 196 credits in the movies and television to his name. He is best remembered as Lt. Commander Quentin McHale from the 1964 TV sitcom *McHale's*

Navy. This should have been a natural role for Borgnine, as he ended his ten-year career in the US Navy in 1945, where achieved the rank of Gunner's Mate 1st Class. He also gave a strong performance in the original *Poseidon Adventure.* You'll find him forceful, although not all that lovable in *Moving Target.*

The tennis legend/tennis pro played by Charles Pitt is the same Charles Pitt that is featured in the 1979 movie *Skatetown USA.* He couldn't have played a more lifeless, pampered geek than he did in *Moving Target.* The only passion that he reveals in *Moving Target* is lust, and he is barely able to convey that.

Mike Francis is responsible for the music in this film. Some of it is good. Some of it is annoying. I don't know if this is the same Mike Francis that played saxophone for the western swing band *Asleep At the Wheel.* They won the Country Music Award for Vocal Group of the Year in 1987 and 2000 (a). There is also a remote chance that the Mike Francis responsible for the music in this entertainment vehicle may have been Mike Francis alias Francesco Puccioni who arranged the pop song *On and On* which was a top 40 hit by Steven Bishop in 1977(b). The two Mike Francis named here are not one in the same

The automobiles were like the fashions featured in this film. If the Amish drove, they would have driven the bland sedans that were seen here. The van was certainly decorated in a colorful fashion, although it didn't scream of horsepower or styling significance. Linda Blair looked nice in her tennis shorts and top, but other than that, (and the multiple shots of Lindemulder in her underwear) most of the clothes looked like they were designed by a closet gay Amish guy, who liked color, but nothing stylish.

Despite the lame acting by Janine Lindemulder (on the edition of *Moving Target* that I possess, she is listed as Janine Linde), Charles Pitt and Gabriella Georgelli, *Moving Target* has a surprise ending and you'll be shocked to discover who the murderer is.

Silent Assassins
1988

This was a first for a couple of moviemakers. It was the first of Linda Blair's three (to date) martial arts movies. It was also the first movie that Phillip Rhee produced. It was a noticeably low budget film. The action, plot and acting more than compensated for what it lacked in extravagant props and special effects.

Sam Kettle (Sam J. Jones) is a cop who loses a couple of colleagues in the line of duty. It is the result of a most diabolical man who is working to obtain a biological patent that is to be used in a most diabolical fashion. Kettle and his wife, Sara, (Linda Blair) are in the process of moving to Colorado when all of this shapes up.

The second criminal act performed by the sinister Kendrick is the ambushing of two government agents who are protecting the brilliant old biochemist (Dr. London) who developed the lethal biological potion. This occurs when a lovely dark woman emerges from a Mercedes convertible. (Phillip Rhee said that in an effort to make the movie within its budget, they had to cut the top off of the Mercedes because it was too expensive to find a genuine Mercedes ragtop.) She drops her keys. She bends over to pick them up in the parking lot. The agents are ogling over the opulent attraction. They drop their guard. She rises up, pulls a gun and drops the two of them in less than four shots. She is obviously the best shot in the movie.

The next tactical maneuver is the kidnapping of the aged but brilliant Dr. London (Bill Erwin) and an Oriental debutante's niece, Joanna (Joanna Chong). Her parents and two other bodyguards are also brutally butchered in the melee. The surviving duo is whisked off to a fortress.

Her uncle Jun Kim (Jun Chong) is obsessed with rescuing his niece. He does all that he can to enlist his talents with Sam the cop. After rescuing Sam, he is welcomed to the call. The deadly chase would be on but they aren't sure whom they are pursuing. They also know that this criminal organization has something to do with a government agency that was supposed to have been dissolved ten years ago.

Kim suggests that Oyama (Mako) might have some clue as to the identity of the villains. He thinks that the secret Asian society of Iga might be responsible for the crimes. His nephew Bernard (Phillip Rhee, who also is listed as one of the producers of *Silent Assassins*) reluctantly enlists his expertise in the quest to rescue the little girl and the highly esteemed Dr. London. It is only after his martial arts studio is turned into a shooting gallery and his girlfriend is poisoned in a Sushi restaurant that he agrees.

Phillip Rhee is a fascinating individual. He is no stranger to the Martial Arts. He possesses a 6th degree Dan Black Belt in Tae-Kwon Do. He has also earned a 3rd degree Black Belt in Hap-Ki Do. He produced all of the *Best of the Best* films. He is a very underrated actor. He brought a wealth of character to *Silent Assassins*, as the Yuppie operator of a Martial Arts studio. He plays a strong part with rugged, sublime charm.

Kim (Jun Chong) interjects determination and some humor to the making of this film. He and Bernard are outstanding in their display of the Martial Arts. The deliverance of lines and timing of the cast is great, especially for such a low budget film. Sara (Linda Blair) blends some humor, passion and reality to the plot as the wife of a dedicated cop. She truly loves the lug, even though he can't stay committed to any of their commitments, save his marital vows. The dialect flows flawlessly in this film.

Silent Assassins isn't for the weak of heart as there is some graphic violence and bloodshed displayed. Some forms of torture are implemented on the kidnapped Dr. London. Arms are severed. Guts are slashed and spilled open. In one case, a man loses his head in the bloodiest of ways. The widest array of weaponry is put on display here. Sabers are brandished and knives are slashing. Automatic guns blare, as do high-powered handguns of enormous proportion that come equipped with silencers. A human claw is fruitlessly brought into fisticuffs. Even the most lethal weapon of WWI is brought out; shovels were the weapons of preference in trench warfare, as they could be raised into the neck of descending attackers as they jumped into the trenches. This action would sever their head from their neck. These shovels were integrated into the fighting in *Silent Assassins*.

Alexis Rhee plays Joanna's slain mother. She is a brilliant scholarly woman. She is a certified hypnotherapist and a certified Microsoft network engineer. She is an accomplished classical violinist as well. It's a darn good thing they didn't cut her hands off in *Silent Assassins*.

There is the usual surprise conclusion to this Linda Blair film. It questions the intentions of government officials of the day (The Ronald Reagan Right Wing Radical Regime) and rightly so. How dare Hollywood question the motives of the Ronald Reagan regime! How dare the girl that played Regan in *The Exorcist* be cast in a movie that would question the infallibility of Ronald Reagan's right-wing radical regime in 1988! How dare the powers that be that made *Silent Assassins* leave us hanging as to the outcome of Dr. London! How could they wrap this film up without letting us know if Sam and Sara ever moved to Colorado? When and if Sara and Sam Kettle moved, did they have children? Could they possibly be in line to be the next generation Ma and Pa Kettle?

I know that twenty years have passed since its release, but I think that we need a sequel so that we will know what happened to these good people and then we can rest easy.

SEE IT!!

Grotesque
1988

This was Linda Blair's first attempt in the film industry on the other side of the camera. She was one of the associate producers of *Grotesque.* Lincoln Tate was the other and both of them appeared in the film. According to an interview in Fangoria magazine, she thought that the movie should have had a more exploitive title. When she realized that it would have cost more to fight for the change than she made doing the film, she wisely left well enough alone. I wonder what name she would have blest this frightful flick with.

It wasn't the first time that Linda Blair chose to hang onto her money instead of lining the pockets of the legal gurus. She was arrested eleven years prior to the releasing of *Grotesque* for conspiring to purchase and distribute cocaine and for possession of amphetamines. Linda's cohorts were dog breeders and the phone taps indicated that dog was the code word for cocaine. (In the 25 years that I've disc jockeyed in taverns I've never heard of cocaine referred to as "dog".) Although there was a real dog discussed, Linda's legal team went for a guilty plea instead of challenging the charges. It may have been more economically feasible to do so and it would keep her name out of the papers, which may have led to even more scandal had the trial dragged on. In an interview on the October 25, 1999 edition of *E-The True Hollywood Story* she claimed the arrest ruined her acting career. Perhaps she is speaking from financial point of view, as it was many years before a name studio would bankroll an effort featuring her in a lead role. Although she has failed to reach the cinematic heights of *The Exorcist* again, she has done some outstanding acting. I don't know if the arrest is wholly to blame for the stagnation of her career; if it is part of the cause or if she just hasn't been surrounded by the caliber of professionals at all levels of film making that was present in her blockbuster performance at the early age of 14 in *The Exorcist*. I do know that she has not been in the revolving door at a rehab center as so many of her Hollywood colleagues have. She hasn't had any messy divorces and she hasn't been involved in any dirty custody battles over children. She has stayed focused on her legacy as a person and has stayed true to her ideals, once she ascertained their identity. She may be looking at herself in the mirror today and feeling better about herself (inside and out) than many of us.

Many of the crew that was involved in the production end of *Grotesque* was also cast in it. Linda was the featured female Lisa and Lincoln Tate appeared in the flick, although his role isn't listed on the IMBD web sight, he probably was used as one of the posse that was searching for the killers. Mikel Angel and Joe Tornatore, who also directed this grotesque gateway to horror, wrote the script and played the part of Charlie. Like, Lincoln Tate who played the role of officer Blaine. Joe Tornatore would later appear as the fight trainer in the critically blasted Blair un-classic *Bail Out*. His acting wasn't limited to Linda Blair films. He played the black-gloved gunman in the 1973 classic *The Sting*.

I don't know if Donald Tornatore is related to Joe, but I am assuming that he is. In over 50 years of life, this is the first time that I've heard the name Tornatore. It is a name that resonates with a ringing ruggedness. It should have been used for a movie character. Donald played the role of the Ghoul in *Grotesque*. Bob Apiza played the role of Patrick. He did a decent job. All he had to do was amble around, grunt and look repulsively disgusting. (How many of us have gone to class reunions and found old dates filling this bill?) Donald was seen as one of the stadium workers in *Night Force* (film featuring Linda Blair from 1987). Robert Zoller played the sheriff in *Grotesque* and he looks so familiar. He shouldn't because this is the only acting role that he ever did professionally. He was also the property master for this film.

Let's go a little deeper into some of the stars and extras involved in Linda Blair's movies as long as we've touched the family lines. Nels Van Patten plays the part of a murdering laugh happy lunatic (Gibbs) in *Grotesque*. He has a sinister laugh and is Donna's beau. She makes a very cutting remark regarding his manly performance, which should be heard from the film, as it fails to carry the same weight written. Nels is the son of TV's *Eight Is Enough's* Dick Van Patten and his lovely wife, Pat. His acting brothers include James and Vince Van Patten. Nels is the oldest of the acting Van Patten brothers, being born in 1955. Like his brother, (Vince) Nels was tennis pro. Farrah Fawcett was one of his students. This is the only film that features Linda Blair and Nels Van Patten together to date.

James Van Patten shows up in two movies with Linda Blair. He played Hoppy in Blair's best musical (*Roller Boogie*) and the part of Steve Worthington in *Night Force*. He was born into an anointed acting family in Brooklyn, New York on 7 October 1956. He was a mainstay on television during the 1970s. He played parts on westerns like *Bonanza* and *Gunsmoke* in the early 1970s. Perhaps his most notable role on the silver screen may have been that of Dr. Hefner on *Saw IV*. His physical appearance reminds me of a young Billy Ray Cyrus.

Vince Van Patten is the youngest of the acting Van Pattens from Dick's lineage. He played the part of Marti Gaines' (Linda Blair's) boyfriend Seth in *Hell Night*. Born in 1957, Vince's professional acting career goes back to the days of *Gunsmoke*. He appeared in an episode on this western classic in 1972 and another in 1973. The kid must have looked like the real cowboy because he was given a part on the *Bonanza* TV show in 1970 and 1972. If you were glued to the tube in the early 1970s you may have seen him in *The Courtship of Eddie's Father*, *The High Chaparral*, *Cannon*, *Nanny and the Professor*, *Ironside*, *Marcus Welby MD*, *Adam 12*, three episodes of *Medical Center*, *Barnaby*

Jones and *Love American Style.* His first TV role came as Stevie on *Dial Hotline* in 1970. The handsome man was a grizzled veteran of the TV screen before he was twenty. He is two years Blair's senior and he was well acquainted with Tinseltown at an early age. Like Linda, he has managed to keep his name off of the sheets of scandal that Hollywood's inksters love to spill. Linda has kept her nose clean for over 30 years.

This economical chiller was released on 9 September 1988 as Linda was fast approaching the 30-year marker and was about 15 years since *The Exorcist* was released. *Grotesque* didn't have the intrigue, but the head spin administered by Patrick was every bit as unnerving as Regan's.

Here's a little synopsis of the chiller: Lisa (Linda Blair) and Kathy (Donna Wilkes) her college compadre are heading to Lisa's parents' home in Big Bear Lake, California for the weekend. It is a cozy community where everyone knows their neighbor and the scenery is sweet. It is somewhat isolated and insulated from the rush of the rest of the world.

Lisa's dad works in the make up department of Hollywood. He is the man responsible for feature creatures in the scary movies that keep us awake after we go to bed at night. He is also planning on escaping to his beautiful home for the weekend. Her dad's brother works the other angle of creation and lives in Big Bear Lake too. He is one of those plastic surgeons who make people look better. Her father is a man who truly loves his work. He delights is scaring his guests. Kathy understands and appreciates his mischievous attitude. The only family member that isn't introduced, but is spoken of is Patrick. The first time that I saw this movie I wondered if he was the family dog. They are all enjoying the good food and fun as host and guest when the strange bunch of rowdies that were encountered on their way home show up uninvited.

(This is the second of three films that deal with the special effects aspect of film making that feature Linda Blair. The others are *SFX The Retaliator* (1987) and *Monster Makers* (2003).

The intruders of both sexes wore earrings and leather jackets and featured facial paint. If one of your children brought them home to introduce them as your future in-law it would scare the devil out of you. They heard that there were a lot of drugs or a stash of cash in the house. They quizzed the family and their guest. There was no money and there were no drugs. This response wasn't the one that the intruders were looking for and they began to use force to obtain the information that they were looking for. (How often do we attempt to force events our way when we know that it is impossible?) The father is bludgeoned. The mother and guest are murdered. The view was grizzlier, more morbid than a rabid bear could have left.

Lisa is able to escape by jumping out of an upstairs window. (She makes a similar escape in *Witchery* (1988).) She runs through the snow-covered woods to elude the pursuing intruder.

It is about this time that we are introduced to Patrick. This creature redefines ugly. A 600-pound woman with a pimple-roni face wouldn't flirt with him at bar time. Imagine a guy with a five- pound skin tab. What would your face look like if you went bobbing for apples in battery acid? Imagine the offspring of a courtship between Mr. Bill and Roseanne Barr. I think that you've got the picture of Patrick. He limps over to Lisa's dead dad and says, "Papa". He is angry.

Patrick goes unnoticed as one of the great mass murderers of cinematic horror. He grabs a very large and muscular Eric (Robert Z'Dar) and puts him into a bear hug. The back snaps and Eric ends up lying limp and lifeless on the floor. He grabs the head of his next victim and spins it like a yo-yo. Patrick catches up to his third victim and slams her into a tree. Oh! To wrestle like a pro! Gibbs is his fourth victim and he is placed into a claw hold. His couldn't hold out much longer after the move was applied and Gibbs moved onto the next life. The sultry Donna is hoping that she can use womanly persuasion to save her lovely life. Patrick embraces her face, chokes her and then breaks her neck as well. He is not just an angry young man. He is a monster.

One of the eccentric rowdies catches up to Lisa and tries to kill her. Patrick catches up to the punk at about the same time. I don't need to tell you what happens to him.

The local storeowner stops by the house the following day to go fishing with Lisa's dad. He stumbles onto the carnage left by the marauding misfits. He is appalled and notifies the authorities. They gather up a posse, like the ones you would find in the old TV westerns. They are searching for the murderers and Lisa. This is the only part of the film that is difficult to accept. First off, they used Dobermans for search dogs. I may be wrong, but aren't hounds usually used to sniff out and search for the escaping crooks? Secondly, the dogs' owners are usually leading the dogs in this search instead of the dogs leading the men. This may be a film first. Whatever dog or method was used, it was fruitful as the two surviving villains were apprehended and Lisa was found alive, but not well. She was beaten and left in the harsh blizzard elements in no more than her pajamas.

The male suspect, Scratch, (played by Brad Wilson) is interrogated by the police. It is the typical good cop/bad cop routine. He doesn't confess, although he doesn't give a very convincing story. The female suspect, Shelly (played by Michelle Bensoussan in her only professional acting experience) is not falling for those hoaky police interrogations either.

Lisa's Uncle Rod is brought into the movie at this point. The only way to convict the two suspects is with Lisa's testimony and she is in critical condition. She is all that remains of her uncle's family, as far as the community knows. Tab Hunter plays Uncle Rod.

Tab is most famous for his role as Joe Hardy in the classic musical *Damn Yankees*. Director Stanley Donen said this about Tab, "He couldn't sing. He couldn't dance. He couldn't act. He was a triple threat." Hunter was born Arthur Andrew Kelm 11 July 1931 in New York, New York. He was a pretty good actor at the age of 15, when he convinced the Coast Guard that he was old enough to join. He was one of the lady-killers of the silver screen during the 1950s. His athletic persona, blonde hair and flat stomach kept demand for his services up until Troy Donohue replaced him with a similar image. Tab lost his brother Walt in Viet Nam in 1965 and his brother left behind seven children. Tab was stricken with a heart attack while skiing in Taos, New Mexico in 1980 and had a stroke in 1991. He has recovered from both. It is coincidental that Taos is where Sweet Hostage was filmed in 1975. There are some other coincidences regarding Tab Hunter and Linda Blair being cast in this film together. His moniker was "The Sigh Guy" (because the women sighed whenever his name came up) and Linda Blair is known as "The Scream Queen." What are the odds of this pair (The Sigh Guy and The Scream Queen) being cast in the same low budget movie? Blair's attraction to musicians is legendary, but I'll bet to this day she didn't know that Tab Hunter's song *Young Love* held down the number one spot on the Billboard Charts for six weeks in 1957 (a). Of course, its charting would have been two years before Linda Blair was born.

As previously mentioned, Linda Blair movies have the most unpredictable endings. I'm going to leave you hanging as to what becomes of the two suspects.

Witchery
1988

This is low budget gore at its finest. It holds true to William Friedkin's (director of *The Exorcist*) ideals (a). It did scare you. It also provoked me. I gained a great disdain for witchcraft after seeing this film. It also made me reflect and be grateful that our society is no longer greatly influenced by the occult practices of the Dark Ages.

It was an unnerving production. Linda Blair plays the role of pregnant Jane Brooks. This is a unique portrayal by the polished actress. It is the only time that she is ever seen as a mother in waiting. It is interesting to note that the father of the baby is never mentioned in *Witchery*. A woman in black dress mysteriously rescues her from an industrial accident. This may have something to do with the plot.

Her parents are interested in purchasing an abandoned hotel on a deserted island off the coast of Massachusetts, where the filming took place. Jane is from a family of four, father, mother, kid brother and herself. The parents are considering the purchase of this ramshackle of a wreck for investment purposes. Mrs. Brooks has aspirations for turning this place into an exclusive nightclub. It is only fifty miles from Boston. Their architect (The Taylor firm) is unavailable, due to a broken leg. Mrs. Brooks (Anna Ross) has her husband call a party that the Taylors recommended as an architectural consultant.

Linda Sullivan is the young professional played by Catherine Hickland. We are introduced to the new architect as a beauty bathing in the shower. So many Blair films portray their women as squeaky-clean. This is the 6th film (I am counting her bath tub appearance in *Savage Streets*.) of her career that features a young woman in the shower. *Born Innocent, Fatal Bond, The Chilling* and *Bail Out* would be the only subsequent film featuring fine feminine physiques lathering their lusciousness. The shower scenes in Born Innocent and Bail Out are the only ones that have any relevance to the plot.

Linda thinks that the phone is ringing while she is in the shower. Her boyfriend informs her that the phone did not ring. The same lady in black appears in the mirror as Linda dries off from her shower. It mysteriously rings right after this and Mr. Brooks is on the line. He tells Ms. Sullivan that the Taylors recommended her. She does not know the Taylors. There is already a mystery going on and the producers still haven't sunk the bank into this condemned creation.

Their real estate agent was coincidentally unavailable and his son was given the opportunity to show this old place that was steeped in character. Rick Farnsworth plays the son, Jerry Giordano. Jerry may be many things, but he doesn't come off as a very good real estate agent.

Meanwhile, back at the abandoned mansion on the isolated island, a young photographer named Gary (David Hasselhoff) and his companion, Leslie, (Leslie Cumming) are snapping shots of the old hotel. Leslie is a student of the occult and desperately desires a picture of the witch's light. They are successful in this endeavor.

The lady in black has a constant presence throughout these sequences. Hildegard Knef plays the lady in black to a tee. She rambles on in German. This may be one of the reasons that *Witchery* debuted in West Germany. It is revealed that she is the house ghost. She was once regarded as the darling of the silver screen. She came to the island and spent her final days. We will never be certain if she spent them alone or in the company of others. Many witches were said to have been burned there. This island is of particular interest to Leslie.

Our whole crew is on the island and what a diverse cast of characters we have! There is the greedy, bossy demanding Rose Brooks. She meets her Waterloo in a most gruesome fashion on this island. She is taken captive by the evil ones and her lips are sewn shut, but her ultimate demise doesn't occur here. A close-up of her red high heels adds to the desperateness of her futile struggle.

Jane purchased a toy tape recorder for her younger brother, Tommy (Michael Manchesster). They, too are stranded on this island from hell. Jane is taken into another dimension through the bathtub and witnesses two wretched looking souls tugging over a baby doll.

The realtor and the architect fall to their lustful desires. Gary's girl, Leslie doesn't fall for the seductive persuasion of her heart throbbing companion. She refuses sex throughout the movie. Linda and Gerry discover the consequences of their lustful weakness. She is strapped to a chair and savagely ravaged by ghules. He is burned after being nailed and bound to a cross. Again and again the old lady in black is there to witness the misfortune of others.

Linda shows up in the room with the bill of a swordfish sticking through her slashed throat. Mr. Brooks and Gary are the poor souls that make this discovery that keeps us wondering what kind of misery will soon befall these castaways. There are so many strange twists of fate that are brought to us in this heaping helping of horror.

Leslie thinks that she has a dream where she is seduced. She wakes up screaming and Gary finds her. He holds her. She is dressed in a common blouse and blue denim jeans. Rose's ring is found at the base of the fireplace. The guests are desperate to escape in the tumultuous weather. The water is far too rough to take Gary's rubber dingy back and the boat that brought them is gone after the mysterious murder of its captain. The boys fire a flare gun. The only one to witness the flame is a wheelchair bound girl on the other shore. A skeptical father dismissed her discovery.

Jerry's father is concerned enough to notify authorities. He is initially treated with skepticism. However, the sheriff gives in and the two of them search the island in a helicopter. It is to no avail.

Freddy Brooks is the next victim and it looks like the score of casualties is going to keep on growing. None of the deaths are normal. None of the deaths are peaceful. Most of the casualties fall victim as lone souls in a haunting atmosphere.

Would you believe that Linda Blair leaps through another upstairs window in *Witchery*? It was not, however, the same window that she escaped through in the movie *Grotesque*.

Witchery does shed some light as to the methods behind the murderous madness of this movie. It reveals that the three gates to hell are greed, lust and the blood of a virgin. The mysterious maiden in black informs us of four things that are also needed to complete the formula for her diabolical scheme:

1. Fire from the greedy
2. Lust from the harlot
3. Fruit of the woman in labor
4. Blood from a virgin

Jane mentions three doors to the dark side near the end of *Witchery*. She appears possessed in this scene. They are:

1. Lust: Linda for the lust
2. Greed: Rose for the greed
3. Ire: Ire of the persecuted bitch

Add Jane's baby and the blood of the virgin which came from Leslie and

that completes the formula.

We are also harshly reminded in Romans 6:23 "For the wages of sin is death;"

German film veteran Hildegard Knef is the mysterious lady in black. She began her seven-decade career in films in the 1944 German film *Traumerei* She also played The Countess Liz in Ernest Hemingway's *The Snows of Kilamanjaro*. She was Catherine the Great in the 1963 version of *Catherine of Russia*.

Hildegard was born in Ulm, Wurttemburg, Germany 18 December 1925. She began acting at the age of 15, but with a war going on and hers' the losing side, there were some tough choices to make and unconventional behavior was sometimes needed to survive. She dressed up like a boy after the Russians invaded the land of the invaders so that she would not be raped by the marauders. She was sent to a prisoner of war camp. It is amazing how some of our great actors and actresses gained their most convincing experiences because of the military. (See Tab Hunter in *Grotesque*.) She played Marina in the German film *Die Sunderin*. The Roman Catholic Church registered a most rigorous protest to the nudity portrayed in this film. The nudity spoken of was brief, yet powerful and enhanced the plot of the story. It was the first nudity used in the German film industry. *Die Sunderin* takes a hard, honest look at the social and sexual scenes of the German people during the Second World War. In 1959 she received the German Film Award in Silver for Outstanding Individual Achievement as Supporting Actress in *Der Mann, Der Sich Verkaufte*. Hildegard passed away 1 February 2002.

Witchery is a well thought out, low budget wonder. It has a very deep plot and it is well researched. The acting is good. If you like suspenseful gore, you'll gobble this goblin right up. As usual, you'll never guess who lives through this movie or its outcome. It will surprise you.

As an afterthought, I found this movie much too unnerving to view twice. It is even more disturbing than *The Exorcist*.

Rain Man was 1988's most memorable movie, but *Die Hard* and *Naked Gun: From the Files of Police Squad* were worth the price of a ticket (average price for an American movie ticket was $3.50) as well. George W.W. Bush was elected to the Presidency and you still buy a gallon of gas in America for under a buck.

The Chilling
1989

This is one of Linda Blair's first attempts to join the throngs of Hollywood in an effort to capitalize on the science fiction craze that gained momentum during the 1980s. It featured a bizarre mix of veteran cast members. Linda Blair was the unchallenged Queen of Scream at the time and science fiction was a new, although somewhat relatively connected, genre for her. Troy Donohue is brought back from the dead. (His career had been dormant for some time.) Donohue plays the unethical capitalistic entrepreneur who operated a cryogenics business that was selling body parts from the dead that were supposed to be brought back to life at a later date. Dan Haggerty, best known as "Grizzly Adams", plays the role of the senior security guard.

The son of Joe Davenport Sr. (Jack De Rieux) is involved in a series of robberies and is shot by the police and Joe Jr. is brought to United Cryogenics to be interned in the same building as his recently deceased mother. Joe is permitted to visit the tombs of his family. One of the workers at United Cryogenics, Mary Hampton (Linda Blair), accompanies him and is disturbed that the tomb shown is not that of Mr. Davenport's kin. She discretely brings this to the attention of her boss, Dr. Miller. Mary doesn't yet know that Dr. Miller is involved in the human parts business. He removes body organs for transplants and is getting money for the preservation of the dead, as well as receiving good money for the body parts.

Part of Mary's job is to comfort the families of the deceased. She is very sincere in her approach and her customer relation skills are well developed. Mary is living with an abusive alcoholic. Mr. Davenport is a wealthy tycoon and he is attracted to the sweet woman.

Sergeant Vince Marlow (Dan Haggerty) is in charge of security at United Cryogenics and is friendly with Mary. Normally it would be a sleeper of a job, but not on this

Halloween. Kansas City is smacked with a wicked thunderstorm. The power goes out and the bodies began to thaw. Kansas City is confronted with its most unusual dilemma. Vengeful, bloodthirsty zombies are emerging from their vertical caskets.

The Chilling offers a new weapon in fighting zombies. When shotguns fail, and the Doberman is silenced, it is the indomitable forklift that snatches the potential victims from the jaws of death. If Grizzly Adams only knew that his career would come to rescuing the possessed girl from *The Exorcist* while behind the wheel of a forklift.

It is interesting that *The Chilling* features three highly recognizable stars in Haggerty, Donahue and Blair, but the rest of the cast has a short list of credits. Only Jim Duggan and Robert Colbert have more than 10 more acting credits to their name as of 2009. Of course, it doesn't take a wealth of talent to play the part of a protester or Zombie. Many of the supporting cast claims *The Chilling* as their only movie credit.

Dan Haggerty would later be dealt real life dilemmas with life support systems. In 1991 he was involved in a motorcycle accident and was in a coma for a while. His survival was a triumph. In an unfortunate twist of fate, Samantha, his wife of twenty years hit a deer while on a motorbike in 2008, and was placed on life support. When the family accepted that there was nothing more that could be done to bring her back to a normal life, the plug was pulled. (a)

This was one of Blair's three movies from 1989. As usual, this film features a woman in the shower. As usual, the final scene will surprise you.

Bail Out
1989

I hope that the crew had as much fun making this movie as I did watching it. Although the critics have bashed *Bail Out*, **it accomplished what most films fail.** It was entertaining. It was not runner up to *Casa Blanca*. It won't go down as one of the greatest movies made about abduction, but it was fun to watch. Its success is owed to the capable character actors and a meandering plot that kept the ticket buying patrons on their toes and in their seats. The people that played the part of the good guys and the kidnapping victim were all likeable sorts.

A bail bondsman named Haronian is entrusted with bringing the daughter of a wealthy businessman to court on time. The bondsman is a tightfisted penny-pincher who hires tennis pro Roger "White Bread" Donaldson (David Hasselhoff) to handle the job. Annette Ridgeway (Linda Blair) was the daughter. What should have been a court appearance where a plea is to be entered was turned into a major abduction. Her father had hired a couple of private detectives to bring her home. They were ambushed by Columbian drug dealers and Annette was whisked away. This all took place, as Donaldson was about to fetch her.

Another of Haronian's top affiliates, Mason "Blue" Walcott (Tony Brubaker) was a retired pro football player and is a top man at bringing in the bandits once they had paid their bail. He was what you might call the muscle behind the movement. The other man called to bring in the missing maiden was Casper

"Bean" Garcia. He was a married man with a handful of hungry youngsters waiting for the meal money that the Bean would earn hauling in the bunch out on bail. He is a weapons expert. He possesses a penchant for acquiring guns, grenades, teargas and a bazooka. This trio of opposites banned together and used their resources to find where the Columbian mob was hiding Annette. It was an example what the American society was supposed to be, a real racial mix. The white tennis pro and the black football player and the Hispanic handyman were a team that wouldn't get a handicapper to bet on them, but would win every time.

It was discovered that Annette's boyfriend was set up by the Iranian mob and her father may have been involved.

A bold, ingenious plan was devised and its daring paved the way for the springing of Annette from the hands of horror. Donald is persuaded by Annette to pull into a motel so that she can shower. After being abducted and rescued she felt she could use some freshening up. She showers and convinces Donald that he may be in line for a little extra reward after he showers. Annette bolts, taking his clothes and car with her. She heads back to her father's home, where the original abduction took place. Donald is left waiting for his partners to rescue him with nothing to wear but a towel.

It is only fair to warn the reader that the motel scene is the only one that features any nudity. Annette and Donald are greeted by a completely nude motel clerk. The bubbly clerk with the beautiful body is Debra Lamb. She is a veteran Los Angeles exotic dancer and an accomplished fire-eater (a). If this scene and the foul language were omitted from *Bail Out*, it would have been a decent family film.

Back at the Ridgeway mansion, the Columbian crime leader is waiting for Annette and she is kidnapped again. Her father is played by the veteran Canadian actor John Vernon. He is best remembered from his role as Dean Vernon Wormer in the 1978 classic, *Animal House* as well as the same character in the TV series Delta House. He played the principal in *Savage Streets* and the warden in *Chained Heat*. He also was the mayor in *Dirty Harry*. He could be seen as Maynard Boyle in the 1973 thriller *Charlie Varrick* and was featured in a 1975 episode of *Gunsmoke*. Interestingly enough, John appeared in another 1979 film: *Afghanistan—The Last War Bus*. It seems ironic that 30 years after *The Last War Bus* was done about Afghanistan our nation is deeply imbedded there in a warring fashion. The veteran actor passed away in LA, the first day of February 2008.

Zalazar was the corrupt Columbian waiting for the return of the Ridgeway girl in her own home. She is hauled to a remote outpost in Mexico. "White Bread", "Blue" and "The Bean" used their expertise to discover their whereabouts and pursued the banditos.

Roger invents a way to gain access to the captured creature. The Bean and Blue assist in the rescue coup. It is clever, imaginative and you must see the movie to discover its degree of effectiveness.

Some of the automobiles featured in this Blair/Hasselhoff vehicle are interesting choices. The Bean drives an old orange Plymouth Duster with a hood scoop and the driver's door that falls off when it is opened. The best description that can be offered is that it resembles the Bundy family's mighty Dodge on the classic TV sitcom *Married With Children*. If you soup it up with the Halloween paint scheme and a hood scoop and then trash it, you have the look of the vehicle of the Garcia family. Roger Donaldson cruised in a sporty Chrysler LaBaron convertible. These were tight, little cars with that sported a gutsy four cylinder with an available turbocharger and was also available as a 6 cylinder. I drove one and it had remarkable thrust for such a small car. There is one other interesting automotive sidelights in *Bail Out* is the Excalibur that Haronian is seen driving during the opening scene. It is the same make of car that Blair is seen gallivanting about in *Roller Boogie*. To my knowledge, she is the only actress to appear in two films featuring the Excalibur.

There are some light, humorous moments in *Bail Out*, a.k.a *W.B., Blue and the Bean*. It had all of the ingredients that were needed for a network television series. There was the diversity of the lovable rescuing crew and their abrasive boss. *Bail Out* did an outstanding job of bringing the diverse American classes into a functional team of fun loving achievers. It also had the potential to promote a woman in a leading crime fighting role. This is another one of the Blair movies that features an unusual ending.

One of the greatest military forces in history sent thousands into a highway tunnel that local gorillas sealed off and planted poisonous gas in. This event contributed heavily to the withdrawal of Soviet troops from Afghanistan in 1989. The Berline Wall came down this year. Serial killer Ted Bundy was executed this year. Prince and Madonna were hot on the hot wax charts. The hot wax charts were switching over to the compact disc forum and in a short time we would never view album covers again. *Driving Miss Daisy* and *The Little Mermaid* were very popular at the box office. Betty Davis and Lucile Ball bid adieu in 1989 as did American composer extraordinaire Irving Berlin. The voice of Warner Bros. Cartoons, Mel Blanc also passed away. That's all folks.

Dead Sleep
1990

This 1990 film (release date was 1992 in the USA) was Linda Blair's first Australian film. It was based on a true story of mental health care gone amuck Down Under. It was shot down under in Brisbane, Queensland, Australia. *Dead Sleep* takes an American filmgoer some getting used to. The cast has a British (or Australian) accent. The cars all drive on the other (for Americans) side of the road.

Linda Blair plays the part of nurse Maggie Healey. She begins her new job at a facility for the mentally ill. The highly esteemed Dr. Jonathon Heckett (Tony Bonner) is the man behind the method used to treat the mentally ill. Dr. Heckett's theory on treatment for his mentally ill patients at Elysian Fields is to put the patients into a deep sleep. He is an enthusiastic proponent of bringing peace into the patient's life through the deep sleep therapy. Maggie is excited about being of service to the patients at the Elysian Field and working with the highly esteemed doctor.

Maggie's old boyfriend comes back into the picture and it seems as he hasn't changed his murky ways. He manages to con his way into her apartment for the night and steals her rent money before departing. He will also be treated by the famous

Dr. Heckett. The fate of her old flame is not a desirable one.

Vassey Cotsopoulos (Tina Fuery) is a former patient railing on the authorities to reform this deadly method. She is blown off time and time again.

Maggie quits her job after one of the patients dies. Maggie then makes an appointment with one of the authorities at the complaint bureau in regards to the issue. She notices Vassey is there and the receptionist conveniently lost her appointment. Vassey is furious and nastily remarks that this is the fourth time that this kind of thing has happened. While the receptionist deals with Vassey, Maggie rushes into the regulator's office and wants to discuss her allegations with the chief. He has the complaint in his pile but refuses to discuss the matter because the $10 fee isn't attached to the complaint. It sounds as if American Government Bureaucracy has finally caught fire down under.

Dead Sleep plays like a daytime soap opera. I won't delve into the plot any further, as it is predictable.

It is noteworthy that this film was released in 1990. Linda plays a part that most of the shining stars of the firmament of filmland would shun. It has never been fashionable for the movie industry to take on the role of challenger to the medical field. She has championed other causes that weren't popular with her contemporaries. She spoke of society's ineptness to deal with troubled teens in *Born Innocent*. She exposed our distorted view of the alcoholic in *Sara T. Portrait of a Teenage Alcoholic*. Thirty years had passed since the horrors of the Holocaust the world stood by while a large group of Israelis were hijacked and threatened with death. Linda played the role of a young Jewish hostage in *Victory at Entebbe*. The wake up call issued by Tinseltown would not be embraced by the big names of the big town again in the rallying fashion that *Victory At Entebbe* did. She took on the plight of American political prisoners and the American government's disregard for them in *Red Heat*. I am not sure if Lind Blair is a non-conformist reformer and found these roles attractive or if these films were the only jobs available to her at the time. She gains my gratitude and respect for accepting these challenging roles just the same.

In *Dead Sleep* there have been remarks about the inconsistency of dress between the male and female patients. There are a few shots of women's breasts in *Dead Sleep* and none of the men are topless. (I think if the women in Elysian Fields were as old as the men, their blouses would have remained intact.) If the girls could have kept their shirts on, this too could be a family film.

Dead Sleep is not of the same caliber as the afore mentioned movies that Linda starred in. It does make the viewer contemplate the treatment of the mentally ill. Shock treatment is nowhere near as widespread as it once was and I am not sure that it is even implemented at all these days. Although, I do know one woman who claims to have received shock therapy and she didn't endorse its implementation. I am aware of the widespread use of prescription drugs made available to the mentally ill. In an interview (May of 2010 on WMTV in Madison, WI) many of the heroin addicts claimed that their dependency began with prescription drugs, not marijuana. *Dead Sleep* seems to be abundantly available on the Internet for a reasonable price.

Zapped Again
aka
Zap 2 It
1990

I missed the original *Zapped* movie that featured Scott Baio and Heather Thomas. As is usually the case, the sequel falls short of the original's effect. This 1990 spoof of *Zapped* is ridiculously fun to watch and would seem pointless except that is brings back the ability to make us laugh. Laughter is the tonic that softens life's pains as we savor its gains. It reduces stress. Wait until you see what Linda Blair has up her stress in this shelf duster.

A high school boy begins life in a new school setting and is bullied from the start. He has the same dreams as most high school boys. His mother (played by Shannon Wilcox) is a real estate agent. Women of this field spring up in Linda Blair movies so very often. (It should be noted that Elinore Blair (Linda's mother) was employed in the real estate field.) Todd Eric Andrews play the role of the new boy, Kevin Matthews. Kevin does his best to make friends in his 6th new high school and finds himself face-to-face with a bullying jock dubbed Wayne (played by Reed Rudy) and then with his henchman Cecil (David Donah). Kevin's impromptu interview with work out clad curve master Amanda (Maria McCann) ignites the ire of Wayne. A brief brawl ensues and Kevin is escorted to Principal Burnhart's (Sue Ann Langdon) office by Coach Kirby (played by football legend and

Yankton College alumni Lyle Alzado). It looks as if Kevin is riding the same old bicycle that took him to the other schools.

He finds some after school work at Wonder Wiener; a fine dining establishment catering to sausage connoisseurs the world over. It is here that he meets Lucy (played by Kelli Williams). They become fast friends and she is looking for something more than that and he is as clueless as *The Cat In the Hat*. Amanda has caught his eye and it seems as though (and as is usually the case in life), she has her heart set on football hero Wayne. There is more light-hearted romantic comedy in *Zapped Again* as Coach Kirby is hot for Miss Burnhart. And then there is Cecil.

Kevin discovers a bizarre potion in the wall of the science room behind the picture of Einstein that gives him the power to levitate things as well as unzip and unstitch. So, of course there is going to be some women displayed in topless array, but only in their briefs' moment. This less than legendary light-hearted spoof is laced with one-liners and background jokes. You may not laugh out loud, but there are some choice chuckles in this one. You also may decide to watch it without the kiddies.

Zapped Again also takes on a more serious tone when viewed pass the eye and into the heart and soul. It points out that there is still a difference in the treatment of students because of the image that they portray. It would be so nice if all of the male students were high school quarterbacks and the girls were all Honor Roll cheerleaders. It would be wonderful if all of the children at high school had wealthy parents that could afford the finest clothing of the latest fashion.

There is truth and surrealism brought to life in the scene where the Science Club accepts the challenge of the Key Club to participate in the Penguin Run. Elliot (Ira Heiden) is upset because nobody has ever defeated the Key Club in the Penguin Race. Elliott is the president of the Science Club and the Key Club just took over their meeting room. If the Science Club can win the Penguin Race they get their meeting place back. Elliott would just as soon stay with the status quo. The geeky guys and gals of Emerson High have just rolled with the punches whenever the more well to to students rubbed their noses in the dirt that they dealt them. Kevin won't hear of it. It would be nice if we could make all of this right in real life. It just doesn't work like that. In real life the runner who drops out of half of his races receives the track team's MVP. It wouldn't be because his parents are teachers? Would it? Did you ever notice the high school's football team has had as quarterback the likes of the village's attorney, the plant manager of one of the area's leading manufacturers, and the President of the Booster Club? Maybe these kids were best qualified, but I still think that there may have been some politicking involved. If you truly believe that talent and desire are the deciding factors in who performs in your school's programs, look and see what family the stars come from.

As an interesting family oriented sideline, Shannon Wilcox played the mother of Kevin in *Zapped Again*. In real life she is the mother of Kevin's girlfriend in *Zapped Again*, Kelli Williams.

Linda Blair does a great job as a Home Economics teacher in *Zapped Again*. Naturally, her soufflé collapses and her law for the sagging soufflé is, "When the meal is ruined, it's time to order pizza."

Karen Black (from *Airport 1975*) appears in a cameo role as a substitute teacher at Emerson High School and she is up to the task that comes from the quick thinking Kevin.

Kevin is played by Todd Eric Andrews. The pride of Hastings, Nebraska was born in 1966 and is best known for either the part played in *Zapped Again* or *I Know My First Name is Steven* where he is featured as Cory Stayner, the murderer of two women in Yosemite National Park.

It was surprising to see Lyle Alzado as the romantic rogue numbskull. His passion for Miss Barnhart brought some unique humor to this film. Lyle is best known for his job as defensive tackle for the Cleveland Browns and Oakland Raiders during their glory years. He was one of the reasons for those years of glory on the Bay and the shores of Lake Erie. He attended college at Yankton, a small community in southern South Dakota. I don't know how the Brooklyn born boy found his way to the greener parts of South Dakota, but it is my guess that it had something to do with a football scholarship. He was one of the starting tackles on the 1983 Super Bowl Champion Oakland Raiders. His roughhouse demeanor in *Zapped Again* is typical of the man who said, "I never met a man I didn't want to fight." He was a spokesman for Hanes underwear and also appeared as Bronk Stinson in the 1987 Ernest Goes to Camp classic. Mr. Alzado died in 1992 from cancer, which he linked to the use of steroids.

The Princess of His Pursuit in *Zapped Again* was the pert Miss Barnhart, played by Sue Ann Langdon. She also played Miss Rose Barnhart in the original *Zapped*. She was born Sue Lookhoff in Paterson, New Jersey 8 March 1936. She has defied the Hollywood odds and is still married to Jack Emrek just like she was in 1959 the year that Linda was born.

There is one thing about our attractive Scream Queen that has puzzled me. This movie brings the question to the surface. Linda began modeling for catalogues at age six and soon after did stints as an adorable little girl in commercials (Downey fabric softener and Gulden's Mustard come to mind.) She terrified the clergy and the rest of us (U.S.) as an early teen. *Zapped Again* begs her talent as a teacher. I was curious as to the type of education that Linda received. My curious question is this: Did she ever attend public schools? If she did how did she feel about them? In the event that she did spend a great deal of time in the public school system how did those in her environment treat the girl of 5000 threats from *The Exorcist?*

Linda returned to her public school in Connecticut upon the completion of *The Exorcist*. She continued the relationship with the same boyfriend she had before leaving to film the classic. She said that her classmates had no idea at the time of her return (to school) as to what film she was working on. She did receive the President's Award for Physical Fitness, which is no easy task, as the competing individual hat to run the 600-yard and 50-yard dashes under a certain time. They would also have to run a shuttle run under a prescribed time, throw a softball so many feet, do a flexed arm hang and if memory serves me well, 100 sit ups. Linda was surely a healthy looking young lady. Her present physique bears testimony of the results of the Vegan lifestyle.

This isn't one of the movies that you'll want to rush out and rent, but it does have some laughs in it that accompany some strange romantic twists.

Bedroom Eyes II
1990

This is Linda's first shot at the erotic thriller. It is a 1990 release and you'll notice that most of the women's daily fashions from the era are what promoted the creation of Viagra and other male enhancements. Two of the characters are carried over from the original *Bedroom Eyes.* Stockbroker Harry Ross who is played by Wings Hauser and his ex-wife JoBeth who is played by Veronica Hart. The plot weaves and intrigues. There are a number of shady characters.

A very shapely Carolyn Ross (Kathy Shower) does all that she can to entice us into the voyeurism that Harry gets sucked into. Her attire isn't as typical as the loose fitting fashions that plagued the early 1990s. She sports a number of teddies, including one that could have been used as a translucent evening dress. She is the usual busty, blonde bobble head that has been shoved our way by Hollywood. You can count the number of these sizzling sex symbols that have been forced onto our screens the same way you can count the number of cubes in a tavern's ice tub. There have been so many of these mannequins paraded our way that we barely notice them any more. Carolyn is an artist/model and two times Harry. The man she cheats with is fellow artist Matthew Sotto (Kevin Thomsen).

Harry and broker buddy Vinnie Fasano (Joe Garidina) get involved in some inside trading. Harry's ex-wife, JoBeth, pays the boys at the brokerage house a visit after her recent release from prison. Jo Beth was the first of Harry's three wives.

Harry's second wife was killed in an automobile accident, and he meets a woman who bears a striking resemblance to his late wife. Sophie Stevens is played by the thirty-one year old Blair. She does a great job of messing with our heads. Is she the sweet woman that she seems to be? She and Harry have a very hot love scene after Harry catches Carolyn with Matthew. I've never seen anything like it in any movie. She seems very interested in him. He seems interested in promoting her art and offers to introduce her to his current wife who is involved in art as a model and a dealer.

With a title like *Bedroom Eyes II* you shouldn't be surprised to see about a half dozen sex scenes. None show genitalia, but they are more graphic than you would want your teenager to see. Madness, murder, and mayhem splatter the screen and the art that the three artists put on canvass looks every bit as good as the art at the junior high art fair.

Wings Hauser had to be the best kept secret in the acting business. He has a strong screen presence. Veronica Hart is the consummate villain. She is a perfect fit in the role here. Linda Blair is naturally herself in *Bedroom Eyes II*. There is a genuine disarming charm about Blair that cannot be taught nor feigned. When Sophie tells Harry that she would really like some company for supper, it is genuine and natural. This attribute comes through in so many of her films. The rest of the cast could join the junior high art fair.

The music that is piped into Bedroom Eyes II will keep you up at night, as if the steamy love scenes won't. The music is mixed into the movie at a volume level that makes its attempt to enhance the scene ineffective. The only exception to this is the music of Tosca that plays in Sophie's apartment while Harry is visiting. Sophie explains how the art reflects life and how life reflects the art.

I wonder if Linda Blair owned a maroon Mercedes two-door

coupe during the late eighties and early nineties. The one that Harry drove in this film looks a lot like the chopped Mercedes convertible used in *Silent Assassins*. The 1980s and 1990s was the automobile era of the personal luxury car and what better example of such a car than the Mercedes two door.

Maybe one of the reasons that the first love scene between Linda Blair and Wings Hauser seemed so natural and sincere was their off-screen romance. Or maybe one of the reasons for their off-screen affair was because of the love scene in *Bedroom Eyes II*. Is art imitating life or is life imitating art? This relationship did last for a few years. They complimented each other well in *Bedroom Eyes II*.

Hauser is twelve years Blair's senior. In real life, Hauser was born in Hollywood. Gerald Hauser gets his nickname from playing wing back in high school football. He launched his show business career at the age of 5 on a radio commercial. He also did some musical recording prior to his acting success. His father, Dwight Hauser was a writer, actor and producer. The rumor mill had he and Linda Blair as romantically involved for a time. He's either a real lady's man or just hasn't met with the right magic until now. He is currently married to his fourth wife, Cali Lili Hauser. She is a veteran actress and a shirttail relative of Edward G. Robinson. She and her husband have teamed up to make films together.

This is interesting because the Internet Movie Data Base lists Cali Lili Hauser as Wings' wife on their web sight. According to *Who's Dating Who?* on 14 February 2009 Hauser dated Linda Blair from 1990-1994. She would have been 31-34 at this time. It is a time that many women come to terms of long range plans for husbands and children as this time in their lives generally expires within the next five years. The love scenes in *Bedroom Eyes II* and *Gang Boys* are especially intense. It is said that Blair and Hauser fell in love and began dating after the movie and ended their relationship in 1994. According to an old magazine article that comes from a periodical that runs a section dubbed "couples" Blair was smitten by the hunky Hauser on the set of *Bedroom Eyes II.* The article featured photos of Blair and Hauser and they were taken by Roger Dong with Joanne Kaufman and John Hannah collaborating on the article. Wings was married to actress Debra Lock at the time.

Things changed about a half-year later. Lock and Hauser became solo acts and Wings discovered a lump on his breast. Hauser holed up on his boat off the California coast and preferred the solitude. Like the least likely contestant for the role of Regan in *The Exorcist,* Linda arrived oblivious to the concept of rejection. She greeted the ailing Wings armed with herbal remedies and vitamins. The Princess of Photogenic Faces also brought a teddy bear.

Bunches of Blair movies feature stuffed animals. There is a stuffed hound dog on the physiatrist's shelf in *The Exorcist II.* There is a stuffed yellow bird in the motel bedroom scene in *Fatal Bond.* You'll also notice a couple of stuffed monkeys embracing each other in one of the earlier scenes of *Roller Boogie.* It is the scene that features Linda modeling her roller skating attire for the first time. She is wearing a body hugging blue top/shorts ensemble with the spaghetti straps accented with a flattering red belt.

Wings was featured in a thriller of a film entitled *The Watchers* that was filmed in the Amazon jungle at this time. He and the nurturing Blair roughed it in this prehistoric environment for six weeks. Linda D. Blair surprised "Wings de Hauser" by enduring the experience where they shared a hut with no electricity or door for six weeks.

The stonehearted culprit that played JoBeth is accomplished adult film veteran Veronica Hart. The University of Nevada alumnus has been involved in over 150 adult films. She won the AFAA award for Best Actress for her work in *Amanda By Night* in 1981 and for her character in *Roommates* in 1982. She picked up another AFAA award for Best Supporting Actress in *Foxtrot* in 1982. She showed up as the mother of Crystal the maid in *A*

Woman Obsessed.

As movies go, *Bedroom Eyes II* offers a plot that will keep you guessing. The problem with this movie is that it doesn't flow well enough to keep you interested. It is another of the films that Linda Blair was in that was filmed in Canada. Toronto is the host city to *Bedroom Eyes II*. It is also the town that hosted a young Rick James (who dated Linda Blair) during his early learning years of the pop music culture. James was emerging as a talented upstart. Toronto was one of North America's most progressive and gleaming cities during this era. Many young artists were making their bones in the largest city of the Canadian nation during the late 1970s and early 1980s.

Repossessed
1990

This is one of the funniest sequels that you will ever see. *The Exorcist II-The Heretic* was good, but not in the same class as the original. This was one of the ten movies Blair did in a three-year span and may well have been her best comedic effort. Leslie Nielson co-stars as Father Mayi. He is the priest who drives the devil out of the victim in this flick that features Regan being repossessed years after her first exorcism.

In *Repossessed*, she is a married woman with two irritating little snotbergers for children. Her husband is a most tolerant soul. The devil enters her body as she watches television.

After dousing her spouse with the patented pea soup, she knows what she has to do. A young priest (Anthony Stark plays Father Luke Brophy) is called in to perform the ritual.

Things take a turn for the bizarre. Ned Beatty stars as the fledging TV evangelist Ernest Weller with a dog loving diva-ding bat for a wife. Lana Schwab portrayed Mrs. Weller perfectly. When the religious community realizes the ratings bonanza and the cash that it could generate, they plan on televising the exorcism.

Blair is the possessed Nancy Aglet. She wears a blue dress

and the writers capitalize on that combination. This screamer features laughs galore. It also features wrestling announcer Mean Gene Okerlund and once Minnesota Governor Jessie "The Body" Ventura. A couple of the Blair Bunch is seen on the screen as well. Bob Zany is seen giving a movie studio tour. Murray Langston is the man in the car. Both were in *Up Your Alley*. Julie Strain (the aerobics instructor) would show up in *Sorcery* as well as *Naked Gun 33 1/3* with Leslie Nielsen. *Repossessed* is Strain's first screen appearance.

Leslie Nielsen and Linda Blair is a match made in, well heaven isn't the best term to use in *Repossessed*, but they worked well together in this madcap misadventure. Leslie was born 11 February 1926 in Regina, Saskatchewan, Canada. Among other Canadian born stars that worked with Blair are Al Waxman and Michael Wincott (*Wild Horse Hank*), John Vernon (*Chained Heat, Savage Streets, Bail Out*) and Murray Langston.

At one time Nielsen was the spokesperson/model for a Wisconsin Savings and Loan firm. He is most famous for his misleading appearance as the serious looking citizen with the bent sense of humor in many movies. He was Dick Steele Agent WD-40 in the laugher *Spy Hard*. He played Lt. Frank Drebin in *Naked Gun 33 1/3 The Final Insult* and *Naked Gun 2 ½ The Smell of Fear* and in the lesser-known *Naked Space* as Captain Jameson. He is the son of a Welsh mother and a Danish father. His dad was a member of the Canadian Royal Mounted Police. His brother Eric was once the Deputy Prime Minister of Canada. At age 17 Leslie joined the Royal Canadian Air Force. He has over fifty movies to his credit (including Captain Harrison in the original *Poseidon Adventure* that also featured Ernest Borgnine) and loved playing the bad guy. He considered it a challenge. His philosophy was that the worse the villain looked the better the hero appeared. Celebrated film critic William Ebert dubbed the naturalized American citizen as "The Laurence Oliver of Spoofs (a)" His face is as familiar as our old TV screen. It has been seen on *Ironside, Cannon, The Mod Squad, Colombo, The Red Skelton*

Show, M*A*S*H and *Hawaii Five-O* and countless others. Many people watch movies just to see this lovable, laughable icon of the silver screen. His first camera appearance came in 1950 on television's *Actor Studio*. Who could have guessed that it would launch the career of one Hollywood's most recognizable individuals?

Another subliminal anecdote in *Repossessed* is Mrs. Aglet's first name. It is Nancy, and her first name in the original Exorcist was Ragan. Nancy Reagan was the First Lady at the time of *Repossessed's* release. There are a number of other comical political skits. The Oliver North scandal and the Chappaquidic incident involving Ted Kennedy are also mentioned in *Repossessed*. Nancy even questions the Bible's verse (Geneses 1:26) that man was created in God's image. Nancy asks how you would explain Pee Wee Herman if this were true? I don't think that the line was meant in a heretical sense, but jabbed at our serious side with some humor.

Father Brophy is blessed with a unique means of transportation. He is spotted in a Nash Metropolitan. They rivaled the Volkswagen as the consummate economy car of their time. The earliest ones were sold by Hudson dealers. Hudson and Nash motor companies merged about the same time as the introduction of the Metropolitan and comprised American Motors, which would be selling these cars made in Great Britain. (They were originally manufactured in Britain until about 1960.) They had an 85-inch wheelbase and were less than 150 inches long. These little devils rolled around on thirteen-inch wheels and were only 54 and one-half inches high. They weighed in as lightweights at 1800 pounds and originally came with the gutless 42 horsepower engine. They came in two-door coupes and convertibles. By 1960 the 90 cubic-inch engine was introduced and it sputtered out 52 horsepower. They also sported continental kits and in 1960 improvements were made for outside trunk access, a glove box door, seat adjusters and window vents. These two seaters were incredibly small and had a 55 horsepower engine. It boasted a capability to get up to 40 miles per gallon. Among the options offered were the radio, heater and white-wall tires. Having the cute little car transporting the priest to do battle with the big, bad Beelzebub was surely a deliberate paradox.

Due to some brief upper frontal nudity in the opening ten minutes or so, and the film's content, this probably isn't a show for youngsters under 16. The theme of demonic possession might be a bit heavy for some people. You might want to use your discretion.

Much like *Zapped Again*, this movie is best if not taken seriously. It is far too funny to analyze. Everything from the theme to the backgrounds is lent to your laughter. This may have been the movie that Linda Blair was looking for to put her role in the classic *The Exorcist* into her personal perspective. You'll love the music and the outrageous outfits that Father Mayi dons to look like the celebrated musical legends of the 1990 era; none of who probably ever performed *Devil With a Blue Dress On* in concert.

There were progressive signs of change in the times in 1990. 1990 saw New York City sware Darrell Dinkins in as its first Black mayor. Lithuania and Ukraine declared their independence. These events would have been considered impossible 40 years ago.

Sting joined professional wrestling's Four Horsemen, which included Ole and Arn Anderson and Ric Flair. Egypt and Moroccan troops landed in Saudi Arabia to help prevent an Iraqi invasion. Turmoil in the Mideast is still a current topic 22 years later.

Fatal Bond
1991

Veteran cinematographer Vince Monton directed *Fatal Bond* masterfully. In this edgy thriller, he takes a quick thinking, successful hairdresser (a lady named Leonie Stephens who is played by Blair) and matches her up with a tall, rugged rogue from the wrong side of the tracks (Joe T. Martinez is played by Jerome Ehlers.) This is a tale based on an Australian serial killer.

Monton only directed four films to date. I don't know how long it took to film *Fatal Bond*, but you'll remember that it took 224 days to film *The Exorcist* and great attention was paid to detail and it was that great attention that helped make *The Exorcist* so compelling and gripping. It must have taken awhile to shoot *Fatal Bond*. Monton not only takes the bright hairdresser and has her fall helplessly in love with the bad boy. He utilizes Leonie's hairdos to enhance each scene. In the shots where she is bonding with Martinez, her hairstyle gives her a youthful, carefree persona. Her hairdo accents her apprehensions when Joe is up to no good. The hair frames the face that houses Leonie's emotional experiences. This is noteworthy because the lead character IS a hairdresser. *

Monton gets the most out of Blair's acting ability. He uses her gate to bring power to the scene of what may well be another murder. He takes advantage of Linda's 33 years and portrays her as the appealing, young lover and the complicated creature held captive by a man she is irresistibly attracted to. She has the signs of age slowing creeping across her face as she begins to realize what manner of man Joe really is. He brings out Linda's lifetime of emotions from her spirit into the person of Leonie Stevens so well that you beg to ask if she is really acting or reliving. Her patented laughter and carefree conversations are brilliantly brought into this spellbinding who-done-it. If you ever listen to a Linda Blair interview, you'll find that she cleverly weaves whimsy into a conversation that has a pointed purpose.

The adorable child model has reached the age of no return and *Fatal Bond* is the first flick that states this conclusively. Blair continues to capitalize on those big, brown eyes. Although she is still attractive, she no longer features the flawless face of the captivating cutie in *The Exorcist II*. It isn't to say that she has outgrown the role of the sultry seductress. Again, Monton has featured Leonie Stevens as a sizzling seductress in the motel room in the scene on their first night on their new adventure. But he also portrays her as second best eye candy to a number of other women in *Fatal Bond*. The director does this deed with a purpose.

How can a brilliant, well-grounded artist become an impetuous companion of the likes of a Joe T. Martinez? How can a person with a secure job, their own apartment, a nice car and good friends give it all up on a whim? How can one person have such an affect on another? In all of the parenting manuals and all of the lectures that the clergy offers us with the noblest of intentions there is no way to explain being "in love". It is a journey that all of us take and we board the boat blindly. Some of us get lost on the way. Some jump ship and become shark bait. To some, love becomes another four-letter word. Yet, some of us return with a life filled with the character building experiences that bring us boundless and true happiness. Where will Leonie's lesson on being in love leave her?

Monton's attention to detail can be witnessed in the motel love scene. He creates a heart pounding illusion of passionate sex between Joe and Leonie. The only part of their bodies that are exposed in a way that might draw attention from the local chapter of the church league is the exposing of one of Leonie's breasts. She is wearing what appears to be a silky nightie that is never removed. Joe has part of his shirt unbuttoned and you don't see much of anything other that his Adam's apple. This unparalleled love scene is successful because of the sounds and facial expressions of Leonie. A television set lends credence to the scene, as Joe is tardy in his entrance into the motel room where a frustrated Leonie is feigning sleep as she waits. The TV set never gets turned off through the whole ordeal. You'll notice that the bedsprings squeak, but even this isn't overstated. This scene offers something that few thrillers do. The couple is passionate about each other outside of the bedroom. Their characters and their relationship with each other are carefully constructed before this scene. It doesn't come across as mechanical screen sex. You get the feeling that there is an explosive passion between them. Blair does a superb job. Ehlers makes sure that she doesn't do it alone.

It is obvious that Leonie is the good-hearted hottie with an unflagging belief in Joe. Joe is dark, edgy and mysterious. This makes him all the more attractive. He is mixed up in a car stealing operation. He even offers a confusing preference in his choice of beverage. Joe loves to drink beer, but there are two scenes that feature the leading man stealing milk. He is as fearless as he is quick.

Jerome Ehlers bears a striking physical resemblance to screen giant Robert Mitchum, more so than Chris Mitchum (Robert's real son) did in *SFX The Retaliator*. Ehlers is a real lady's man, but it seems as though he prefers the princesses of the prom to the infatuated hairdresser. Joe has an encounter with a high school age cutie who turns up dead the next day. Martinez is an impatient man and wastes no time waiting, especially for a fight.

The new couple's relationship is strained when Leonie reads of the murder the next day in a newspaper on the way to Joe's hometown. Joe wants to see his brother about work and Leonie is eager to embark on her hairdressing career in her new locale. On the journey they stop off at a campground and enjoy intimacy. It is the usual scene. The guy gets so worked up that he rips the panties off of the other lover. If you look closely in this particular portrayal, you'll see that Leonie actually hands Joe a pair of underwear during the counter scene. It is pretty well disguised.

How did the young lady die? There was a violent struggle. Is Joe the only suspect? Did the boyfriend that is introduced forty minutes into the story do the deadly deed? The police know about the murder. Are they doing all that can be done about solving the crime? Why is Bree (the first victim) Boon's mother weeping at the funeral and her father just seems cold? Her parents were divorced and she was residing with her father.

Joe refreshes his old acquaintances. They are operating a garage outside of town where they chop and paint the cars that they steal. Donal Gibson plays Rocky Borgetta, who seems to be the leader of the ring. He fits in like a baby fits a diaper. He is smart and even-tempered. He does his utmost to be discrete. Former European heavyweight boxing champion Joe Bugner plays Claw Miller. Joe's brother Jack is said to be having an affair with Claw's girl. Claw is a rugged looking ruffian. He seems to care about things even less than Joe does. I watched one of the Joe Bugner-Mohammad Ali fights years ago. Bugner slugged the champ so hard in the gut that the impact literally lifted Ali a good half foot off the canvass. Bugner's character looks every bit the slugging soldier in *Fatal Bond*. If I were Joe's brother Jack, I would have run from any advances that his girl made towards me. Claw Miller is one tough tater. Claw does the bodywork in the shady business that the Martinez brothers are mixed up in.

Bugner was born in Szorag, Hungary in 1950 and left with the rest of his family during the unsuccessful uprising in 1956. Joe is six-foot four and the former European heavyweight champion went the distance with Mohammad Ali twice. Bugner won a world title at the ripe old age of 48, six years after the release of *Fatal Bond*.

Leonie struts home alone after Joe embarrasses her at a restaurant where they were supposed to meet with the realeter. She discovers another female victim and does all that she can do to keep the authorities from implicating the man she is so fatally bonded to.

Jerome Ehlers is about a year older than Linda Blair and has a long resume of television and movies to his credit. He played the role of Captain Halliday in the 1995 version of the TV movie *Sahara*. He is a native Australian and does well in his portrayal of the lean, tough decadent who develops a bond with Leonie that is a bit deeper than his casual observances of lovely young creatures of the fair sex.

It is about this time that the police finally locate the whereabouts of Joe. A team of crack detectives led by Detective Chenko (played by Caz Lederman) arrives via aquaplane to further the investigation. Bree Boon's father, Anthony, also arrives in town to pursue his own vendetta. Mr. Boon happens across Leonie at the scene of the second fatality.

I don't dare tell you anymore, as it would deny you the satisfaction of seeing the outcome yourself.

Monton utilizes the music in *Fatal Bond* as well as anybody since Francis Ford Coppola did in *American Graffiti*. The band at the bar in the opening of Fatal Bond has an appealing sound. The song goes thusly:

It'll be a hard act to follow.

> It'll be a tough axe to grind.
> It'll be a bitter pill to swallow
> If you're born in those times.
> It'll be a heartache tomorrow.

It'll be a heart break to find
That the devil took the high road,
And you're following behind.

When it all falls around us,
When it's taken just too much
When we've tried to go further
Than the world ever can.
When the heavens have found us
To be taking just too much
To be playing with fires
That we don't understand.

It'll be a hard act to follow,
The righting of the wrong
The closing of the stables
When the horses are gone. **

You couldn't ask for a more appropriate opening number for a movie like *Fatal Bond*. The band was Manual Days and the Black Hats featuring Kevin Johnson who also penned *A Hard Act to Follow*. I was humbled in the process of gaining permission from Johnson to use the lyrics in this work. Kevin has taped TV and radio specials in Ireland, Switzerland, and Germany. He has tasted fame and success as a songwriter, singer and performer at home (Australia) and abroad. He wrote songs about his youngest son Scotty and his eldest son Shane. After viewing the lyrics of his *Rock and Roll I Gave You the Best Years of My Life*, my heart was touched. I spent my teenage and early 20s playing drums for bands that came up short and couldn't lose that feeling that rock and roll invades you with. I spent 25 years as a disc jockey, yet Johnson's lyrics in the song *Rock and Roll I Gave You the Best Years of My Life* pull parallel emotions from deep within me that I have been unable to put into words. Mac Davis charted this song in the USA in 1974 where it reached number 15 (a).

Johnson's works of art comes straight from the heart and this song hits me right at home. Kevin Johnson hailed from a small town in Queensland Australia. His mother could play the violin and attempted to teach him the stringed instrument to no avail. His interest in music was awakened in his teens. He purchased and mastered the guitar. He worked for the Queensland Public Service: Department of Main Roads and played some of the local clubs after working hours. His talent and acceptance awarded him great success thereafter.

The opening ballad reminds me of Bob Dylan's brand of blues. A different band is playing on TV in the motel room rocking out a tune that fits the mood of the seemingly jilted and abandoned Leonie Stephens to a tee. Some of the lyrics go, "I want it. You give it. I take it." Once again, the music is subtly blended into the action in the fashion of George Lucas from American Graffiti. The closing number tells the tale of the journey taken.

It must be noted that this story takes place in Australia. It is Linda Blair's second filming in the land down under. *Dead Sleep* was the first. Both were based on true stories. It is the land of one of Linda's first loves, Rick Springfield. There are some things that will take an American viewer time to adjust to. Australians drive on the other side of the road and their steering wheels are also on the other side of the car. They also have an accent that sounds somewhat British, although I am sure that the English will contend that it isn't all that similar. Their cuisine is certainly different than what Midwestern Americans might be used to. Take note of the daily special at the first restaurant. It is pumpkin soup and leg of lamb. By the same token, they have a beautiful country. There is lush landscape seen in these scenes. There are rich greens and a fine blue sky that is bordered beneath by a sky blue ocean. The only thing that those of us from the Midwest might not find as familiar is the brown-green grass. For these reasons, it seems as though Australia is as welcoming and familiar to me as the United States.

You will get a good argument from the rest of the world about what *Fatal Bond's* producers perceive as hot cars. Maybe it's the Australian taste. Maybe it's what they had at their disposal in the 1990s, but Joe's 1962 Valiant "S" series doesn't compare with America's version of the high horse powered, big block hot rod. It is the vehicle that Joe outruns the cops in. This Chrysler made Australian flavored Valiant is also known as "The Rocket Car." It is the Down Under's version of the Plymouth Valiant 200 Series Signet that was produced by Detroit's Chrysler Corporation for the USA. The American version fancied a blacked out grille and bucket seats as standard equipment. The Australian version in *Fatal Bond* has a sun visor located on the outside of the auto, but otherwise looks quite like its American cousin. The Valiant was one of the first efforts of Detroit's Big Three to utilize aluminum in cars. Aluminum was preferred because it was lighter than the other metals that were used in making cars at the time. The slant-six cylinder was standard in the Valiant, and it has a history of rugged endurance. The grille was also made of weight saving aluminum. The Australian Valiants were made at the Tonsley Park manufacturing facility in Adelaide, Australia. These compact cars were put on Dodge frames down there and were better received than they were in the States. The other hot rocket on wheels is the mid 1960s Citroen Goddess. They were popular for their sporty shark-nosed front ends and their comfortable ride. Claw Miller drives an Australian derivative of a Ford pick up truck.

This is probably Linda Blair's best acting effort since *Sweet Hostage*. The only flaw that can be seen is her inability to cry in front of the camera. When her crying is heard, it is real. When it is seen, it seems like a symphony of phony tears. She masters many scenes and works well in *Fatal Bond*. This film gives concrete credence to the acting ability of Linda Blair. This spellbinding dramatic romance features the 5 foot 2 Blair and the 6 foot 3 Ehlers. It not only works, but it convinces the viewer that the love and mutual passion is real. I am still of the opinion that

Blair wasn't awarded more prominent roles in the film world after she left her teens is because she is only 5 foot 2. This movie proved that actors who portrayed their characters from their heart could overcome the difference in stature. These twisting tales are woven together like a perfect sweater and *Fatal Bond* flows much better than *Bedroom Eyes II*. Linda Blair was a perfect fit for the plot in *Fatal Bond*.

The taste in cars differs. The taste in music is excellent. The cast and crew did a great job on what appears to be a shoestring budget in bringing this unusual drama our way. It is one of the better Blair movies.

*One of the reasons that I paid so much attention to the hair is because one of my daughters is a licensed cosmetologist.

** From Kevin Johnson's album *In the Spirit of the Times*. Used by kind permission of Kevin Johnson Enterprises, PO Box 216 Woollahra NSW 1350 Australia. All rights reserved.

The Heart of the Lie

There were very few things in the great state of Wisconsin that created a buzz in the news arena like the Laurencia Bembenek story. In 1982 a Milwaukee policewoman was sentenced for the first-degree murder of her husband's ex-wife. Her husband was also on the Milwaukee police force. There was a lot of story to tell in this case. If you have ever met a policeman from the Milwaukee metro area you'll find them to be very dedicated and professional. They come across as a close-knit crew of no-nonsense people who put their lives on the line every time they show up for duty. Despite all of its charm, Milwaukee has its share of dangerous criminal activity.

The "Bambi" story had its share of supporters on both sides of the verdict. There were rumors of the stunningly attractive undercover policewomen attired in provocative outfits jumping into cars at stoplights in hopes of busting someone for soliciting. Was there anything to the rumors? I could never say for sure, but it seemed strange that they spread half way across the state to my ears. How hard would it be for a centerfold to convince an unsuspecting soul to pay her for favors?

The Milwaukee Brewers won the American League pennant in 1982. It had been a long drought for Milwaukee's baseball fans. The team was transformed into a winner in 1979 with the very popular George Bamberger at the helm. The city that endeared the old Braves from Boston was last in a pennant race in 1959. So when the man affectionately dubbed "Bambi" (Brewers' manager George Bamberger) turned the organization that was eternally developing prospects for next year into winners, his name was on the joyous lips of every Brewers fan that ever downed a cold one. Although he wasn't managing the Brewers in 1982, his name was still spoken with a fondness. Another Wisconsin characteristic is the enthusiasm that jumps out during deer season. One of the unwritten rules of deer hunting in Dairyland is that you do not shoot at the young deer, which are called Bambi. Bambi was something that was not only used in reference to the accused in the movie, but it was something that was fondly associated with scores of deer hunters and baseball fans.

The Women's Movement was in full swing at this time. The fact is that women can do anything that men can do, except provide the other half of the necessary materials needed to procreate and hold the priesthood in some churches. Some people were experiencing difficulty in accepting this. (Some people had difficulty in accepting the fact that no matter how hard guys try; they just aren't the same in the role of mom as mothers are.) It may have been very hard for some of the old hardliners in the Police Department to accept the changes that were going on. From a practical standpoint, about half of the population is female, so it makes sense to have a somewhat proportionate number of female police officers. These were some of the factors that play into the Laurencia Bembenek story.

The entire state of Wisconsin was intrigued and shocked at the murder of Christine Schultz and the story that went with it.

It is so unfortunate that this movie was made for TV ratings. The story in itself should have provided enough romance, sex, intrigue, violence and conflict to cause it to soar to the top of the ratings race. The real story gives us a centerfold turned cop. It lends us the murder of a policeman's wife where three of the leading suspects are cops. The two children who are left without their mother should give a tug on even the toughest of heartstrings. There should be hypnotic excitement as the convicted woman escapes jail and finds refuge in Canada. I was disappointed that I didn't get emotionally involved with *Heart of the Lie*. I live in Wisconsin and love the events that Milwaukee provides us. There are the Brewers and the world's largest outdoor music festival (Summerfest.) It is a community with strong ethnic ties and the Italians, Poles, Germans and Irish all have their own festivals during the summer. Yet, for some reason, this film reads like a newspaper. The heart and soul of The City That Means Beer is overlooked. The personality of Milwaukee is never seen. Its landmarks are as absent as the love that should have been shown between Detective Fred Schultz and either of his three wives. It provides us with just the facts. It gives us verbs and nouns. It may be presented in this fashion so that the viewer can put himself (or herself) in the juror's box.

Lindsay Frost is Laurencia "Bambi" Bembenek in this Lifetime Network made for TV movie. She has been seen on such television programs as *Without a Trace, The Unit, Boston Legal, Crossing Jordan, Frazier, Bull, Nightmare Café* and others. She didn't come across as centerfold material in *Heart of the Lie* (aka *Calendar Girl, Cop Killer, The Bambi Bembenek Story*). One of the few times that she was dressed in a provocative way was when she was about to escape from prison. Wisconsin State Prison workers would not have seen a prisoner in such attire in a maximum-security facility.

Emmy Award winner Timothy Busfield played the part of the dashing, debonair hunk of masculinity Detective Fred "Disco Freddie" Schultz. Busfield won his Emmy for Outstanding Supporting Actor in a Drama Series in 1991 for his role as Elliot Weston in *Thirtysomething*. He got his start in the comical classic *Stripes* in 1981 as the man with the mortar. Busfield does not come off as the heartthrob of America in *Heart of the Lie*. Schultz comes off as a cop of shaky character. He is not all that charming.

He is mean to his ex-wife. He is a drunkard and an exhibitionist. When you think of the ultimate Lady's Man of the 1980s, John Travolta or even Elvis might come to mind, but this chubby carrot top? Come on! This red headed officer gives the police department a black eye.

Linda Blair would have been about 30 when this disappointing project was assembled. . She is seen as Officer Jane Mader. Jane was a classmate of Bambi during their training at the police academy. She is the first interview for Pittsburgh reporter John Garner. Once more, we get just the facts. Mader is a friend of Bambi and maintains her activity as a Milwaukee policewoman. She is the one who introduces Schultz to Bambi. Her main concern is for the protection of her career.

Even after all is said and all is done, I was left with questions regarding Christine Schultz's real killer. Bembenek did file a sex discrimination suit against the Milwaukee Police Department and that wasn't brought out until after the trial and recapture of Ms. Bembenek. This movie did pose some questions and maybe the reason that the characters seemed void of any emotion was so that we would examine just the facts after the trial. Here are some of those facts that cause us to question:

1: The cops sent Detective Cushman with Fred to check his own gun. Fred Schultz was still a suspect at the time.

2: Detectives Cushman and Schultz failed to write down the serial number of said gun "Two veteran cops don't write down the weapon they're inspecting in a murder case."

3: Detective Schultz meets with superiors, supposedly to check the gun and they too fail to get the gun's serial number.

4: There is no record of the meeting.

5: Detective Cushman destroyed his notebook after he wrote his report regarding the murder.

6: The person that was seen leaving the scene of the crime was wearing a green jogging suit. Bembenek claims that she never owned a green jogging suit. The picture of the green jogging suit that the District Attorney displayed to the jury was in black and white.

7: There were eight people that said they saw a man in a green jogging suit and a ponytail running near Chris' (the victim's) house. One of those sightings was on the day she was killed and one of those witnesses was a cop.

8: There is also some speculation as to whom the mysterious dark wig in the toilet of Bembenek's old apartment belonged to.

Laurencia Bembenek maintained her innocence. Only she and the real murderer know who did kill Christine Schultz and we will never know if they are one in the same. She will never be able to tell us in any hyped up interview exclusive either, as the tormented woman died 20 November 2010 from complications due to liver and kidney ailments. There are other contradictory issues regarding this case. Although Fred Schultz testified that he and his partner, Michael Durfee were on duty investigating a burglary at the time of the murder, he later recanted his story and said that he was actually drinking at a local bar. Dr. Elaine Samuels was the current Medical Examiner assigned to the trial. She claimed that the hairs on a brush in Bembenek's hairbrush were consistent with those found on the victim. Upon further investigation by an hair analyst from the Wisconsin's crime lab, this evidence was questioned. In a letter quoted in the Toronto Star (1991) Samuel refuted her initial claim and stated, "I recovered no blonde hairs of any length or texture... All the hairs I recovered from the body were brown and were grossly identical to the body of the victim...(I) do not like to suggest that the evidence was altered in any way, but find no logical explanation for what amounted to the mysterious appearance of blonde hair in an envelope that contained no such hair at the time it was sealed by me."

There was also the confession to the murder by Frederick Horenberger, who was the boyfriend of Bembenek's old roommate, Judy Zess. He was a career criminal who helped Fred Schultz on a remodeling project. Horenberger would never publicly admit to his participation in the murder. Verily, he denied involvement in it. A number of his fellow inmates signed affidavits that claimed that Horenberger claimed to have killed Mrs. Schultz. These claims were made while Horenberger was doing time in prison. We will never know any more of what Frederick Horenberger's involvement, if any, in the crime in question was. He is no longer available for comment. He committed suicide in 1991 following involvement in a robbery, hostage-taking stand off. It makes you wonder about the choice of friends and associated that law enforcement professional Fred Schultz chose to let into his circle of friends.

Another unnerving bit of evidence that seems to have been conveniently disregarded was the testimony of the oldest surviving son, who was also the best witness at the murder scene. He claimed that it was a man with a red ponytail that was seen fleeing the residence. When was the last time that you saw a centerfold looking masculine?

Of course on the other side of the table, you have a woman who was said to have wanted the victim dead, as the support and (or) alimony that was paid to her by Fred was denying her the lifestyle that she desired. She and Fred were the only people that would have had access to the gun used in the murder. If you reside in Wisconsin there are some things in this investigation that raise eyebrows. There have been things that have gone on in the Dane County Wisconsin Courts that raise questions. Just north of Dane County, in Columbia County a young man was convicted of murdering his wife in early part of the first decade of this century. There was no victim to be found. There was no murder weapon found either. The convict is serving a life sentence. In Portage, (Columbia County) Wisconsin case, a man was arrested on drug related charges and after he was handcuffed behind his back and while in police custody he managed to find a gun under his bed and fatally shoot himself in the head. The state's witness and expert on such matters said that he (the victim) would have been able to accomplish such a preposterous feat if he was double jointed. I wouldn't be at all surprised if the same witness and expert on the matter believes in Santa Claus. The expert was actually a consultant for the Wisconsin State Patrol. It was also never established that the victim was double jointed.

I found that the Ed Lauter who played Lieutenant Driscoll is a seasoned, veteran actor. He has nearly 200 (to date) film credits to his name. I found the reason for the immediate sour taste in my mouth was a familiar association that any of us who saw the original *Longest Yard*. Ed Lauter played the warden in that classic B movie. He comes off just as uppity, heartless and arrogant here. It is surprising that Ed got his start in show business as a stand up comedian (1). Ed was born 30 October 1940 in Long Beach, Long Island, New York. He attended CW Post College on an athletic scholarship, where he participated in the Big 3: baseball, basketball and football. Ed is six-foot two. He and Burt Reynolds are the only actors to appear in both film editions of *The Longest Yard* (1974 and 2005). Lauter states that one of the greatest tools that an actor can employ is imagination. He feels that it is essential.

There are many things about Bembenek that seem to bring a triumphant spirit to an oppressed woman. She was considered to be a model prisoner while serving time in the Taycheedah Correctional Institute. She earned a degree from the University of Wisconsin-Parkside. It made her one of the few convicted killers to earn a degree while serving time in prison.

In spite of her model behavior, she did indeed escape with the assistance of the brother of one of her fellow inmates and headed to Thunder Bay, Canada. After the new of her freedom, signs and slogans, "Run, Bambi Run!" were echoed throughout the state proclaiming to be America's Dairyland. As a side note, Laurencia did not like the nickname "Bambi".

It doesn't seem all that long ago that all of these events occurred. So many of the people that were involved in them are no longer with us in this world. Yet, it does make us wonder if our system may need a little tweaking if we are to remain the bastion of freedom and the model of justice that the rest of the world holds in examplarary esteem. With all of that being said, I wonder today how the children of Fred and Christina Schultz have faired after the tragic loss of their mother and becoming stepchildren to two different women. Divorce traumatizes children under regular (How can anything in a divorce be classified as "normal"?) circumstances. When the murder of their mother is thrown into the mix you cannot help but to feel that the other victims of the crime were overlooked.

Although *Calendar Girl, Cop Killer?/The Bambi Bembenek Story* fails miserably to entertain, it does provoke us to ponder.

A Woman Obsessed
a.k.a.
Bad Blood
1993

This is a tale of an accomplished heiress/artist. (The role of Arlene Bellings is played by Georgiana Spelvin.) Arlene fancies a young man as her husband reincarnate. The fact that the young man (Ted Barnes is played by Gregory Patrick) is her son lends to an intriguing plot.

Ted happens to see a portrait of a young man with a striking resemblance to himself. Arlene Bellings introduces herself as the painter and invites attorney Ted Barnes to her mansion for a visit. Of course his young wife is welcome.

All is normal in the next scene as Ted and his wife (Evie, played by Linda Blair) are playing beach volleyball with Ted's parents. Mrs. Jack Barnes (played by Carolyn Van Bellingham) is put into the awkward position of explaining how Ted got to be part of their family. It's a longwinded albeit interesting tale. Ted and Evie are excited about the prospects of meeting his generic mother. The happy couple climbs into their BMW and head to Arlene's mansion in the exclusive part of town.

A party is thrown in his honor as the portrait is unveiled. This is the beginning of the end of the "The Happy Hour". Arlene is a very possessive person and isn't willing to share Ted with anyone else. She is a most jealous jewel. Lust and murder circumvent the air. The eye popping, jaw-dropping maid Crystal (played by Christina Veronica) makes an unsuccessful play for the hunky beefcake and the keeper of the house deals with her in a most severe fashion. Arlene does her utmost to dispose of the unsuspecting Evie. Ted is even more unsuspecting than Evie and he also becomes prisoner of his mother's lust.

Arlene's departed husband was a philandering fool who was

murdered by her father. The rest of her world is to pay dearly for it. She is ruthless and cold. She is calculating and conniving. She serves as the matriarchal head of the most dysfunctional family ever seen on film.

Linda Blair plays professional real estate agent Evie Barnes. In real life, Linda's mother Elinore was a real estate agent and was also an outstanding seamstress to boot. Evie Barnes has many noble traits. She is faithful and fun loving. She is positive and good hearted. She is pretty, although not as steamy as Mrs. Bellings' maid. Blair is cast as the consummate victim again. It wasn't the most challenging part for Blair to play, but she made the best of it and her performance did lend to the believability of the production.

Elinore Blair was the mother of three children, Linda, Jimmy and Debbie. Mrs. Blair was a real estate agent and an outstanding seamstress. The old adage, "Like mother, like daughter" is reproved here, as Linda worked with her mom in designing some of the gowns that she wore to the Golden Globes and Academy Awards. Linda designed and Mom sewed. At one time she owned her own line of clothing "Linda Blair's Western Ware". It just rolls off your tongue. If you are fortunate enough to have some old Lynyrd Skynyrd or Molly Hatchet albums, you might take delight in knowing that a young Linda Blair designed some of the stage attire of the band members (1). It appears that despite the turbulent teenage years that saw Linda being involved with Rick Springfield and the hassles of Hollywood, the charming Connecticut cutey did have a good relationship with her mother. This is a credit to the both of them. Elinore died after a seven-year bout with cancer in 1994. Linda would have been 35. Linda was aware of her mother's health during the filming of *A Woman Obsessed*. She was curiously interested in the treatment of the laboratory animals used in cancer research, and this was one of the many things that contributed to her interest in animal welfare and animal rights. Miss Blair is perhaps more compassionate than her former beau, Rick James, credits her for in his song *Cold Blooded.* (If you take note of the tune's lyrics, James isn't necessarily bashing Blair.)

The guests at the Bellings mansion are surprised by their hostess' real intention. She is plotting a diabolical scheme to have Ted compensate for all the time that he has spent with the parents who adopted him illegally. Once Ted becomes a prisoner of Arlene's heart and mansion, things turn to terror. Ted is portrayed as an outstanding physical specimen in the start of the movie and I am bewildered as to his ineptness in regards to escaping the whacked out widow.

His adoptive parents investigate their son and daughter-in-law's disappearance. Arlene tells them that Ted and Evie went into one of the nearby towns to do some antique shopping. Mrs. Barnes isn't convinced of her family's sudden fondness of antiques.

The senior Mr. and Mrs. Barnes show up for Arlene's wedding the next day. They don't know that she is marrying Ted. Troy Donahue plays Ted's father, Jack Barnes. He is the Hollywood veteran that unseated Tab Hunter as the Heartthrob of America during the late 1950s and early 1960s. He was also featured as the demented capitalist in *The Chilling.*

Some pre-nuptial fighting takes place and its outcome would be predictable for any genre of movie except one that would be selected from the Blair Bunch.

Bad Blood or A *Woman Obsessed* isn't a must watch, but if you think your family is dysfunctional, you'll appreciate how normal it is after comparing it to this family flunkey of a film.

Schlindler's List was probably the most memorable movie that you saw in 1993. The Toronto Blue Jays took the World Series Pennant north of the border and the Dallas Cowboys rode the Buffalo Bills to an embarrassing 52-17 defeat. Five people were arrested and another was sought in the bombing of the World Trade Center in New York City.

Gang Boys
aka
Skins

Life is full of decisions that would have made things better. ***Gang Boys* is a classic example of a racing tire gone flat.** Wings Hauser should have decided which virtue and what venue should have been the theme of *Gang Boys*. All of the ingredients are there for a fine film, but by the time the cook put them all in the pot, the recipe was ruined.

Let's start with a teenage homosexual boy that is brutally beaten and forced to have sex with a woman. If there isn't something in that sentence that doesn't light someone's fuse, fish aren't made to swim. He has an attractive nightclub singer for a mother and she is divorced from a cop who found that his true love is in the bottle. Just for kicks, let's say the boy was beaten by Neo-Nazi thugs. This should be enough for an intriguing story.

Unfortunately, there are too many people and distractions thrown into the mix. The Nazis in *Gang Boys* are totally undisciplined. Their music is awful and unintelligible. Their meeting place is void of class. This is brought to the forefront of the movie numerous times and once, certainly two times, would have made the point.

The ex-cop leaves his life of lush in Baja to return to his old family and hopes to exact justice on the perpetrators that savagely brutalized his son. He and his son begin to bond as he attempts to dry out. This should be a heartwarming experience for the viewer, but it just doesn't have the affect that it should. It is good to see the two of them chumming it up, but there doesn't seem to be any real bonding between them. I don't know if this is to imitate the empty apologies made in life or if there just isn't enough depth to the two characters.

The rekindling of the married couple is easy to see happening and it was appreciated, but they didn't have to go to all of the time and trouble to shoot an explicit love scene to seal the deal. If Maggie (played by Linda Blair) had just greeted her ex (Joe Joiner was played by Wings Hauser.) in the same nightie that they shot the scene in and given him a heartfelt hug and fell into the bed, that would have been convincing enough. They spent four minutes with the love scene and the movie was only eighty-six minutes long.

Wings Hauser wrote, directed and starred in *Gang Boys* aka *Skins*. It was a most ambitious endeavor. There were many worthwhile messages that he attempted to convey. He made the mindset and ambitions of the skinheads perfectly clear in one of the scenes. It's done when Bentz (Cole Hauser) delivers a monologue pertaining to being a determined leader and the association with Adolph Hitler and his ideals. Wings portrays the skinhead culture as something that is sick and fearsome. They rule the streets of Hollywood with fear and violence. It may not have been so disturbing had the Nazis not implemented these tactics during their reign of ruin in the 1930s and '40s. Theirs is a policy of divide and conquer. It is a policy of bullying the smaller segments of society, smashing them into submission and then moving onto the next segment. They meet with less resistance, as those who dared to resist are put out of commission. In *Gang Boys* they start with the homosexual and then move onto the Jew (They rape a Jewish woman and make her husband watch.) and then the Negro (They kill a Black policeman). Nazi Germany made the same steps during their rise to power. Many people turned a deaf ear and a blind eye, because it was always the other fringes of society that were victimized. First it was the Communists, then the Jews, then the

Jehovah's Witnesses, then the members of labor unions and before the silent opponents knew it, they were next if they didn't enthusiastically step into line with the ruling Junta.

Hauser touches on society's inability to understand the gay community. He sings the song of marital reconciliation. He demonstrates the horrors of alcoholism and the rough road to recovery. He mercilessly slams us for our apathetic attitudes. There are many good messages that Hauser tries so valiantly and yet so vainly to convey.

One of the most piercing lines that Linda Blair has ever delivered is this one, "Getting sober and staying sober are two different things...your dad is a very intelligent man at some things, but he's a genius at finding reasons to drink. And when he drinks, he really hurts people." It has to be a difficult message to give to a son who is recovering from a beastly beating by the Nazi thugs. It is a difficult message for a wife whose former husband is trying to recover.

Wings manages to get the whole Hauser family into the act in this cinematic endeavor. Wings Hauser is the returning husband, Joe Joiner. He is the alcoholic ex-cop, ex-husband. Joe is returning to the things that should be the foundations of a good home and a good society. His son in true life, Cole, plays the Skinheads' leader, Benz. (Cole also starred in the riveting movie "Paparazzi".) He is ruthless, heartless and ambitious. He never meets with an opponent that is able to put him away. The woman that sings *America, the Beautiful* is Wings Hauser's daughter, Bright. This is her only movie credit to date. Cali Lili Hauser is the Skinheads' pass around party plate (named Kix) and in real life is the wife of Wings. Of course, this movie was released in 1992 and Cali Lili and Wings weren't united in marriage until 1 June 2000, so that could explain all of the risqué business in the film without either of them raising an objectionable eyebrow at the time.

Cali is an extremely photogenic NYU alumnus. She earned her master's degree as a teenager. She was able to skip many grades because of her intellectual brilliance and received a scholarship. She is a shirttail relative of the great Edward G. Robinson. She and Wings are building a songwriting company. She does the lyrics. He does the music. Let's hope that they put out something better than Bright's version of *America the Beautiful.*

Here is the song list from *Skinheads*:

Fear the Mask by the Outpost

Since You've Been Gone by Linda Blaire

Walking' On the Right Side of the Devil by Wings Hauser

Real World by Gary Falcone and The Outpost

Follow Me In the Rain by Robyn Kirmsee

Time To Need a Friend by Dee Dee Funk and Sherwood Ball

Comin' Back Again by Sherwood Ball

America the Beautiful by Bright Hauser

Time to Need a Friend was probably the best song in the batch. It truly was a fine tune and is prototypical of the 1990s love ballad.

Skinheads took too much time in too many of the wrong places to give its noble message the strong impact that was desired. The plot wanders and weaves. Bentz didn't need any more time for us to dislike him, but most of the other characters don't have enough time to develop into people that we develop any bond with. Some of the scenes are too abstract to comprehend. Watching this is like going on a mission without a map.

Double Blast
1994

Linda accepted the council of both of her parents and lent her talents to all genres of acting. She did some singing in *Gang Boys* and sang part of Carol King's *It's Too Late* in *Sara T: Portrait of a Teenage Alcoholic.* She played the part of Rizzo in the Broadway remake of *Grease.* In *Gang Boys* she plays the role of nightclub singer Maggie Joiner in a movie that is laced with sex and violence. In *Double Blast* you can bring the children out of their rooms, put on the popcorn, pull up the chairs and enjoy a movie with the whole family. There are no disturbing scenes in *Double Blast* and the cast is perfectly matched for their parts. The plot isn't on par with *Rocky* or *The Maltese Falcon*, but like Thanksgiving at Grandma's, there is plenty to enjoy even if you don't like turkey.

Double Blast was released the same year (1994) as *Gang Boys* and it is about as far at the other end of the movie spectrum as Australia is from New York. In this film a geological expedition discovers a significant find. The leading authority on the translation of this discovery has no idea that he is mixed up with scoundrels and prefers death to revelation.

The rest of his expedition is as crooked as a snake and finds that the only other qualified scholar on the writings of such ancient properties is Professor Claudia (Linda Blair). Her kidnapping is witnessed by the son of world champion kick boxer, Apollo Cook.

Dale "Apollo" Cook is a native of Tulsa, Oklahoma and is one-year Blair's senior. He is best remembered for his role in *American Kickboxer 2* where he plays himself. If you like kickboxing, *Double Blast* has plenty of it. He plays the role of the father of a son and daughter in this matinee classic. Both of his children are well schooled in the martial arts and join in the fun.

Ten-year-old Lorne Berfield is Jimmy, the son of the great kickboxer. He is the older brother of Young Artist and Young Star Award winner Justin Berfield. In *Double Blast* he is an inquisitive firecracker waiting to explode. When he witnesses the kidnapping of the professor the plot explodes.

This is the only professional appearance of Crystal Summer in front of the camera. She is Lisa, the older sister of Jimmy. Her character added spice to the mix, but her ability in this film seemed limited.

The most entertaining actors in *Double Blast* are the villains. Robert Z'Dar brings some light-heartedness to the heavy character Mongoose. Claudia reprimands him and sternly inquires if his mother would approve of his mean spirited activity. He refuses a command from his superior because he says that he loves his mother and she most certainly would not approve. Born Robert J. Zdarsky 3 Jun 1950 in Chicago, Z'Dar reappears as Mongoose in *Double Blast*. He played the evil Eric in *Grotesque*. He has an intimidating stature, being a heavyset man in a six-foot two frame. He got his start in show business as singer, keyboard artist and guitar player for the band Nova Express. You may have seen them open for Jefferson Airplane, The Electric Prunes (whose *I Had Too Much To Dream Last Night* marched to the #11 slot on the Billboard top 40 in 1967 (1)) and The Who. He is an alumnus of Proviso High School in Hillside, which is the same high school that graduated some of the players in the original band Chicago. Robert was also was one of The Second City's finest, serving as a police officer in Chicago for a short time. His most famous part came as Police Officer Matt

Cordell in *Maniac Cop*. Z'Dar relishes his roles as the heavy. His views on being the villain are similar to Leslie Nielson's. He says that it is important to be as intimidating as possible, be it physically, emotionally or mentally. He also enjoys being the bad guy because it is boundless in its interpretations. There are no limits to how creative you want to be. He prefers to change his appearance for each part that he is awarded with. In *Double Blast*, his imposing appearance adds to the comic effect of the children outfighting him.

Adding equal comic effect to this family film is Chuck Williams' character Boggus. He comes off as a leftover hippie with a craze for Karma. He can be counted on to say the wrong thing at the wrong time every time. He is incessantly trying to bring calm to the tense situations. His long, unkempt hair clashes with his long trench coat. You too will wonder if he is a gangster or a misplaced hippie. In this movie he has a skit with the newly discovered helmet that is high humor.

Martin Sheen's younger brother Joe Estevez plays the miscreant ringleader, Nadir. Estevez' resume is plenty long and features *Terminal Exposure* (1987), *Lockdown* (1988), *Fatal Justice* (1993), and 147 more video productions to date. He makes an interesting star next to Linda Blair, as Estevez doesn't appear to tower over Blair. His character parallels global leaders who toy with the rest of the world and don't have a clue as to how to bring their efforts to fruition.

You'll see these two children (Lisa and Jimmy) trounce the best of the underworld's enforcers. You'll see a grown man wear a pair of balloon pants fit for a clown because he is unable to find anything else after a couple of kids dispose of his usual pair of trousers. You might join my daughter's squealing laughter when Linda Blair's character responds to hypnotism.

I am not an accomplished student of the martial arts, but there is plenty of kickboxing going on in *Double Blast*.

There are many madcap misadventures that transpire before the rescue is made sure. I'm not really sure how everyone in the movie is needed, but it is light-hearted fun and flows well. Your family should enjoy being *Double Blasted* into the evening. There were some serious, memorable crimes committed in 1994. Mrs. O.J. Simpson was murdered. It is my guess that more people saw the televised trial of Simpson than viewed any two movies released that year. Olympic Nancy Kerrigan was attacked and beaten for one and all to see. Tom Hanks won an Oscar for his work in Forrest Gump. It was a year of high crimes, good times and two Linda Blair movies.

Sorceress
1995

You had best send the children back to their other activities because this movie should make most adults blush. Just because so many of Linda Blair's R rated movies feature shower scenes doesn't mean that they are clean viewing. We get another look at the occult in *Sorceress* and it is a perverted one at that. Most of the female stars seem to be plucked from the Silicon Valley of the Dolls. Sorceress was filmed in the Netherlands.

Julie Strain plays the role of Erica Barnes. Her husband is passed over for promotion at a prestigious law firm. She is hooked up in an occult crew that sports a young and buxomly Amelia Reynolds (Linda Blair) and the gorgeously proportioned Maria (Toni Naples). A little evil voodoo is exacted resulting in the disabling of Amelia's husband.

Julie Strain was the Penthouse Pet of the Month in June of 1991 and their Pet of the Year in 1993. Despite her impressive credentials (40D-27-38)(1) Julie did have a difficult time breaking into the movies because she is six-foot-one, nearly a full foot taller than Linda Blair. The two of them do not appear in the same scene together in Sorceress. *Femme Fatale's Magazine* ranked her as #20 of Sci-Fi's sexiest 50. She was a member of the Pleasant Hill High School track team and does most of her own stunts. Strain has been in many adult movies and has also been seen in the Leslie Nielsen comedy *Naked Gun 33and a Third: The Final Insult* as Dominatrix. Coincidentally, her first film appearance was as the nude girl in the locker room in the Linda Blair spoof, *Repossessed.* Here are some of her other film appearances: *The Bare Wench Project* and *The Bare Wench Project II: Scared Topless, Zombiegeddon, Thirteen Erotic Ghosts,* and *Planet of the Erotic Apes.* This gives you an idea of Julie Strain's type of movie role. Her role as Erica isn't all that much in *Sorceress,* but the character is vital to the plot.

Toni Naples is the other sorceress in said movie. She is also the executive producer of this not for you family flick. She was "Dream Girl" in the 1983 comedy *Doctor Detroit.* She is the good friend of the Barnes family and she is the soul that introduced Erica Barnes to the witchcraft craze. She was born Karen Chorak in Los Angeles seven years prior to Linda Blair. They both look about the same age in *Sorceress.*

Rochelle Swanson is the lovely Carol in *Sorceress.* She was cast aside for the more buxomly Erica by Larry Barnes as his choice for a wife. She picks up where she left off after Erica's untimely death. She is a beautiful actress with a resume similar to, but with fewer accomplishments than Julie Strain. She is victim of the voodoo performed.

Larry Poindexter plays Larry Barnes who is suddenly a widower. He sees his best friend and comrade at the law firm become a victim of voodoo curse. He is the desire of his beautiful workmate Carol. He is clueless to all of the witchcraft going on around him.

This is a tale that zigs and zags with victims, vixens and villains. It sports a scene that I've never witnessed before; lawyers and their wives having a house painting party. Even that runs amuck.

Edward Albert plays the role of Howard Reynolds, Amelia's (Linda Blair) lawyer husband. Edward is the son of the legendary Eddie Albert of TV's *Green Acres* fame. His mother was the Mexican actress/dancer Margo. Edward attended Oxford University and studied psycology at UCLA. His big acting break came cast opposite the leggy Goldie Hawn in *Butterflies Are Free.*

He learned to respect diversity from his polished acting father and his dancing donna of a mother who was of Mexican descent. He owned a ranch in the Malibu area and developed a great appreciation of nature from this association. Edward faded from the limelight after his father developed Alzheimer's disease. He cared for his father as best he could. Edward the Younger would leave this world after succumbing to lung cancer, only a year after his dad died in September of 2006

Howard Reynolds is promoted instead of his associate, Larry Barnes at a prestigious law firm. His bewitching wife takes revenge on Howard and he is crippled in an automobile accident. Larry confronts his wife, Erica, about this. She becomes defensive and angry. They end up on the balcony and she lunges at him. He sidesteps her and she goes over the rail to her death.

Her spirit seeks revenge. Amelia Reynolds also seeks revenge. What could be more savage than a couple of witches in a grudge match?

Larry's old flame rekindles the romance and is put under a spell after donning the necklace that Erica wore when she plummeted to her untimely death. She becomes the vehicle of vengeance.

If you're expecting the appearance of Edward Albert as Amelia Reynold's lawyer husband to give credence to the quality of this film, you'll be disappointed. It is a good thing that *Sorceress* has the patented Linda Blair surprise ending.

Prey of the Jaguar
1996

This is the last of the three martial arts movies that feature the scariest kid of all time. **It isn't the type of film that would inspire a couple to cuddle up with for a getaway weekend, but you can bring the children in for this one.** The review that I read on this movie was negative and nasty, but I found that *Prey of the Jaguar* is aimed at the juvenile audience and it seizes its young, targeted prey. Not too many fourth graders write movie reviews. My nine-year old daughter liked this one more than I did.

Linda Blair stars as half of a police partnership alongside Roger Reed (played nicely by Tom Badal). This may be one of the most authentic male/female police pairs on film. Maxwell Caulfield plays the complex Derek Leigh. Leigh is a young retired government agent. His past catches up with him and his family pays the price.

Derek's son was going to dress up as "The Jaguar" for Halloween, "Because he has gloves so the bad guys can't trace his fingerprints... And he has darts and other stuff... He puts sleep stuff on 'em and he uses them instead of regular bullets. The jaguar can't fly. That's what's so cool about him. He's just a normal guy who makes his mind and body really strong so that he can wage a war with the evil minds and bodies of the underworld," as young Jeremy Leigh said.

A drug kingpin that was brought to justice by Leigh escapes prison and murders the younger Leigh and the rest of Derek's family. Trevor Goddard plays the escaped drug lord Damien Bandera to a tee. He has nerves of steel and a conscience to match. He is as ruthless as he is skillful. After the elimination of Leigh's family, Bandera aims for the man who helped put him away. Bandera even feels that Derek Leigh was also responsible for his father's fatal heart attack.

Leigh's old government agency wants to bring him back to

life and work for them again. Leigh feels that the agency has become like the people that they used to pursue, and declines the offer. You'll see that the SOC (the government agency that Leigh used to work for) isn't what it used to be.

Leigh trains like the superhero character his late son wanted to be. He seeks out old acquaintances and is refreshed on the latest secret agent technology and martial arts. He wants to serve his country, relieve his conscience and to avenge the murder of his family.

You'll see loads of fighting and shooting in this one. It is a mixture of James Bond and John Wayne with a little Bruce Lee thrown in.

You will never see a prison transport team stop to aid an accident victim as they do in *Prey of the Jaguar*. They would most likely radio that in. On the clock prison guards are a jumpy bunch and I doubt that Bandera's escape would have been executed in this fashion in real life. Some of the usual question that I so frequently ask during this genre of movie are brought out again: Are professional hit men really that bad at shooting? Are they such awful fighters that eight of them can't bring down one man in a street fight?

There are some other Hollywood consistencies that creep into this family friendly film. Leigh's wife is expecting when she is murdered. It seems that the entertainment industry likes to play on our emotions by bringing a baby or a pregnant woman into the plot and playing their condition up. It is as though the crime is that much more heinous because they were expecting. We have been living in a society that has permitted abortion for over 35 years, so the pregnant condition of the female victim should not affect us any differently than if she were not with child. Were these two murders any worse than the killing of the roofers in *Prey of the Jaguar*?

I am always amazed at the ability of the Karate experts in the good guy's corner. The well-trained criminals never seem to be equal to the skills of the white knights of Kung Fu. It doesn't even matter that they outnumber the superhero a dozen to one. *Prey of the Jaguar* does pull away from the stereotypical Tinseltown production in a refreshing way. It beats Michael Moore to the punch. This film belts the government and its spy agencies in the breadbasket. It was nice to know that even in 1996 someone in the movie industry would dare to ask if the government had become like the evil factions that they were battling. They even portray Derek Leigh as a vigilante who fights his government. It is filmed in California. It portrays Officer Cody Johnson (Blair's character) as someone who is hip to the ways of the Jaguar and does all that she can to bring justice its due course.

I really don't want to delve too deeply into *Prey of the Jaguar*, as it is a film for the juvenile viewer. Yet, I must admit that I enjoyed this one more the second time that I watched it. All in all, it was done as nicely as a martial arts/cop movie can be done.

"The way of the Jaguar is one of strength, stealth and speed."

In 1996 Israel elected Yonni Netanyahu's brother, Benjamin as its Prime Minister. You will remember Yonni from the movie *Victory at Entebbe*. Dallas defeats the stalwart Steelers from Pittsburgh in the Super Bowl. The New York Yankees beat the Braves of Atlanta in the World Series. They last beat the Braves in the Fall Classic in 1958 when they were the Milwaukee Braves. Janet Jackson signs for a record $80 million with Virgin Records. Ella Fitzgerald, George Burns and Gene Kelly took the last bus out of town in 1996.

Monster Makers
2003

Have you ever been faced with the dilemma of inclimate weather on Halloween and the children can't go out to trick or treat? What do you do with kids who wake up with nightmares after seeing a horror movie? *Monster Makers* is the perfect answer. It is a movie about monsters and is scary, but not to the point of sleepless nights in Seattle.

Dexter Brisbane (George Kennedy) is a retired producer of horror movies. He hires live-in nurse Shelly Stoker (Linda Blair). This single mother and her fine young son Tim, (played by Tim McCallum) move into the old, spacious Brisbane mansion. Tim is a brilliant buff of movies featuring creepy creatures and scary monsters.

Tim isn't all that popular at the new school. One of the resident ruffians has it in for this new kid on the block. Brisbane wants to sell the junk in the basement and tells Tim that he can have whatever he wants from the collection. Tim discovers an old film, titled *Monsters On the Loose,* in the trunk in the cellar. It is an unreleased Brisbane monster film that was recorded on a revolutionary tape made of radium acetate. The tapes have a unique quality to them. If the film receives a huge electrical surge, the characters come to life.

Tim invites a sweet young girl from his new junior high school over to view the holy grail of horror movies on Halloween. Tina Corman (played by Ashley Edner) is also the crush of the local bully that has it in for Tim. Shelly has to work a double shift at the hospital and leaves the house and Dexter in the hands of the capable youngster. Dexter takes a few too many (but not a lethal dose) sleeping pills. Lightning strikers during the movie while Tim and Tina are viewing it and chaos culminates around the cast and crew.

The feature creatures of the shelved film are energized from reel life into real life. Vermin pops from the screen as a guy who is down on his luck. He was wandering around a nuclear test site during a test. Whenever he smells garbage, bad things happen as he is transformed into the diabolical personage in *Monsters On the Loose*. Another escaping character is a mismatch of maniquin parts dubbed "Maninkin." The third frightful fellow from the old movie is Revenant. He is evil personified that can and does take over any body at any time. His presence isn't as disgusting as the evil personified in "The Exorcist", but he is a force to recon with. The film industry has never experienced a trio like this. You literally need to see the movie to discover the demise of these demons.

This is a great family film. It isn't as riveting as *The Exorcist*. It isn't as lame as *The Chilling*. It isn't as bloody as *Grotesque* It is more fun to watch than *Bail Out* and it is as heartwarming as *Up Your Alley*.

George Kennedy is a veteran versatile actor. He previously teamed up with Linda in *Airport 1975*. He is the only actor to appear in all four of the Airport movies. He won an Oscar as the best supporting actor for his part as Dragline in the 1968 classic *Cool Hand Luke*. He has also been featured in most of the *Naked Gun* movies. The burly buck played the role as a slave ion the 1960 *Spartacus*. He was born in 1925 in New York, New York and served in the U.S. Army for sixteen years. It would prove to be time well spent. He served under General George Patton and would get to play his top commanding officer in the 1978 movie *Brass Target*. In his later military career, George served as Armed Forces Radio and Television officer. He served as a military consultant for the TV series *The Phil Silvers Show*. Kennedy has done work in more than 200 movies and television episodes. He is highly sought after and plays a great straight man in comedy and serves as the typecast military man in many movies. He is great in his comic role in *Monster Makers*.

A younger veteran actor stars in *Monster Makers*. Adam Baldwin adds this creative creature feature to his resume. He has been seen as Stillman in *Ordinary People* (1980) He played the part of Animal Mother in the 1987 war movie *Full Metal Jacket*. He does a swell job playing police officer Jay Forrest. Jay is forced to make a transition from 1951 when Brisbane's shelved *Monsters on the Loose* was made, to 2003 when the film comes to life. You need to think about this a little bit. The roles of policemen have changed during this time and so has the equipment that they would use. They didn't have cell phones or microwave ovens or computers back in the day. How would you explain these gadgets to someone who is living in the golden age of radio? How would you explain a panel truck to the mini van generation?

The Dodge mini van is the featured automobile in *Monster Makers*. Its inception was rejected by the Ford Motor Company in the 1960s and Lee Iococca took it to Chrysler when he left. The creation of the versatile family wagon helped turn the Chrysler motor maker around. They featured removable seats. Station wagons of the previous generation had seats that folded down, but they didn't sport the headroom of the mini van. The mini van had a rear door that would open all the way. You didn't need to roll the window down to open it and that was a huge feature because those rear windows developed shorts in their electrical system and wouldn't always roll all the way up or all the way down. If the door was slammed with the window partially down, the glass had a tendency to shatter. With the mini van, you just open up, load up and climb in. They came with two doors up front and featured sliding doors in the middle of the van. You could get them with the sliding door on one or both sides. The min van has a split personality. It can be the family sedan. They can comfortably seat six and you could squeeze seven into these three seaters. In a matter of five minutes, you can remove the two back seats and use it as a cargo van. They rode like a car, although not quite as smoothly as the station wagon. The sport utility vehicle has been slowly replacing the mini van. I have loaded both, and prefer the mini van.

A forty-four year old Blair stars in *Monster Makers*. She

looks very good and you can drop the prepositional phrase "for her age." One of the reasons for her sleeker appearance is her Vegan lifestyle. She struggled mightily during her twenties and thirties to keep her girlish figure from expanding as she made the transition into womanhood. She looked very much a desirable damsel during these years. It was nice to see a female star that looked good without looking like a starved blonde bobble head. She is a Vegan and has authored a book (*Going Vegan*) on the topic. She also practices yoga and her daily routine caring for the critters provides a vigorous physical workout. To her credit, her trim body is well toned and that is most unusual for the thin Hollywood sect.

This is also the second time that she plays the part of a mother. Her first parental portrayal was Jenny Bellows in *Ruckus* (1981). She decided not to have children in real life and the reason is sound. She knew that she would not be able to do the work that she has accomplished (both on screen and with her World Heart Foundation) and do a creditable job rearing children, too. She said you cannot stand up for others as effectively as she does and raise a family (a). I salute her realistic view on the subject. If women buy into the demands of today: having a career, doing charity work, raising a family, keeping a household in functioning and safe order, and teaming up with their husbands, they would need about four more hours in a day, and they still wouldn't be able to get enough sleep to stay healthy and effective in all of the mentioned catagories.

The monsters in this movie are unusual and their demise is unique. You'll enjoy the lighthearted romances in *Monster Makers* as well as the stars and the plot that they illuminate, even after the third viewing.

I.M.P.S.
The Immoral Minority Picture Show

This is a compilation of comedy shorts done in an irreverent matter where the film industry takes some time off and laughs at itself. Some of it is gut-busting hilarious. Some of it is raunchy. Some of it is in bad taste. It is not the classic "Art Reflecting Life" nor "Life Reflecting Art". It is "Art Reflecting Art." This movie went unreleased for nearly twenty years and that hurt the potential fan base, as many people have never seen such television as *Hill Street Blues*. It takes an irreverent swipe at the powerful right-wing radical group that ruled the reigning Ronald Reagan roost during the 1980s into the early 1990s. The crossword puzzle buffs will be quick to note that an imp is a little devil. Is it any wonder that Linda Blair wanders into *I.M.P.S.?*

I.M.P.S. features a comical "warning" in an introductory note.

The cool Black dude is part of the ongoing opening scene. He is sporting the portable boom box radio that preceded the ipod. The progression of the portable music box is interrupted by mini-skits of comedy. The, "I'm sorry the boss is tied up right now," is among them. Marie-Alise Recasner is the flight attendant saying, "Soya Norah", to the air passengers as they arrive safely. She gets in one of those parting shots that anyone who has worked with the public would love to sneak in if they could only get away with it. Recasner is another of the actresses that has appeared on both *General Hospital* and in a movie featuring Linda Blair.

The credits continue to roll into the bedroom with Tracy Vaccaro who plays the sizzling seductress "Marlene" who is looking for a few good men. Tracy was *Playboy's* Miss October 1984 and was Mrs. Fred Dryer for five years. Fred was the star of the television series *Hunter*. He is also remembered as the star of the Los Angeles Rams defensive line for thirteen seasons. The credits finally disappear and who should appear, speaking of imps and lucky numbers like 13?

Linda Blair is the "Don't Girl". She is told not to answer the phone, or the door. She isn't to do anything. She is funny and I will always feel that she loved the comedy genre best. She concurs with me in an interview article in the 3 December 1999 issue of *Femme Fatales*. Her interviews are exceptional spontaneous entertainment and her sense of humor always seems to be keen and in high gear. In *I.M.P.S.* a new version of Jason chases Linda into the next skit.

Squire Fridell is the interviewing news scooper in the next segment of this pointless rolling gag. It is officially titled, *Sale on Professional Men*. Jennifer Tilly is the hot tamale drooling over the wares of the auction. Tilly is a seasoned professional. Some of her most memorable work manifests itself in the horror end of the cinema-scope. She played Tiffany in *The Bride of Chucky* and *The Seed of Chucky*. Tilly also is featured in Disney's *Haunted Mansion* (2003) in which she played Madame Leota. She received an Oscar nomination for her role as Olive Neal in Woody Allen's *Bullets Over Broadway* in 1994. Jennifer did a bit in the comedy *Liar, Liar* in 1997 that also featured a young Jim Carey. She was nominated for the Blockbuster Entertainment Award as Favorite Supporting Actress in that one that all of my daughters liked.

1997 smiled on the talented California native, as she won the International Fantasy Film Award for Best Supporting Actress by Fantasporto for her roll in *Bound*. *Bound* is a somewhat controversial film that features two lesbians (One of them is Violet who is played by Jennifer Tilly) attempting to steal millions of mob dollars and pin the blame on Violet's beau. The Fantasporto Awards come from a film festival held in Porto, Portugal. It salutes newcomers to the film industry as well as films that it considers fantastic. It must have been a corker as it won the GLAAD Media Award for Best Film of 1996. In case you were wondering what the GLAAD Awards were for, they weren't for sandwich bags. The letters stand for Gay and Lesbian

Alliance Against Defamation. It was nominated for five Academy Awards.

As we return to "The Sale of the Professional Man" we find Barbara Basson auctioning off a handsome professional malefactor with all of the trimmings. Tilly is one of the bidders. Both Barbara Basson and Jennifer Tilly were featured in a number of episodes of the TV series *Hill Street Blues*. The versatile Tilly is three months older than Linda Blair.

Ed Berke and Doyle Baker do a unique skit in an elevator. Baker played "Wilson" in the classic 1955 *Blackboard Jungle* and hadn't been featured in film for 30 years until *I.M.P.S.* rolled along.

We are introduced to the Three Mile Island Family. I wonder if it was this clan that inspired *The Simpsons* or if it was *The Simpsons* that inspired the Three Mile Island Family. Fred Willard plays the part of the patriarch who works at the Three Mile Island nuclear facility. Fred has been around almost as long as Linda Blair. The first of his (to date) 211 film credits began in 1966. Fred is twenty years older than Linda and she had already been doing commercials and (or) catalog shoots for a couple of years. Willard has run the gauntlet of television series. You could see him in *Get Smart, Love American Style, The Bob Newhart Show, Laverne and Shirley, Fernwood 2 Night, Family Matters, Roseanne, Saturday Night Live, Mad About You* and surprisingly, the older Fred grows, the greater his demand. A couple of light comedies that feature this young man of 71 are the original *Fun With Dick and Jane* and *The Silver Streak*, which featured the kings of screen comedies during the 1970s, Richard Prior and Gene Wilder. If you've ever watched American TV you would recognize Willard's face if not his name.

Adult actress Marilyn Chambers plays herself in *I.M.P.S.* She does the American Express gig. She lusciously appears in a teddy and endorses the product amidst a naked crowd (no genitalia exposed). Paradoxically, she and Linda Blair were at one time linked to *Ivory Soap*. Linda played the part of the speaking preschooler who informs her mother that she needn't use *Ivory* anymore because it is gentle enough for babies and she (Linda) was no longer a baby. (This commercial appears on You Tube and it'll rope you in if you like watching cute kids on TV). Chambers was the model on the box of *Ivory Soap Flakes* who held the baby in her arms. The *Ivory Soap* people replaced her as she entered the new area of entertainment. Chambers and Blair both grew up in Connecticut. Marilyn passed away 12 April 2009 at the age of 56 as the result of a cerebral hemorrhage. It was the same year that *I.M.P.S.* was released.

I'll never offer to buy a lady a drink after watching Bruce Weitz use the classic line in *I.M.P.S.* *Hill Street Blues* and Kansas City Chiefs star Ed Marinaro is the friend who urges Bruce to introduce himself to the lady. The lady at the bar is Colleen Camp. She must have played the role of a policewoman more than any other actress on record. She also released a record *One Day Since Yesterday*. I don't think that it fared too well, as it isn't listed on the Billboard Top 40 Hits 6th edition.

The experience of film veteran John Carradine is summoned for the role of host in the skit *Great Moments in Polish History*. Normally this wouldn't be a challenging role. You must see the movie to appreciate all this legend must endure to accomplish the expectations that this job has in store. John has over 300 film and television credits to his name, beginning in 1930 when he played a reporter in *Bright Lights*. He played the part of a Roman soldier in the Oscar winning *Cleopatra*. This gem set the immortal Claudette Colbert as the Egyptian queen. Working with Claudette Colbert and Linda Blair gives us an idea of the span of Carradine's career. Carradine was Long Jack in the film adaptation of Rudyard Kippling's 1937 *Captains Courageous* that netted Spencer Tracy the Oscar for Best Actor. *Captains Courageous* also starred Hollywood heavyweights Lionel Barrymore and Mickey Rooney.

In 1939 John went to work with distinguished director John Ford in the classic western *Stagecoach*. He teams up with one of

Hollywood's most celebrated horsemen, John Wayne. Carradine played the part of Hatfield, and Thomas Mitchell earned an Oscar as Best Supporting Actor for his convincing portrayal of Doc Boone. *Stagecoach* also received the coveted Oscar for Best Music Score. It was truly one of the greatest representative Western films. John was doubly blest to work with two of the Silver Screen's finest representative riders from each sex, John Wayne and Linda Blair. In 1939 he appeared in nine films, the most noteworthy being *Drums Along the Mohawk*. He is teamed up with the beautiful Claudette Colbert and Henry Fonda in this Western.

The next year found Carradine in one of his best character acting roles. He played Casy in *The Grapes of Wrath*. Director John Ford won an Oscar, as did Jane Darwell for her role as Ma Joad. John Carradine teamed up with Henry Fonda in this saga of a displaced Oklahoma family searching for a new home and a new life in California. This John Stienbeck classic set the table for *Up Your Alley*. I remember quizzing my reserved father as to the authenticity of the desperate poverty and need that *The Grapes of Wrath* portrays. The survivor of the Great Depression affirmatively responded. Like Grandpa Joad, my uncle was buried in an unmarked grave during this gripping era. *Up Your Alley* is a little less gripping, but it did broach the fate of our homeless and less fortunate. If you ponder the possibilities of an actor getting to star in movies from the greatest writers of all time, John Carradine defies the odds. He was in Kippling's *Captains Courageous*, John Stienbeck's *The Grapes of Wrath* and graced us with his bit as Bret Harte in *The Adventures of Mark Twain* in 1944, and in 1955 he played "The Duke" in the TV adaptation of Mark Twain's *Huckleberry Finn* on Climax Theater and again in 1960 as the slave catcher from the same classic. He also starred as Gordon in the Robert Louis Stevenson's *Kidnapped* in 1938.

The Grapes of Wrath put Carradine in the big leagues as a character actor. In *The Grapes of Wrath* he played the wayward preacher Casey. His roles would be credited from here on in. They would also be of higher stature for a long time to come. From a theological standpoint, Carradine got to play the Aaron, the brother of Moses in *The Ten Commandments*. He got to play King David in the 1978 *Greatest Heroes of the Bible*. He was the narrator for the film *Genesis* the same year that the Beatles charted in the Untied States (1964). He starred as the friend (Porter Rockwell) of Latter-day Saint Prophet Joseph Smith in *Brigham Young* which was released the same year as *The Grapes of Wrath*.

Carradine was in many of the horror genre that Blair is so celebrated for. His first gig was in 1935's *Bride of Frankenstein* in an unaccredited role. He played Norbert in *Whispering Ghosts* (1942). It was a horror/comedy that featured; believe it or not, Milton Berle in the leading role. That in itself is a scary thought. He did a lot of edgy horror types in the 1940s. Among them are: *Revenge of the Zombies* (1943), *Voodoo Man* (1944), top billing in both 1944 flicks *The Mummy's Ghost* as Yousef Bay, and in *Bluebeard* as Gaston Morrell, and saw action as Dracula in *House of Frankenstein*. He was cast alongside such sinister stars as Lon Cheney and Boris Karloff in Frankenstein's humble abode. The next year he was in *The House of Dracula*. It is intriguing what the public turned to for entertainment as the Second World War was being rapped up. It wouldn't be until 1956 that Carradine would return as a frightening face on film on the television series *Matinee Theatre.* Again it would be as the dark Dracula. He would appear with Lon Cheney Jr. in *House of Black Death* about the same time as the Ford Motor Company introduced the Mustang, 1965.

It would only be fitting that he showed up in two episodes of the TV *Munsters* and the 1966 theatrical non-thriller *Munster Go Home!* This Carradine character was not at all bashful about the roles that he would tackle. If you have the creativity to imagine *Billy The Kid vs. Dracula* you have license to see this movie with John in it. Your imagination may be on par with Bob Logan, the creator of *Repossessed*. How about seeing JC in the 1968 reel(ly) not so classic *The Astro Zombies?* The next year this versatile veteran of film was in *The Mummy and the Curse of the Jackals.* By the end of the 1960s Carradine went across the border and did *Las Vampiras, La Senora Muerte* and *Pacto Diabolico* (Pact with the Devil). He plays Satan and speaks in Spanish in this ditty that preceded *The Exorcist* by four years. He was the butler in *Blood of Dracula's Castle* before the 1960s closed its books on history. Some of his more recent activities on the super silver screen include: *Buried Alive* (1990), a minor role in *Evil Spawn* (1987). In 1986 He teams up with the steamy Sybil Danning in *The Tomb* She was one of the top (or topless) stars in Blair's *Chained Heat* in 1983. If you reach behind that dark bedroom door, you'll find John Carradine in *Monster in the Closet*. Stella Stevens was in that one, too. Even Elvis might like to star in *Monster in the Closet* if he could be locked up with her. In 1985 he is paired up with Tina Louise (Ginger from the TV show *Gilligan's Island*) in *Evils of the Night*. In 1981 he was featured in the Saturn Award winning classic (as the best horror film) *The Howling.* He could be found on *Frankenstein Island* in 1981, the year after he was in the *Monster Club* and *The Boogeyman*. He closed out the 1970s with Yvonne de Carlo and John Blyth Barrymore in *Nocturna: Granddaughter of Dracula.*

Like Linda, he got his feet wet in the brown paper bag movies that the censors permitted to the public for the first time during the 1970s. It wasn't just the usual erotica, but eeri-otica for the aging man of many movies. He was featured in *Vampire Hookers* and *Satan's Cheerleaders.*

He teamed up with John Wayne for the last time in 1976 starring as the undertaker in *The Shootist.* Legends like Lauren Bacall, Richard Boone and Jimmy Stewart contributed to this unforgettable movie. It would be Wayne's last. He passed away 11 June 1979. *I.M.P.S.* would be Carradine's final film appearance. He died in Italy 27 November 1988. *The Shootist* also brought an aspiring child veteran back to the screen, Ron

Howard.

William Sanderson is cast as Carl in the *I.M.P.S.* episode of *Alienski.* Sanderson is one of Hollywood's most recognizable souls. He is Sheriff Bud Dearbourne in the TV series *True Blood.* He is probably best remembered as one of the local brothers featured on the television series Newhart. He was "Larry" in the brotherhood of Larry, Daryl and Darrell. Some of his other television appearances include "Weirdo" on *Starsky & Hutch,* "Willie McCracken" on *Quincy MD,* "The Rev" on *Knight Rider,* "Cousin Eb" on *Married With Children,* "Larry" on *The Coach,* "Dickey Crowe" on *Maximum Bob,* "Mayor" on *Walker Texas Ranger,* "EB Farnham" on *Deadwood* and "Dr. Karl Russom" on *Batman.* He is also featured in John Candy's final film *Wagons East.* Sanderson played the role of the backwoodsman in most of the roles that I have seen him featured in. Don't be mislead by the roles he is acting in, he holds a Bachelor of Arts degree from Southern Methodist University and a JD law degree from Memphis State. One of Memphis' true sons, William enlisted for a two-year stint in the US Army. He says that it is better to be typecast than not cast at all.

You will also see Sunny Johnson in the role of Missy the cheerleader. Sunny was born in San Bernardino, California 21 September 1953. According to the Internet Movie Data Base she was blest to make her screen debut on the TV series *Charlie's Angels.* She played the role of Marie in the episode *Angel Baby.* According to her obituary on UPI June 21, 1984, her first role was on the TV series *Baretta.* From what she has to feature as a lovely creature as Missy the cheerleader in the episode *Hanukah Horror* she certainly would have fit right in with the other celestial bodies on the oft watched classic drama. The following year (1978) she would be featured on the big screen in one of Hollywood's comic classics. She played Otter's co-ed in *Animal House.* She landed the role of Jeannie Szabo in *Flashdance.* She was a well-built blonde who certainly portrayed an alluring lust object in her cheerleading outfit in *IMPS* and I couldn't help but wonder why her acting credits were so short. She died at the age of 30 from a ruptured aneurysm in Los Angeles. I found it interesting that this movie would have begun filming as early as 1984 and not be released until 2009.

Although *IMPS* doesn't sport a cast of thousands, it features some of the most recognizable faces on film during the 1980s and '90s. You'll see Barbara Bosson, Ed Marinaro and Bruce` Weitz from the old television police drama *Hill Street Blues*. Jennifer Tilly, Marilyn Chambers, Colleen Camp, John Carradine, Julia Duffy, Audrey Landers, Ron Hayes, Michael Preminger and Paul Sylvan made appearances in this DVD only cult release. *I.M.P.S.* was never shown on the silver screen. Sybil Danning (who played Erika in *Chained Heat*) is on the same bill as Blair again.

The humor offered is o.k. but I wouldn't pay the full price for this one. If you can pick up a discounted copy of *I.M.P.S.* it will bring a little laughter to your home.

Scream
1996

Linda Blair returns to the genre that catapulted her to fame in this unforgettable horror who done it. Her refined talents are sculpted to the screen with such other eye-catching notables as Drew Barrrymore, Courtney Cox, Neve Campbell and Rose McGowan. Although she is seen more in this movie than Mercedes McCambridge was viewed in *The Exorcist*, Linda isn't listed on the cine's credits. She is featured as the reporter who is giving us the grim news of the grisly murders. Instead of donning a corona, the original Scream Queen is attired in an orange blouse and short black skirt in her professional appearance as a reporter in the scene that enlightens us to the school body's reaction to the tragic deaths of two of its slashed students. Could the color scheme of her clothing lend to the Haloweenish plot of this notable flick? There are a couple of other notable stars that show up in *Scream* but are not seen on the credits line. Henry Winkler, the "Fonze" of *Happy Days* fame, plays principal Himbre. He should have been credited, as his role is integral to the plot and he is featured for more than a full minute. Director We Craven is the janitor in a very brief appearance.

I am not certain if it was Linda Blair in the scene in the

orange blouse, but the lady did cut the cutey's figure and persona. I am sure of her appearance in the black and white print dress. She approaches the Jeep squad car that Sidney Prescott is escorted to school in. Linda plays the role of the obnoxious reporter who charges her way to the vehicle and shoves a microphone into her face. The reporter then begins blasting questions Sidney's way.

This is a truly twisted tale. Casey Becker and her beau are murdered and gutted early in the movie. Casey answered the phone and is asked a number of bizarre questions. The caller stays unidentified throughout Scream. Their murders initiate a rash of cult like slayings. It seems that the dastardly deeds are always done by someone slithering in a black tunic and a horrifying black and white mask.

The murderous mischief and mayhem are serious enough to warrant the closing of school. This is reason to party. Sydney and Tatum's boyfriends are quite jubilant about the whole deal. You would think that they would be in some kind of mourning after the untimely demise of their schoolmates. Billy Loomis (Skeet Ulrich) and Stuart Macher (Matthew Lillard) are the strange brew beaus of the leading ladies. *Scream* shares a common thread with 2000 movie smash *Erin Brockovich*. It seems that all of the men in this movie are tough talking morons (Principal Himbre) or whacked out weasels like Billy and Stu.

The party responsible for the murder is indiscriminate about the work that is their pleasure. This is not for the weak of heart. It is scary. It is gory. It bleeds red like the ink of 2009 General Motors Corporation.

With the closing of school and a curfew imposed the high schoolers resort to having a party at Tatum's house. The killing creatures are creative. The suspects are countless. There are numerous references to horror movies gone by in this one. For some reason, Jamie Lee Curtis' name surfaces and one of her movies is shown playing on the TV at Tatum's house while the party continues, without the hostess. As far as I know, this is the only movie that features both scream queens in it. Curtis' image appears on a rented movie video on the TV screen at the house party. Randy Meeks (done well by Jamie Kennedy) is the movie buff. He discusses the vitals of horror movies. You cannot have a virgin as a victim, for example.

Tatum's brother is local sheriff's deputy and he is interested in one of the leading ladies (Gale Weathers who is played by Courtney Cox.) She is the local TV reporter of interest and lends a great deal of depth to the story of deaths. She has written a book about Sydney's mother's murder. Sydney's mom was murdered and Weathers wonders if the wrong person is about to die in the electric chair for something that he hasn't done. The strongest damning evidence came from Sydney, who said that the man convicted ran from the house of the murder in an easily identifiable jacket. Weathers claims that anybody of that build could have worn that jacket while leaving the crime scene.

I was taken aback by the lack of affection between the dating couples in *Scream*. The males show little respect for their sweethearts and their manners would put Emily Post into shock. Fat, ugly girls with zits the size of Texas could have faired better than the ladies in this flick. Surely Neve Campbell and Rose McGowan could have found more attractive guys if they would have looked. Billy and Stu are really strange from the get go.

There was a nice romance that became of the local yokel deputy and the refined reporter. I really thought that Gale Weathers was just playing Deputy Dwight Riley (who is played by David Arquette) to gain access to the hands on action and intrigue. Was I surprised! According to the Internet Movie Data Base, the plot was changed because the public didn't want Deputy Riley to die. He and Courtney Cox (who plays the leggy lady playing reporter Gale Weathers) were married in San Francisco in 1999. Although Arquette doesn't look the part, he is one of only two non-professional wrestlers to hold the WCW Title. He pinned Eric Bischoff on 27 April 2000 for the title. He is the grandson of Cliff Arquette, better known as Charlie Weaver, from *Hollywood Squares*. David comes from a French-Jewish family that sports other notable actors: Rosanna, Patricia, Richmond and Alexis Arquette. David, Leiv Schreiber, Courtney Cox and Neve Campbell are the only four stars to have appeared in all of the *Scream* movies. Arquette would have been two years old when The Exorcist hit the screen as he was born in 1971, when Viet Nam was in full swing and Three Dog Night's *Joy To the World* was the hottest thing on wax.

If horror is the apple of your one bloody eye, I think that the *Scream* sequels will keep you guessing and too scared to get up and out to the lobby for more popcorn. This may be the only movie that approaches the dubbing of Cult Classic that Linda Blair appears in since *The Exorcist*, and she isn't even listed in the credits.

The Blair Bitch Project
1999

The *Blair Witch Project* was a poorly filmed hoax of cinema that left the viewer frightened and unsure. It was much ballyhooed and just about any creature with vision on planet Earth saw it and have most likely forgotten about it since its introduction to curious movie going fools who fall for the trendy.

The movie capitalized on Linda Blair's name. Was it coincidental? Would the horror movie going public flock to the theaters for a film dubbed, "The Sarandan Witch Project?" Certainly not. The name Blair carries clout in the scary movie business 25 years after *The Exorcist* was splashed on the silver screen. Ever the clever creature, Linda didn't go after millions in court. She didn't hold a bitter press conference shaming the crew. She didn't call Carol King for advice on such matters. True to her heart, she did some inner searching and decided to have some fun with this (*The Blair Witch Project*) movie. She consulted with some friends and did a parody and appropriately named it *The Blair Bitch Project*. Of course it starred Linda Blair. It provided her a vehicle to do comedy on her terms. Slapstick was the flavor of the day, but you'll also get to see some cleverly laid lines. There was a subliminal reference to one of the lines from *The Exorcist*, just as there was in *Ruckus*. She makes a remark to her rock chucking soundman regarding his mother. "Your mother chucks rocks in Hell!" is the quote.

Some of the humor is raw. Some of it would leave some people uncomfortable. I wouldn't recommend it for a day care facility or if your girlfriend and her Minister father wanted to come on over and watch a funny movie. But for most people, the bad taste is covered up with some gratuitous shots of the starlet and the witty lines that she spews.

Linda heads off to the woods to find out why so many young children are buried in a Rhode Island cemetery. Many of the opening dialogues are as cheesy as they are funny. She opts to bring along a cameraman. He is a true pothead. His uncanny genius is developing bongs out of just about anything. His camera talent rivals that of the cameraman in *The Blair Witch Project*. She also hires an audio expert. It was too bad that *Dumb and Dumber* was already done. This could have turned out to be its parody with the twist of a hot chick tossed into the mix.

There are more laughs than uncomfortable moments on your trip through this flick. It may seem pointless, but sometimes we need to laugh just to break the tension of everyday life. I guess that is the point of humor.

It is sad that there were only 3000 copies of *The Blair Bitch Project* made. It took me 10 years to get one and it was autographed by the curvaceous cutey that played Linda in the movie. Some of the humor is hidden and you need to dig for it. It gets better each time I watch it.

Other interesting items

The Baby Class of 1959

Born the same year as Linda Blair were: Danny Bonaduce (of the Partridge Family), singer Tony de Franco, country music artist Tanya Tucker (who IMDB lists as being born in Oct. of 1958 but it's close enough to call for me), Marie Osmond, and Mackenzie Phillips who starred in *One Day At A Time.* The other one of the Romano sisters in the 1975 CBS sitcom was the lovely Valerie Bertinelli. She is one year younger than Blair. Linda didn't need to go on the Jenny Craig diet to slim down. She attributes her fit and trim figure to the Vegan lifestyle she adheres to. If I were to move from Wisconsin to Fantasyland, I would like to see both Bertinelli and Blair (age 49 and 50) photographed, clad in bikinis so that we could really tell which system works the best. I'm afraid that I'd study the photos for hours declaring the photo finish a dead heat. Even in their later decades, they can make your head spin. As for Marie Osmond, her darling, adorable face kept her looking lovely for decades.

Of this sampling listed from the baby boomer's heyday, I feel that Linda Blair's success rates at the top of the heap. She began her acting career as a model and did some television commercials. What makes it special is that she is one of the few that can still claim to have entered the visual media industry when the *Dick Van Dyke Show* was only seen in black and white. She did many commercials in black and white before appearing in *The Exorcist.* Sadly, the first color that we think of when we think of Linda Blair is the pea green from her patented soup de jour. Besides being immortalized for her role in *The Exorcist*, Linda had two made for television movies that achieved the highest viewer ratings for their respective years. They were *Born Innocent* in 1974 followed up by *Sara T.: Portrait of a Teenage Alcoholic.* (The second of these is nearly impossible to obtain.)

She has been portrayed as everything from the victim (*The Exorcist, Victory at Entebbe* and *Bail Out*) to the vixen (*Fatal Bond, SFX The Retaliator, Sorcery* and *Bedroom Eyes II*). Her career encompasses nearly every genre of acting. She sang in *Sara T.* and *Skins*. She danced in *The Exorcist II* and *Roller Boogie.*

She was kidnapped in *Sweet Hostage, Victory at Entebbe, Bail Out* and *Double Blast*. She was sported as the pretty reporter in *Up Your Alley* and again in *Scream*. She played a cop in *Night Patrol, Prey of the Jaguar* and *the Heart of the Lie.* She was the cop's wife in *Silent Assassins.* Any hairdresser would love her in *Fatal Bond*, where she plays a beautician from Down Under. In this movie she abandons her career for a man. Men would love her in *Fatal Bond* and not just because she looks hot. *Fatal Bond* may be the last movie on the face of the earth where a woman gives up her career for the man she loves.

In *Ruckus* and *Monster Makers*, she played something that she never experienced in real life. She got to be the mother, and for what it's worth, my daughter absolutely loves *Monster Makers*. In *Witchery*, she portrays the mother in waiting. She plays the farmer's daughter (*Sweet Hostage* and *Wild Horse Hank*) and the lawyer's wife (*Sorcery*). She demonstrates her horsemanship superbly in *Wild Horse Hank* and *Stranger in Our House.* Here is what one of my life's final questions, "Will Linda Blair & John Wayne ride off together in the sunset in the land of Heaven?" John Wayne may be that deserving a horseman and I pray that I am that worthy a man to see such a blest pair of stage studies.

Oh, and I almost forgot. She got to play the role of a nurse in two movies, *Monster Makers* and *Dead Sleep* (which was also filmed in Australia.) She played a doctor in *Moving Target*. She was more than the mere paranormal mortal.

Baseball Hall of Famer, Leo Durocher married a Mormon actress named Lorraine Day. She usually played the role of a nurse. She was allowed to step out of her cinematic stereotype in *The Locket*, "If they could only get her out of that nurse's uniform, they'd find out that woman could act,(a)" stated Durocher. The picture was a triumph...She played an insane woman. It was one of the few times that the studio let her get out of than nurse's uniform and show that she could act. Like the lady of the previous generation, Blair has proven beyond any doubts that she possesses and utilizes her acting ability with the best of them even outside the scream queen genre that she has been typecast in.

That brings up afore mentioned Marie Osmond, born 13 October 1959. She is similar to Blair in more ways than year of birth. Both of them have cover girl faces, framed by a hair color other than blonde. Both of them have successfully battled weight gain. Linda Blair has been remembered almost solely for her role as Regan in *The Exorcist*, even though she has mastered so many more roles without much recognition. Marie is best known for her singing ability, which is excellent, as it has survived the tests of time and personal tribulation. She is also known as one of the singing Osmond family. Like Lorraine Day Durocher, Marie is a member of the Church of Jesus Christ of Latter-day Saints, or Mormon in street terms. Linda Blair claimed that her role in *The Exorcist* was an interesting cross to bear. Marie's true to life character is also an interesting cross to bear. She is the most visible female personality save it be the Prophet's wife in her faith. There have been at least six prophets' wives that died since 1959, yet the lovely Marie still remains. She hasn't had to hire security to protect her from death threats, as Linda did after *The Exorcist*. However, I don't feel that this poor woman has had much of a chance to enjoy a private life since she was in her early teens. Members of the Church of Jesus Christ of Latter-day Saints have been following the events of Marie's life since she approached puberty. She seems to have handled the pressure well, but I'm sure that she would love a day in the sun without the paparazzi or nosy church members. Most of Marie's acting credits are of Marie playing Marie Osmond. Her singing credits on the other hand, far exceed those of Blair's. In spite of their different lifestyles, they have both managed to lead productive lives that have contributed to the betterment of our society as a whole. If I may add one more thing to their credit, I think that they are both happy with the face in the mirror and the person behind it when they smile.

Why is it that Tanya Tucker seems light years older than Marie Osmond and Linda Blair? Blair has never married. Tanya Tucker is about three months older than Blair and met success at the frighteningly early age of 13 (same age as Blair was when shooting *The Exorcist*) with her smash hit record *Delta Dawn*. Tucker dated country music superstar Glenn Campbell during the late 1970s and early '80s. She didn't receive a credited role in the box office until 1979 for her role as Sharon Singleton in the made to TV movie *Amateur Night at the Dixie Bar and Grill*.

The girls of Hollywood grew up fast...even in the 1970s.

Linda Blair's Co-Stars and their awards

Anthony Addabbo in *Calendar Girl, Cop Killer?/The Bambi Bembenek Story;*

Jan Adele in *Fatal Bond* won AFI (Australian Film Institute) Award in 1987 for Best Actress in a Supporting Role for *High Tide;*

Benjamin Agundez III aka Beano in *Skins;*

Jason Alabough in *Double Blast* (His only film appearance to date);

Edward Albert in *Sorceress* won the Golden Globe in 1972 for *Most Promising;*

Newcomer, Male for his role in *Butterflies Are Free;*

Lyle Alzado in *Zapped Again;*

Christine Amor in *Dead Sleep;*

Brian Anderson in *Double Blast* (His only film appearance to date);

Dana Andrews in *Airport 1975;*

Tina Andrews in *Born Innocent;* Tina won the Writers Guild of America Award for Original Long Form for *Sally Hemings: an American Scandal* in 2000;

Todd Eric Andrews in *Zapped Again;*

Jennifer Ashley in *Chained Heat;*

Tom Badel in *Prey of the Jaguar;*

Scott Baker in *Woman Obsessed* aka *Bad Blood;* Scott won the Clavell de Plata Award for Best Screenplay for *Litan* in 1982;

Adam Baldwin in *Monster Makers;*

Caroline Barclay in *Bail Out;*

John Barrett in *Double Blast;*

Paul Bartel in *Prey of the Jaguar;*

Peter Barton in *Hell Night;*

Billy Barty in *Night Patrol;*

Belinda Beatty *in The Exorcist II The Heretic;*

Ned Beatty in *The Exorcist II The Heretic* and *Repossessed;*

Billy Beck in *Airport 1975* and *Summer of Fear/Stranger in*

Our House;

Caroline Beck in *Fatal Bond;*

Kimberly Beck in *Roller Boogie;*

Tobin Bell in *Calendar Girl, Cop Killer?/The Bambi Bembenek Story;* Tobin won a Fangoria Chain Saw Award in 2005 for Best Villain in *Saw II;*

Kevin Benton in *Up Your Alley;*

Lorne Berfield in *Double Blast;*

Lloyd Berry in *Wild Horse Hank;*

Dirk Benedict in *Ruckus;*

Karen Black in *Airport 1975* and *Zapped Again;* Karen won the Medalla Sitges en Plata de Lay Award for Best Actress for her role as Marian Rolf in *Burnt Offerings* in 1976 at the Catalonian Film Festival; Karen won the Outstanding Achievement Award for Acting-Female for her role as Sandra in *Firecracker* in 2005 at New York VisionFest; Karen won the New York Film Critic's Circle Award for Best Supporting Actress as Rayette Dipesto in *Five Easy Pieces* in 1971; Karen won the National Board of Review Award for the Best Supporting Actress in *Five Easy Pieces* in 1970; Karen won the Golden Globe Award for Best Supporting Actress in *Five Easy Pieces* in 1971; Karen won the Best Actress Award at the Hermosa Beach Film Festival for her role as Rose van Horn in *Dogtown* and for *Sugar, Fall of the West* in 1998; Karen won a Golden Globe Award in 1975 for Best Supporting Actress for her role as Myrtle Wilson in the *Great Gatsby;*

Greta Blackburn in *Chained Heat;*

Elinore Blair in *The Exorcist* (Elinore is Linda's mother and she played the nurse.);

Rick Blanchard in *The Chilling* and *Skins;*

Verna Bloom in *Sara T: Portrait of a Teenage Alcoholic;*

Margaret Blye in *The Sporting Club;*

Tony Bonner in *Dead Sleep;*

Andrew Booth in *Dead Sleep;*

Ernest Borgnine in *Moving Target;* he won an Oscar for the

Best Actor in a Leading Role in the movie *Marty* in 1956; he won a BAFTA Award and a Golden Globe for the same role in 1956.

Lucy Boryer in *Zapped Again;*

James Bray in *Roller Boogie* (his only movie credit listed on the Internet Movie Data Base);

Melissa Braselle in *Sorceress;*

Stephen Brause in *Double Blast* (His only film appearance to date);

Kevin Brief in *Calendar Girl, Cop Killer?/The Bambi Bembenek Story;*

Kevin Brophy in *Hell Night;*

Tony Brubaker in *Bail Out;*

Bob Bucholz in *Zapped Again* Won 1996 Outstanding Edited Sports Series/Anthologies; Emmy Award for *NFL Films Presents: 1967;*

Joe Bugner in *Fatal Bond*; former European heavyweight boxing champion;

Traci Burgard in *Skins;*

Ellen Burstyn in *The Exorcist;*

Richard Burton in *The Exorcist II The Heretic;* won BAFTA Award as The Best British Actor in 1967 for his role in *The Spy Who Came in From the Cold* and *Who's Afraid of Virginia Woolf;* He won a Golden Globe for Best Motion Picture Actor for his role in *Equus*; *h*e won a Golden Globe as The Most Promising Newcomer-Male for his role in *My Cousin Rachel* in 1953;

Timothy Busfield in *Calendar Girl, Cop Killer?/The Bambi Bembenek Story; h*e won the 1991 Emmy Award for Best Supporting Actor for his role in *Thirtysomething;*

Ruth Buzzi in *Up Your Alley*;   she won a Golden Globe Award in 1973 for Best Supporting Actress-Television on *Rowan and Martin's Laugh In* (1967);

Dave Buzzotta in *Skins;*

MacDonald Carey in *Stranger in Our House* aka *Summer of Fear;* Won three Soap Opera Digest Awards and two Soapys;

Barbara Cason in *The Exorcist II The Heretic;*

Sid Caesar in *Airport 1975*; won an Emmy Award in 1957 for Best Continuing Performance in a *Continuing Comedy* in a Series for *Ceasar's Hours*;

Maxwell Caulfield in *Prey of the Jaguar*;

Steve Chase in *Calendar Girl, Cop Killer?/The Bambi Bembenek Story*;

Jun Chong in *Silent Assassins*;

Matt Clark in *Ruckus*;

Susan Clark in *Airport 1975*; Clark won an Emmy as Outstanding Lead Actress in a Drama or Comedy Series for her role as Mildred "Babe" Didrikson Zaharias in *Babe*;

Lee J. Cobb in *The Exorcist*;

Robert Colbert in *The Chilling*;

Michael Colyar in *Zapped Again*;

Dale Cook in *Double Blast*; he was Light-Heavy Weight Thai Boxing Champion/ WKA Middle Weight Champion/UK Super Middle Weight Champion;

Nicholas Coster in *The Sporting Club*;

Vassy Cotsopoulos in *Dead Sleep*;

Sueyan Cox in *Dead Sleep*;

John Crank in *Double Blast*;

Richard Crenna in *Wild Horse Hank*;

Craig Cronin in *Dead Sleep*;

Gregory Scott Cummins in *Bail Out* ;

William Daniels in *Sara T: Portrait of a Teenage Alcoholic*;

Sybil Danning in *Chained Heat*;

Johnny Dark in *Night Patrol, Up Your Alley* and *Repossessed*;

Don S. Davis in *Calendar Girl, Cop Killer?/The Bambi Bembenek Story*; Don won the Fright-Fest Director's Award in 2003 for Best Supporting Actor for his work in *Savage Island*;

Dove Dellos in *Repossessed*;

Charles Dierkop in *Grotesque*;

Tamara Dobson in *Chained Heat* (listed as the tallest woman to grace the silver Screen in a leading role);

David Donah in *Zapped Again*;

Troy Donahue in *The Chilling* and *A Woman Obsessed* aka *Bad Blood*; Troy won the 1960 Golden Globe Award for the Best Male Newcomer.

Antonia Dorian in *Sorceress*;

Kirk Douglas in *Victory At Entebbe*;

Peta Downes in *Dead Sleep*;

Fran Drescher in *Stranger in Our House/ Summer of Fear*;

Richard Dreyfus in *Victory At Entebbe*;

Kristi Ducati in *Sorceress*;

James Duggan in *The Chilling*;

John Dunbar III in *Calendar Girl, Cop Killer?/The Bambi Bembenek Story*;

Vic Dunlop in *Up Your Alley* and *Night Patrol*;

Richard Dysart in *The Sporting Club*;

Alan Edwards in *Dead Sleep*;

Jerome Ehlers in *Fatal Bond*;

Bill Erwin in *Silent Assassins*;

Joe Estevez in *Double Blast*;

Erik Estrada in *Airport 1975*;

Richard Farnsworth in *Ruckus*;

Norman Fell in *Airport 1975*;

Rebecca Ferratti in *Silent Assassins*; was Playmate of the Month June 1986;

Robert Fields in *The Sporting Club*;

Richard Fitzpatrick in *Wild Horse Hank*;

Louise Fletcher in *The Exorcist II The Heretic*;

Carey Fox in *Roller Boogie* and *Hell Night*;

Bill French in *Dead Sleep*;

Lindsay Frost in *Calendar Girl, Cop Killer/The Bambi Bembenek Story*

John Fujioka in *Prey of the Jaguar*;

Monique Gabrielle in *Chained Heat*;

Beverly Garland in *Airport 1975* and *Roller Boogie*;

Kathleen Garrett in *Calendar Girl, Cop Killer?/The Bambi Bembenek Story*;

Willie Garson in *Repossessed;*

Benjamin Gates Jr. in *Prey of the Jaguar;*

Teo Gebert in *Fatal Bond;*

Grant Gelt in *Calendar Girl, Cop Killer?/The Bambi Bembenek Story*

Donal Gibson in *Fatal Bond;*

Trevor Goddard in *Prey of the Jaguar;*

John F. Goff in *Grotesque;*

Barbara Gordon in *Wild Horse Hank;*

Erna Gregory in *Repossessed;*

Larry Hagman in *Sara T: Portrait of a Teenage Alcoholic;*

Dan Haggerty in The Chilling; Dan won the 1978 People's Choice Award for the Favorite Male Performer in a New TV Program. (*Grizzly Adams*);

Ron Hall in *Double Blast;*

Tom Hallick in *Skins;*

Richard Halpern in *Repossessed;*

Mark Hamill in *Sara T: Portrait of a Teenage Alcoholic;*

James Handy in *Calendar Girl, Cop Killer?/The Bambi Bembenek Story;*

Jack Hanrahan in *Up Your Alley* and *Repossessed*; he won prime time Emmy Award for Outstanding Writing Achievement in Musical or Variety on the television show *Laugh In;*

Mitch Hara in *Skins;*

Ernest Harden Jr. in *Skins;*

Julius Harris in *Victory at Entebbe;*

Lyndon in *Fatal Bond;*

Michael Harris in *Zapped Again;*

Linda Harrison in *Airport 1975;*

Veronica Hart in *Woman Obsessed* aka *Bad Blood* and *Bedroom Eyes II;*

Bobby Harwell in *Calendar Girl, Cop Killer?/The Bambi Bembenek Story;*

David Hasselhoff in *Bail Out* and *Witchery;* David won 1983 People's Choice Award for Favorite Male Performer in a New TV

Program; he won the Hollywood Movie Award for International Star of the Year in 2005.

Bright Hauser in *Skins;*
Cali Lili Hauser in *Skins;*
Cole Hauser in *Skins;*
Wings Hauser in *Bedroom Eyes II* and *Skins*;
Helen Hayes in *Victory at Entebbe;*
Ira Heiden in *Zapped Again;*
Adam Hendershott in *Calendar Girl, Cop Killer?/The Bambi Bembenek Story;*
Paul Henreid in *The Exorcist II The Heretic;*
Charlton Heston in *Airport 1975;*
Brent Hinkley in *Zapped Again;*
Paul Holmes in *Double Blast;*
Anthony Hopkins in *Victory at Entebbe;*
Ned Hourani in *Double Blast;*
Helen Hughes in *Wild Horse Hank;*
Sharon Hughes in *Grotesque* and *Chained Heat;*
Kim Hunter in *Born Innocent;*
Tab Hunter in *Grotesque;*
Fiona Hutchison in *Prey of the Jaguar;*
Jay Irwin in *Calendar Girl, Cop Killer?/The Bambi Bembenek Story;*
Stoner Jackson in *Roller Boogie;*
Conrad Janis in *Airport 1975;*
Kevin Johnson in *Fatal Bond;*
Rory Johnston in *Prey of the Jaguar;*
James Earl Jones in *The Exorcist II The Heretic;*
Jack Jozefson in *Bail Out;*
Lenny Juliano in *Sorceress;*
Peter Jurasik in *Calendar Girl, Cop Killer?/The Bambi Bembenek Story;* he won a Universe Reader's Choice Award in 1996 for Best Supporting Actor in Genre TV series for *Babylon 5*; This award is presented by Sci-Fi Universe Magazine.
John Karlen in *Calendar Girl, Cop Killer?/The Bambi*

Bembenek Story; John won an Emmy Award in 1986 for Outstanding Supporting Actor in a Drama Series for *Cagney and Lacey*; John won a Q Award in 1986 and 1987 for Best Supporting actor in a Drama Series for ;*Cagney and Lacey*;

Marcia Karr in *Chained Heat* and *Savage Streets;*

Nicky Katt in *Skins;*

Stacy Keach in *Prey of the Jaguar;* Stacy won a Golden Globe Award in 1989 for Best Performance by an Actor in a Miniseries or Motion Picture Made for TV for his role in *Hemmingway*; Stacy won a Kansas City Film Critics Circle Award in 1973 for Best Actor in his roll in *Fat City*; Stacy won the Lifetime Achievement Award from the San Diego Film Festival.

George Kennedy in *Airport 1975* and *Monster Makers;*

Ken Kerman in *Calendar Girl, Cop Killer?/The Bambi Bembenek Story;*

Irwin Keyes in *Chained Heat;*

Sue Kiel in *Red Heat;*

Vincent Klyn in *Prey of the Jaguar;*

Sylvia Kristel in *Red Heat;*

Taylor Lacher in *Ruckus;*

Michael Lampa in *Double Blast* (His only film appearance to date);

Burt Lancaster in *Victory at Entebbe;*

Laurene Landon in *Roller Boogie;*

Sue Anne Langdon in *Zapped Again*; 2003 Golden Boot Award; won 1970 Golden Globe Award for Best Supporting Actress Television for her role in *Arnie*;

Murray Langston (The Unknown Comic) in *Night Patrol, Up Your Alley, Double Blast*;

Linda Larkin in *Zapped Again;*

Ed Lauter in *Calendar Girl, Cop Killer? /The Bambi Bembenek Story;*

Caz Lederman in *Fatal Bond;*

Stephen Leeder in *Fatal Bond;*

Steven Vincent Leigh in *Prey of the Jaguar;*

Ryan Lippman in *Double Blast* (His only film appearance to date);

Stephen Liska in *Calendar Girl, Cop Killer?/The Bambi Bembenek Story;*

Peter Looney in *Silent Assassins;*

Myrna Loy in *Airport 1975;*

Richard Lynch in *Night Force;* 1983 Won Saturn Award for Best Supporting Actor in *The Sword and the Sorcerer;*

Heather Jane MacDonald in *Zapped Again;*

Suzie MacKenzie in *Dead Sleep;*

Mako in *Silent Assassins;* Jerri Manthey in *Prey of the Jaguar;*

William Marshall in *Sorceress;*

Jacquelyn Masche in *Repossessed;*

Johnny Mask in *Calendar Girl, Cop Killer?/The Bambi Bembenek Story;*

Tom Mason in *Calendar Girl, Cop Killer?/The Bambi Bembenek Story;*

Maria McCann in *Zapped Again;*

Sean McClory in *Roller Boogie;*

Chad McQueen in *Nightforce;*

Mike McSween in *Prey of the Jaguar;*

Susan Mechsner in *Chained Heat;*

Dorothy Meyer in *Airport 1975* and *Roller Boogie;*

Devon Michael in *Prey of the Jaguar;*

Joanna Miles in *The Sporting Club* and *Born Innocent;*

Jason Miller in *The Exorcist;*

Stephen E. Miller in *Wild Horse Hank;*

Robert Miano in *Chained Heat;*

Bob Minor in *Bail Out;*

Brian Moll in *Dead Sleep;*

Chuck Morrell in *Grotesque* (also produced *Grotesque*);

Pat Morita in *Night Patrol;*

Jaye P. Morgan in *Night Patrol;*

Melissa Moore in *Repossessed;*

Louisa Moritz in *Chained Heat;*

Talbert Morton in *Skins;*

Mary Murphy in *Born Innocent;*

Toni Naples in *Sorceress;*

Ross Newton in *Fatal Bond;*

James Noble in *The Sporting Club;*

Jeanette O'Connor in *Calendar Girl, Cop Killer?/The Bambi Bembenek Story;*

Nancy Olson in *Airport 1975;*

Dink O'Neal in *Calendar Girl, Cop Killer?/The Bambi Bembenek Story;*

Christina Ongley *in Dead Sleep;*

Michael Parks in *Sorceress;*

Luana Patten in *Grotesque;*

Pat Paulsen in *Night Patrol;*

Penny Pederson in *Fatal Bond;*

David Pegram in *Double Blast;*

Cecil People in *Double Blast;*

Roger Perry in *Roller Boogie;*

Haskell Phillips in *Woman Obsessed* aka *Bad Blood* and *Bedroom Eyes II;*

John Pleshette in *Calendar Girl, Cop Killer?/The Bambi Bembenek Story;*

Larry Poindexter in *Sorceress;*

Lee Purcell in *Stranger in Our House* aka *Summer of Fear;*

Nicholas Pryor in *The Sporting Club;*

Fred Olen Ray in *Sorceress;*

Helen Reddy in *Airport 1975;*

Paul Regina in *Prey of the Jaguar;*

Bert Remsen in *Sweet Hostage;*

Michael R. Reynolds in *Wild Horse Hank;*

Alexis Rhee in *Silent Assassins;*

Phillip Rhee in *Silent Assassins*;

Daryl Keith Roach in *Skins;*

Matt Roe in *Calendar Girl, Cop Killer?/The Bambi Bembenek Story;*

Roger Rook in *Calendar Girl, Cop Killer?/The Bambi Bembenek Story*;

Thomas Rosales Jr. in *Bail Out*;

Bill Ross in *Roller Boogie* as Nick (He has 100 credits for his part as an art director, member of the art department, production designer and camera & electrical department in television and the movies.)

Reed Rudy in *Zapped Again*;

Steve Sandor in *Calendar Girl, Cop Killer?/The Bambi Bembenek Story*;

Fred Schiewiller in *Bail Out*;

Lana Schwab in *Repossessed*;

Stan Schwartz in *Woman Obsessed* aka *Bad Blood* and *Bedroom Eyes II*;

Mort Sertner in *Calendar Girl, Cop Killer?/The Bambi Bembenek Story*;

Stanley Sharp in *Double Blast* (His only film appearance to date);

Thom Sharp in *Repossessed*;

Melissa Shear in *Repossessed* and *Up Your Alley*;

Martin Sheen in *Sweet Hostage*;

Carol Shermer in *Repossessed*;

Kathy Shower in *Bedroom Eyes II*;

Harvey Siegel in *Woman Obsessed* aka *Bad Blood* and *Bedroom Eyes II*;

Henry Silva in *Chained Heat*;

George Skaff in *The Exorcist II The Heretic*;

James Sloyan in *Calendar Girl, Cop Killer?/The Bambi Bembenek Story*;

David Smith in *Double Blast*;

Lois Smith in the *Sporting Club*;

Ken Snodgrass in *Fatal Bond*;

Georgia Spelvin in *Woman Obsessed* aka *Bad Blood*; She won Adult Film Association of America Award for Best Supporting Actress for her role as Wanda the Huntress in *Tarz & Jane*

Chetah & Boy in 1975; she won an AFAA for Best Actress in 1977 for her role as Maddy Stone in *Desires Within Young Girls;* she won Adult Film Association of America award for best actress in *Dancers;* she won the AFAA Award for Best Supporting Actress for her role as Henrietta Wilde in *Take Off* in 1978; she won the AFAA Award for Best Supporting Actress as Madeline Church in *Ecstasy Girls;* in 1979; she won the AFAA Award for Best Supporting Actress as Kathy in *Urban Cowgirls* in 1980; she won the AFAA Award for Best Actress as Catherine in *The Dancers* in 1981;

Tim Spring in *Double Blast;*

Dianne Staines in *Dead Sleep;*

Anthony Starke in *Repossessed;*

Stella Stevens in *Chained Heat;* won 1960 Golden Globe Award for Most Promising Newcomer-Female;

Frank Stewart in *Woman Obsessed* aka *Bad Blood;*

Jerry Stiller in *Airport 1975;* in 1998 he won the American Comedy Award for the Funniest Guest Male Appearance In a TV Series (*Seinfeld* 1990).

Larry Storch in *Airport 1975;*

Julie Strain in *Sorceress;*

Crystal Summer in *Double Blast* (Her only movie appearance to date);

Gloria Swanson in *Airport 1975;* Gloria Swanson won a Golden Globe Award for Best Motion Picture Actress in *Sunset Boulevard* in 1950.

Rochelle Swanson in *Sorceress;*

Lincoln Tate in *Grotesque;*

Liz Taylor in *Victory At Entebbe;* in 1985 she won the Golden Apple Award as Female Star of the Year, & The Golden Globe "Cecil B. De Mille Award"; in 1977 she received the USA Hasty Pudding Theatrical Award as Woman of the Year; in 1974 she won the Golden Globe "Henrietta Award" World Film Favorite Female; in 1972 she won the Silver Berlin Bear Award as Best Actress in *Hammersmith Is Out;* in 1972 she won the David

Award as Best Foreign Actress in *Zee & Company;* in 1968 she won the Bambi Award; in 1967 she won an Oscar for the Best Actress in a Leading Role in the movie *Who's Afraid of Virginia Woolf?;* in 1967 she won a BAFTA Film Award for Best British Actress in the movie *Who's Afraid of Virginia Woolf?;* she won the Kansas City Film Critic Circle Award for her role in *Who's Afraid of Virginia Woolf?;* she won the Golden Laurel Award for "Female Dramatic Performance" in *Who's Afraid of Virginia Woolf?;* she won the National Board of Review Award for Best Actress for her Role in *Who's Afraid of Virginia Woolf?;* in 1966 she won the New York Film Critic's Award for Best Actress for her Roll in *Who's Afraid of Virginia Woolf?;* in 1965 and 1966 she won the Golden Laurel Award for Female Star; in 1961 she won an Oscar for the Best Actress in a Leading Role in the movie *Butterfield 8;* in 1960 she won the Golden Globe Award for Best Motion Picture Actress-Drama in the movie *Suddenly Last Summer;* she won the Golden Laurel Award for Top Female Dramatic Performancein *Suddenly Last Summer;* in 1959 she won the Golden Laurel Award for Top Female Dramatic Performance in *Cat On a Hot Tin Roof;* in 1958 she won the Golden Laurel Award for Top Female Dramatic Performance in *Raintree County;*

Benji Thal in *Repossessed;*

Roy Thinnes in *Airport 1975;*

Susanna Thompson in *Calendar Girl, Cop Killer?/The Bambi Bembenek Story;*

Kathy Topia in *Repossessed;*

Donald Tornatore in *Grotesque* and *Nightforce;*

Joe Tornatore in *Grotesque;*

Daniel Trent in *Calendar Girl, Cop Killer?/The Bambi Bembenek Story;*

Vic Trevino in *Prey of the Jaguar;*

Carolyn Van Bellinghen in *Woman Obsessed* aka *Bad Blood* and *Bedroom Eyes II;*

John Van Ness in *Ruckus;*

Jimmie Van Patten in *Roller Boogie* and *Night Force;*

Nels Van Patten in *Grotesque;*

Vince Van Patten in *Hell Night;*

Christine Veronica in *Woman Obsessed* aka *Bad Blood;*

Glen Vincent in *Repossessed* and *Up Your Alley;*

Gustav Vintas in *Silent Assassins;*

Max von Sydow in *The Exorcist;*

Jessica Walter in *Victory At Entebbe* was awarded the Emmy for Outstanding Lead Actress in a limited series for her role as Amy Prentiss in 1975; in 2004 she won the Golden Satellite Award for Best Performance by an Actress in a Supporting Role In a Series, Musical Comedy for her role in *Arrested Development;*

Roger Ward in *Fatal Bond;*

Cameron Watt in *Dead Sleep;*

Al Waxman in *Wild Horse Hank;* Al received the Gemini Award in 1997 for Best Performance By an Actor In a Featured Supporting Role in a Dramatic Program for *Net Worth;*

Joshua Weisel in *Zapped Again;*

Carole Ita White in *Chained Heat* and *Savage Streets;*

Shannon Wilcox in *Zapped Again;*

Donna Wilkes in *Grotesque;*

Chuck Williams in *Double Blast;*

Edy Williams in *Chained Heat;*

Kelli Williams in *Zapped Again;*

Brian Wilson in *Double Blast* (His only film appearance to date);

Michael Wincott in *Wild Horse Hank;*

Brad Wilson in *Grotesque;*

Patricia Wilson in *Stranger in Our House/Summer of Fear;*

Patrick M. Wright in *Roller Boogie;*

Eric Yacoubian in *Double Blast* (His only film appearance to date);

Charles Young in *Silent Assassins;*

Carmen Zapata in *Skins* won The Women in Film Crystal Awards award for Humanitarian of the Year in 1983.

Bob Zany in *Up Your Alley* and *Double Blast;*

Robert Z'Dar in *Grotesque* and *Double Blast*; won Cleveland Indie Gathering Award in 2007 for Best Supporting Actor in *The Waiter;*

Efrem Zimbalist Jr. in *Airport 1975;*

Miriam Zucker in *Woman Obsessed* aka *Bad Blood.*

Linda Blair plays the fatal victim in the following films:

(Please note, if you continue reading this section, it may spoil the outcome of the movies that they are affiliated with.)

In *SFX The Retaliator* (1977) she plays the role of Doris. She is the clever hooker that sneaks off with the boss' money. Her part is concluded when she is shot in the chest.

In the 1988 movie *Grotesque*, she is chased and choked by one of the marauding house invaders. She ultimately expires in the local hospital. I honestly thought that she would survive the first time that I viewed this unique cult classic.

The only time that Linda Blair plays the part of a pregnant woman is in another 1988 shocker *Witchery*. This medium of uneasiness features her as a woman fighting spiritual possession again. It is as disturbing as *The Exorcist*. She ultimately ends her life by jumping out of a window. Oh, and it doesn't end there.

She plays the loving wife in *A Woman Obsessed* aka *Bad Blood* in this 1989 presentation that was just this short of being a box office success. She is slashed and has her throat slit as she is tricked into staying at an artist's mansion.

In *Bedroom Eyes II* (1990), she is shot and stuffed into the trunk of a Cadillac. I'm not talking about the usual black station wagon Caddy that is famous for that last ride. You'll never guess who does the dirty deed.

Four years later and still looking the bit of someone who could turn more heads than stomachs, the poor girl is shot by her husband in the nearly soft porno flick *Sorceress*. After getting her throat slit playing the role of Mrs. Eva Barnes in *A Woman Obsessed* and being shot in the gut by her wheelchair bound hubby in *Sorceress*, is there any doubt as to why one of the screens sweetest ladies never walked down the isle in real life— or *reel* life either for that matter?

Other Credits

Circus of Stars

When I found that Linda Blair was to be one of the stars on this TV special I was certain that she would keep us riveted to the television screen with some of her skilled horsemanship. She provides more surprises than a drunk at a wedding dance. In this episode, she walks more than six-feet barefoot across broken glass. If I hadn't seen it, I wouldn't believe it. The episode that I was able to view was *The Circus of Stars #15* aired in November of 1990. She did look nice in her attire and her waist didn't appear to be all that wasted. She had an ankle length blue translucent skirt that flowed independent and free with a dressy single strapped, one piece black top that was tastefully accented with gold trim and some of the largest earrings that I have ever seen. This live performance kept me on the edge of my sofa seat as effectively as anything of hers that was scripted. She is nearly 32 years old when this episode aired. Her spontaneity and sincerity added to the act. She also appeared on *The Circus of Stars* in 1982 and 1983.

Was she covertly applying for a role in a Disney movie about Cinderella? Her slippers were made of glass, and I think that Linda could have conquered the role at the time.

Real Women/Going Vegan
Lifetime

I also saw Linda do a television spot on Lifetime's *Real Women* with Florence Henderson. Linda was discussing the Vegan life. I was impressed as she kept her cool when quizzed regarding her adherence to the diet. It seemed as though the hostess doubted Blair's sincerity to the Vegan lifestyle. It would have been a more impressive interview and demonstration had she been allotted the necessary time needed to explain her Vegan views. It almost seemed as though the other guests, as well as Henderson were battling over camera time. Linda seems unflappable regardless of the situation.

Blair doesn't just avoid the mouthwatering menus that light up my eyes. She gives some very convincing arguments for her choice. There is the killing of animals to take into account. A friend of mine worked in the slaughterhouse for many years and raised his own beef. He couldn't bring himself to shoot the cow that he wanted to butcher. (Our six-foot –six guitar player did the deed.) She refers to some of the farms as animal factories. Large livestock operations yield large amounts of animal waste. I have seen pictures of the enormous dung piles from such an operation near Chico, California. I (a) I viewed a photo in the local paper of the old stockyards, (in my hometown, Sioux City, Iowa) which were located right downtown and the pile of dung was even greater than that in Chico. There is another factor to be involved regarding the choice to abstain from animal food products. With the modern breeding technologies, our society is breeding animals for food and food only. Some of God's creatures are being genetically altered out of existence. For instance, we breed turkeys to have large breasts. In the process of accomplishing this we have given our turkeys such large breasts that they are no longer capable of reproducing on their own. Around the turn of this century, the red hog and Plymouth Rock chicken were nearly extinct because they didn't afford enough of the cuts of meat we prefer to eat. I also know that Vegans don't eat dairy products. I find it interesting that the weight problems of this generation may coincide with the hormones given dairy cows to help produce more milk. These are certainly points to ponder.

My oldest sister is a vegetarian. She introduced me to Hawaiian pizza, which contained no meat and it was very delicious. She also introduced me to the soybean hot dog, which I wouldn't recommend to a hungry Doberman. Man, did my internal organs seek revenge on me for that experiment! I lived in the Midwest farm area from the time I was eleven. When the wind blows from where the cow goes, you hold your big nose. Sauerkraut was also canned in my neck of the woods, and it wreaks right up there with the cows. I do appreciate Miss Blair's compassion for animals and salute her dedication to the Vegan lifestyle. If you are a woman and consider this form of nutrition, make sure that you get an iron supplement. Linda Blair authored a book dubbed *Going Vegan* and it should help guide you through the transition from the heavy happy eater to the possessor of a slim Jaguar of a body.

She has maintained her current healthy weight for years, and the gorgeous girl starring in the gruesome movie is all of fifty.

Her book, *Going Vegan*, also shed some light on her ability to overcome some of the tougher times that befell her early in her career. In the acknowledgements, she speaks glowingly of her family. She thanks her dear parents and pays tribute to the special talents of her brother Jimmy and sister Debbie. I am a student of the Holocaust and paid special attention to the words that Elie Weisel spoke as he credited his survival in part to the fact that he had his father with him through most of the ordeal. He felt that Anne Frank probably would have survived if she knew that her sister was alive. Family is one of life's most important ingredients. Linda penned her book at age 42 and I was impressed that she would speak glowingly of her siblings after so many years. You don't hear many superstars mention their brothers and sisters once that they (the stars) have reached their moment of fame. It is classy and sincere as is Linda Blair.

I thought that she had a solid family base to support her during the trying times and doubt that they abandoned her during her trials with the press and drug accusations during her late teens.

In her interview with the Biography Channel, she surprised me when she revealed that her parents eventually divorced. She said that her closeness to animals was intensified during the times that her parents would spat. Linda said that she would depart from the house and hang out with her animal pets. I found it refreshing that she didn't turn to drugs and (or) alcohol to soothe that pain. It's just one more thing that makes me question the drug charges of 1977. In the interview, Linda denies having anything to do with the accusations, mentioning that the Florida DA seemed to have a personal vendetta.

Maybe convicting the girl who played the devil would garner him more votes in the next election. It is sad to think that things have come to that.

Talk of the Town
1983

This was a short-lived interview show that came to us live from Las Vegas. It was hosted by Jaye P. Morgan, who was 28 years Blair's senior. Jaye P. Morgan is most famous for her role as one of the judges on the infamous *Gong Show*. Morgan also had a decent career as a singer. In a strange twist of fate, Morgan released her version of *Are You Lonesome Tonight* when Linda was still in diapers, only to have Elvis haul the same song to the number one spot in 1960. Pat Cooper was to be her sidekick in what appeared to be a take off of *The Tonight Show*. Carson had McMahon. Morgan had Cooper.

Linda appeared on Show #1 and I am not sure if there was ever more than one episode. This show also has guest appearances by Rip Taylor, New York's Samantha Fox, The

Unknown Comic (Muary Langston) and of course, Linda Blair.

Some of the format was awkward. The guests were required to descend a stair-like catwalk with Pat Cooper. Cooper donned the huge aviator eyeglasses that were popular at the time and it was somewhat suspenseful to see if the blind man could lead the guests down the steps without anyone falling. Instead of a house band, there was the *Talk of the Town* Dancers. It was also live, so off the cuff was the entertainment de jour.

The Unknown Comic does his stand up routine. Pat Cooper makes a valiant attempt. Samantha Fox reveals some of her secrets while fully clothed. It all seems like the conversation that they all enjoyed together the night before has spilled into the camera of the day.

This episode was as funny as anything that I've ever seen on a live interview program, save it was the night that Rodney Dangerfield teamed up with Johnny Carson and one liners and barbs recoiled in rapid fire. It seems a shame that there are no subsequent episodes available.

It is equally sad that we have such a limited choice of live TV. So many of today's shows have an agenda. They thrive on shocking us with Hollywood's latest scandals and we are sick of it. They are incessant in their attempts to bring us the most pitiful, heart-wrenching real life stories. It seems that the only time a celebrity appears on a live show is when there is a new film in which they are featured, or they are about to launch a new tour. Producers have forgotten how much we love to have the celebrities in our living room engaged in friendly discussion about the pleasantries of life. This may be the reason that I often enjoy watching *Talk of the Town*.

Charitable Work

Linda Blair is a practicing Vegan. She has a deep-rooted love of mankind and their animals alike. She does more than pay lip service to her causes. She has been seen autographing her photos for $5 donations to the food pantry in San Francisco. She is a frequent flyer at the Genesis Awards. She is said to be active in 75 charities.

One of the reasons that she accepted the role in *The Exorcist* was to earn enough money to put her through veterinary school. She has loved more dogs than anyone that I can think of. There are countless pictures of her with dogs during all stages of her life. She is the founder of the World Heart Foundation, which helps place homeless dogs into loving homes. It isn't just a feel good title for her. In viewing many of her photos, you'll notice that she doesn't possess the dainty Hollywood hands of most starlets. She'll let you know that taking care of as many animals as she does is hard work, and her hands tell the tale of truth. She takes care of as many as 50 dogs at her California facility.

While most of us were wondering about the future of the survivors of Hurricane Katrina, she took a plane to the city of New Orleans and rescued as many animals as she possibly could, in hopes of finding suitable homes for them. It is creative thoughtfulness at its highest level.

Countless are the times that she has been clicked cuddling a puppy and both seem to be enjoying the moment. She doesn't just sound the drum for her World Heart Foundation. She has the animals that need homes in her care. Is it any wonder that she has the hands of an industrial worker? If you check it out on the Internet, you'll find that beneath that lovely cover girl smile, are the hands of strength that have done some real physical work. Any artist will remind you that the hands are the same size as the face and they too tell a story. She doesn't just smile for the camera she works for the cause.

She originally contemplated the suffering of animals when

her mother was stricken with cancer. Coping with a cancer ridden relative is plenty to deal with. Linda reached deeper into the eternal plot and was concerned with the treatment of the laboratory animals that were used to help find a cure for cancer. I really feel that this was a pivotal time in her life. I think that she contemplated her purpose and potential during this crisis. There has been a lot of bad ink spilled her way, but to her credit, Linda has overcome many obstacles and has remained true to her ideals. It appears that she has repented of the sins of her youth and devil can lay claim to her no longer.

In Closing

I have enjoyed the experience of viewing Linda Blair's cinematic work. This expedition enabled me to learn volumes about the movie industry and what makes it successful and the surprising small things that can turn a great work in the making into a Frisbee flying to the dump. Linda uses her body language as well anybody. She can strut the angry soldier strut with the best of them and swing the hips like a sexy street sweetie just to keep you interested. It is challenging to find an actress that has implemented her eyes into the plot and mood as perfectly as Linda has for nearly 45 years. I truly believe that her most precious physical features are her beautiful brown eyes. She bats them flirtingly in *Roller Boogie* and flashes an angry fire at Leonard Hatch in *Sweet Hostage* when she responds to the ageless question, "Did you run out of gas?" with a, "Naw. I ain't that stupid."

When I first heard her in *Born Innocent*, I thought that her speech delivery was sub-par. I was mistaken. It seems that her less than resonant voice makes her characters more believable. It makes it easier to imagine her as the new girl in class (*Sara T: Portrait of a Teenage Alcoholic.*) It makes the character of nurse Shelly Stoker seem less spectacular twenty-eight years later in *Monster Makers*. That quality makes it easier for the viewer to identify with the character and that is one of the qualities that makes a movie successful. Her vocal deliveries in *Fatal Bond* catapult the work from just another cheap love story to an intriguing believable tale. It gave her a disarming charm that is a rare find in film. Her voice in *IMPS* enhanced the comic mood of the movie.

You could tell which movies she enjoyed working in as you watched them. In some she did a great job. In others, she pulled out some of her own soul and put it onto the screen. And that enhanced the work of those around her, making some hidden treasures in the process.

From a personal point of viewing, I am an older brother to four sisters and one of them (Linda) was born the same year as Blair. I also have three daughters, spaced fourteen years apart. It is interesting to correlate their life's stages with the progressing rolls of Linda Blair. It seems that in less time than it takes a film to rewind, they have transformed from adorable little girls playing with dolls into college graduates holding down important jobs.

Her works transcend the era of 1965 thru current (2012). Viewing them is chronicling history. It was intriguing to see the times and styles change through the movies. The journey takes us from black and white to color. The concept of art imitating life and life imitating art still seizes my soul. Some of the things seen in 1971's *Sporting Club* would have caused it to be limited to those of eighteen years of age or older during its run. Today, some of it is seen on prime time TV. I don't know if we will ever see the lavish design and attire that the young ladies of *Roller Boogie* brought us in teen movies again. The cars and the music have all changed. Some say for the better. Some say for the worse. Her films give us a sample from Hollywood's box of chocolates from which we may taste and decide which we like.

After watching thirty-eight of Linda's movies and seeing (and reading) countless interviews with her, I must confess that she unknowingly has spent a lot of time in my living room. She will always be a welcome guest.

Bibliography

Ethan Sacks Daily News Entertainment 9 Nov. 2006
The Internet Movie Data Base: Linda Blair
People Magazine: 11 July 1977 p.42
Photoplay: Oct. 1977
The Montreal Gazette: 14 June 1977 p.46

The Sporting Club
The Internet Movie Data Base: Jack Warden
The Internet Movie Date Base: Jack Warden article
By Jon C. Hopwood

The Exorcist
The Exorcist preview on the film
Internet Movie Data Base
The Exorcist preview on the film
Internet Movie Data Base: William Blatty
AMC Filmfest: Most Controversial Films of All-Time part 4 by
Tim Dirks
tv.com/linda-blair/person/40160/trivia

Born Innocent
Einsiders.com features/interviews/ Linda Blair p.2
Salon.com/story/ent/tv/int 25 October 2003

Airport 1975
Internet Movie Data Base: Dana Andrews article by Jim
Beaver
Spec Magazine October 1974 Volume 14 number 7
pp. 22-23
Late, Late At Night by Rick Springfield 2010 p.12
Late, Late At Night by Rick Springfield p.144
Spec Magazine October 1974 Volume 14 Number 7 p.36
Late, Late At Night by Rick Springfield

Late, Late At Night by Rick Springfield p.146
Worldwide Guide to Movie Locations

Sara T. Portrait of a Teenage Alcoholic
Femme Fatales 3 December 1999 Vol. 8 Number 8 p.31

Sweet Hostage
Internet Movie Data Base: Martin Sheen
Salon.com/story/ent/int/25 October 2003 p.3
about.com4-Whell Drive/Offroading
Femme Fatales: 3/decenber 1999 Vol.8 Number 8 p.22

Victory at Entebbe
A State of Blood p.168 by Henry Kyemba
A State of Blood p. 171 by Henry Kyemba
A State of Blood p.170 by Henry Kyemba
A State of Blood pp. 171-177 by Henry Kyemba
A State of Blood p. 53 by Henry Kyemba
Internet Movie Data Base: Elizabeth Taylor

The Exorcist II The Heretic
Interview on the American Movie Classics
22 October 2007
Ted Nash Web Site viewed 16 November 2008
Internet Movie Data Base: Richard Burton
UPI 15 May 1977
Femme Fatales 3 December 1999 vol. 8 Number 8 p.23

1977
People Magazine July 1977 p. 43
The Billboard Book of Top 40/ Hits 6th edition p.568
People Magazine July 1977 p.40
People Magazine July 1977 p. 40
Mahalo.com Linda Blair viewed 20 April 2009
Celebrities 411 Biography/ Linda Blair

Wikipedia / Linda Blair
Fallen Angel p.85 by Michelle Lee
Late, Late At Night by Rick Springfield pp.145-146
John McLaughlin's interview on "McLaughlin's One on One"

Summer of Fear aka *Stranger in Our House*
Femme Fatales 3 December 1999 /Vol. 8 Number 23
Linda Blair's Fowl Play interview with PETA
Vegetarian Era/ Special Interviews from an interview
6 May 2005 The Supreme Master Ching Hai International
Assn.

Roller Boogie
Interview with Rusty White
Internet Movie Data Base: Jim Bray
Internet Movie Data Base: Roller Boogie
The Billboard Book of Top 40 Hits 6th edition p., 198
Singing in the Rain DVD set 2002
Internet ad for the Excalibur
Internet Movie Data Base: Kimberly Beck
You-Tube interview with Cheap Trip 1978
The Billboard Book of Top 40 Hits 6th edition

Ruckus
Wikipedia
Salon.com/story/ent/tv/int/25 October 2003 p.1
Salon.com/story/ent/tv/int/25 October 2003 p.2

Chained Heat
Celebrity Sleuth Magazine
.Internet Movie Data Base: Stella Stevens
Internet Movie Data Base: Where Angels Go Trouble Follows!
Femme Fatales 3 December 1999 Vol. 8 number 8 p. 24
Die Schlechtester Filme aller Zieten; BVA Berlin 2002
Memoirs of a Super Freak/ pp 199-200 by Rick James

Savage Streets
Hub Cap Café 1957 Chevrolet

Night Patrol
Ford, The Men and the Machine p.235 by Robert Lacey
Bentley Historical Library, Gomon papers Box 10 "Racial Record"
Femme Fatales 3 December 1999 Vol.8 Number 8 p. 25
Internet Movie Data Base: Jackie Kong

Red Heat
Femme Fatales 3 December 1999 Vol.8 Number 8 p.25

Up Your Alley
The Exorcist preview on the film
Reno Film Festival on the Internet/ Bobby Logan

Moving Target
Country Music Awards Data Base
The Billboard Book of Top 40 Hits 6th edition p.751

Grotesque
The Billboard Book of Top 40 Hits 6th edition p. 296

Witchery
Preview of the film "The Exorcist"

The Chilling
WENN news 21 Aug. 2008

Bail Out
Internet Movie Data Base/ see Mary Lamb

Repossessed

Internet Movie Data Base/ Leslie Nielsen biography page

Fatal Bond
The Billboard Book of Top 40 hits 6th edition p. 163

Calendar Girl, Cop Killer? / The Bambi Bembenek Story
Internet Movie Data Base/ Ed Lauter

Bad Blood aka *A Woman Obsessed*
1 Movie Model Agency

Double Blast
Billboard Book of Top 40 Hits 6th edition p. 203
The Internet Movie Data Base

Sorceress
Celebrity Sleuth Magazine

Salon.com/story/ent/tv/int 25 October 2003

Nice Guys Finish Last p. 198 by Leo Durocher